D1336367

DO NOT OPEN

LONDON, NEW YORK, MELBOURNE, MUNICH, AND DELHI

Senior editor Claire Nottage
Senior art editor Jacqui Swan
Editors Niki Foreman, Andrea Mills
Senior designers
Sheila Collins, Smiljka Surla
Additional editors Steven Carton,
Julie Ferris, Jenny Finch, Fran Jones.
Additional designers Jim Green, Philip Letsu,
Johnny Pau, Owen Peyton Jones, Marilou Prokopiou

Managing editor Linda Esposito
Managing art editor Diane Thistlethwaite
Publishing manager Andrew Macintyre
Category publisher Laura Buller
Design development and jacket design
Sophia M Tampakopoulos Turner
Jacket editor Mariza O'Keeffe
Picture researcher Frances Vargo
Production controller Georgina Hayworth
DTP designers Siu Chan, Andy Hilliard

Illustrators
Mr Bingo, Khuan Cavemen Co.,
Gilman Calsen, Sheila Collins, Craig Conlan,
Alain Goffin, Hennie Haworth, Headcase Design,
Irene Jacobs, Neal Murren, Led Pants, Ali Pellatt

First published in Great Britain in 2007 by
Dorling Kindersley Limited, 80 Strand,
London WC2R 0RL
Copyright © 2007 Dorling Kindersley Limited
A Penguin Company

2 4 6 8 10 9 7 5 3 1
SD303 – 08/07

All rights reserved. No part of this publication
may be reproduced, stored in a retrieval system,
or transmitted in any form or by any means,
electronic, mechanical, photocopying, recording,
or otherwise, without the prior written permission
of the copyright owner.

A CIP catalogue record for this book
is available from the British Library.

ISBN: 978-1-40532-207-2

Colour reproduction by GRB Editrice, UK
Printed and bound in China by Hung Hing

Discover more at
www.dk.com

DO NOT OPEN

Written by JOHN FARNDON

CONTENTS

Unexplained...

Unthinkable...

DO NOT OPEN

Freaky facts...

Unknowable...

I dare you to open me

CONTENTS

Spine-chilling...

Spooky...

DO NOT OPEN

Strange coincidences...

Classified...

Go on, I dare you...

HOW TO USE

Welcome to Do Not Open, a fact-packed compendium of all the weird and wonderful stuff they don't want you to know about!

From secret services to conspiracy theories, this book will take you on a magical mystery tour of the truth behind the known and the unknown.

Whichever way you choose to read this book, you're sure of an instant hit of cool info. Of course, if you want to, you can just start reading Do Not Open in the old-fashioned way, by starting at the beginning. Or you can just dive in to the book at any point and then follow our special links to related subjects on other pages. So, for example, if you started with UFO, and then wanted to know more about weird extra-terrestrial happenings, just look for the links on the bottom of the right-hand page – they'll take you straight to other interesting alien stuff.

Your journey through the pages will depend on which links you choose to follow. In time, you can probably work your way through the whole book!

Here's an example of just one way you could get from Hoaxes to Everyday surveillance in just six steps.

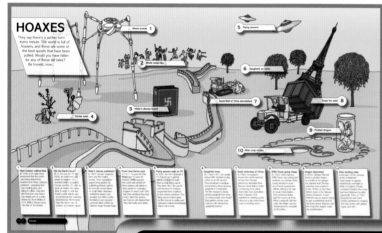

Fact or fiction? For more suspicious stories, check out Anastasia: the lost princess on **pp.138–139** and Crazy zoo on **pp.236–239**.

Hoaxes
Fact or fiction? For more suspicious stories, check out Anastasia: the lost princess on pp.138–139 and Crazy zoo on pp.236–239.

Anastasia
For more lost souls, seek out Bermuda Triangle on pp.40–41 and Haunted places on pp.94–95.

Everyday surveillance
For more undercover investigations, sneak a peak at Secret services on pp.64–65 and Private eye on pp.106–107.

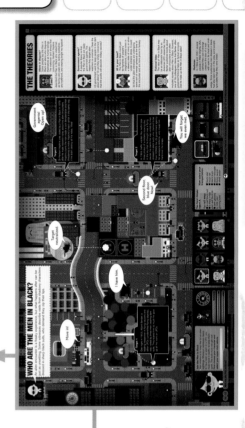

Who are the Men in Black?
Who else is watching you? Find out in Global eavesdropping on pp.22–23 and Everyday surveillance on pp.56–57.

Haunted places
For more spine-tingling stories, see Spooky! On pp.96–97, UFO on pp.200–201, and Vampires versus werewolves on pp.240–241.

UFO
For more encounters of the alien kind, visit Who are the Men in Black? on pp.48–49 and Roswell Alien Tribune on pp.140–141.

Hand-picked pilots

Air Force One crew members are very carefully selected. Each pilot has a long and distinguished flying career, and is thoroughly checked to be sure he poses no security risk.

Presidential suite

The president's rooms are all on the mid-level of the plane, in the aircraft's nose.

Hails to the chefs

Kitchen staff can prepare up to 100 meals at once in two large galleys. The aircraft's freezers contain enough food to keep passengers fed for up to a week. If food runs out, the plane lands and stewards sneak out to local grocery stores, selecting them at random to avoid any chance of the president's food being poisoned.

The upper level is the focus of Air Force One's highly sophisticated electronics. The communications centre is here, with connections for 87 telephones, dozens of radios and computers, and 19 TVs.

The middle level is the passenger area, with galleys, the medical room, and the president's personal suite.

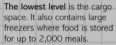

The lowest level is the cargo space. It also contains large freezers where food is stored for up to 2,000 meals.

President's "me" time

The president has his own personal suite of rooms, including a bedroom, gym, shower room, and office. US presidents say they have more privacy on Air Force One than when they are on the ground.

Ups and downs

Air Force One has its own retractable stairs at the front and rear, so it does not have to rely on local airport facilities, which could be a security risk.

Fuel tanks and engines

The four engines and the fuel tanks in the wings are Air Force One's most vulnerable spots. The fuel tanks can hold more than 200,000 litres (50,000 gallons) of flammable fuel, so they are protected with infrared units that can detect the heat of incoming bullets or missiles and fire flares to intercept them.

We've got you covered…

Keeping the president safe is top priority. Dangers could come from inside Air Force One as well as outside. Secret service agents are hidden throughout the aircraft to seize terrorists or would-be assassins should they manage to sneak on board. Most agents hide near the president's suite.

AIR FORCE ONE

You would expect the president of the USA to travel in style. For longer journeys, he takes to the skies in one of two specially adapted aircraft. When the head honcho is on board, the aircraft is called Air Force One. Both planes look like standard Boeing 747s on the outside. Inside is a staggering array of secret technologies and a variety of luxury rooms to ensure the president is kept safe and comfortable at all times. Welcome aboard!

Personnel and passengers
A standard jumbo jet can squeeze in more than 400 passengers, as well as a large crew. Air Force One carries 70 passengers at the most, and has a crew of 26. Besides reporters, the passengers include the president's personal staff and any VIPs invited aboard.

Defence systems
Air Force One is equipped with devices to provide maximum protection. These are the aircraft's most highly guarded secrets, but we know they include "electronic countermeasures" (ECMs), designed to jam enemy radar so that the plane effectively becomes invisible.

Getting connected
On board, the sophisticated electronic communications and defence systems mean the aircraft has twice the amount of wiring of a standard jumbo – more than 380 km (175 miles) of it. The wiring is specially encased to protect it from a damaging electromagnetic pulse that would be sent out by a nuclear explosion.

Can we quote you on that?
Apart from the president's staff and the flight crew, reporters are allowed to travel on board so that the world gets the news directly from the source. Reporters travel in the rear of the aircraft, and have their own phones and computer terminals so that they can send their news reports to editors on the ground.

AIRCRAFT TYPE   BOEING 747

There are two identical Air Force One planes, SAM-28,000 and SAM-29,000.
- Each one is 19.4 m (64 ft) – higher than a five-storey building.
- They have more than 370 sq m (3,983 sq ft) of cabin space.
- Each one weighs a massive 360 tonnes.
- They can fly at more than 1,000 kph (621 mph).

For more secrets in the skies, check out Watchers in space on pp.24–25 and Stealth technology on pp.130–131.

Mind the gaffe!

Different cultures have different traditions and etiquette. What's polite in one place may be offensive in another. When people from different cultures meet and interact, there can be a lot of room for misunderstanding. So, it's worth doing a little research next time you take a trip to a foreign land.

Eyes down

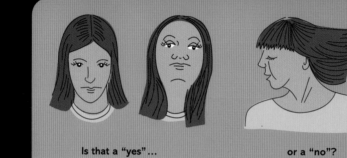

Is that a "yes" ...   or a "no"?

Submissive or shifty

While in some African countries, look downwards when speaking to some of a higher social status is conside respectful, in other places it is seer a sign of dishonesty or sha

Use your head

If you nod your head in Greece or Bulgaria, it means "no", and shaking y head means "yes". It means the oppos in most other places, so, don't say "yes when you mean "no".

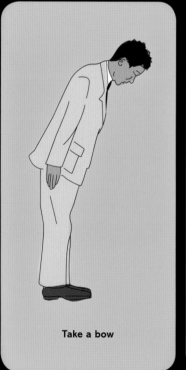

Take a bow

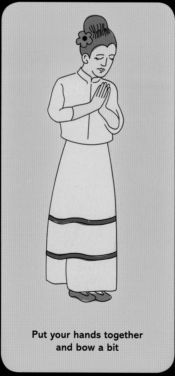

Put your hands together and bow a bit

Shake on it

Nice to meet you

There are many different ways that the people of the world greet each other. A mutual bow from the waist, with the back held straight and hands by the side, is the respectful and courteous greeting in Japan, while in Thailand, the junior person approache the senior, puts both hands together and gives a little bow. In the UK and USA, a firm, right-handed hand shake is the most comfortable, formal way to greet somebody, and in France, a sequence of cheek-kisses, starting with the left cheek, is *de rigeuer*.

Opening presents

Give and take

The etiquette surrounding the giving and receiving of gifts differs between cultures. In many places, it is considered rude to accept an invitation and then turn up empty-handed. When receiving a gift in Japan and Colombia, it is considered rude to open the gift in front of the giver.

Compliments to the chef

Instead of shooting disapproving glances at the person who allowed that burp to slip out after eating, some cultures view a big belch as a compliment to the food. In Canada, for example, the Inuit people interpret a burp as "thank-you, your food was excellent".

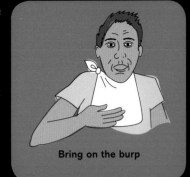

Bring on the burp

Present sense

In some parts of the world people are offended if the receiver doesn't open the gift in front of them. So, if you're a stranger in a strange land, check out the custom before you check in at a party.

Go on, open it

A royal no no

Flip-side of the coin

While disregarded coin "shrapnel" on the pavement is normal in many countries, the act of stepping over, or standing on, bills or coins in Thailand is considered severely disrespectful to their highly revered king, whose face is on every coin and note.

Nose blowing nos

Instead of sniffling and suffering a runny nose in public, it is generally preferable in most places for people to blow their noses and spare those around them from irritating sniffling sounds. However, in other places, such as Japan, it is considered rude and impertinent to blow your nose in public, whether you have the sniffles or not.

There she blows

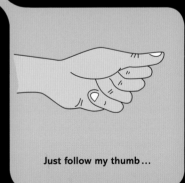

Pointing the finger

And the point is?

Pointing at people is considered rude in many places, and can be especially disrespectful if the person is pointing with purpose, so don't point to make a point! However, it is generally acceptable to point using your finger when giving directions.

Picking nose

Nose-picking

While blowing your nose in Japan is a national *faux pas*, picking your nose in public is socially acceptable. By contrast, many other countries consider picking one's nose as a disgusting and embarrassing habit that should be restricted to the privacy of a person's home, if at all!

Point of thumb

In Indonesia, pointing with the finger is considered rude, no matter whether giving directions or not. Instead, a closed fist held sideways is the preferred pointing method, with the thumb at the top (as shown here) pointing in the appropriate direction.

Just follow my thumb...

 For more interesting facts about the ways we interact, check out Strange vibrations on pp.108–109 and Body language on pp.186–187.

LEAKS AND MOLES

Sometimes secrets get out. Disgruntled employees can reveal dodgy dealings in corporations and governments to the press. Professional spies can infiltrate organizations and unearth confidential information. Let's snoop around the murky, double-crossing world of undercover espionage.

TOP SECRET

Whistleblowers

When an employee discovers the company they work for is up to no good they may "blow the whistle" and reveal all to the press. In 1994, for example, American Jeff Wigand revealed that tobacco companies knew that cigarettes are addictive and include cancer-causing additives long before it became public knowledge.

Another famous whistleblower was Ingvar Bratt. In the 1980s, Bratt released details of how Indian prime minister Rajiv Gandhi accepted payments from Bratt's employer, Swedish gunmakers Bofors, in return for a government contract.

Leaks

Sometimes secret information is released without authorization and without saying who let the secret out. In 1972, US president Richard Nixon's involvement in the illegal break-in at the Democratic Party's election headquarters in the Watergate office building was leaked to journalists by Mark Felt (who worked for the FBI – the US federal investigation agency – and went by the codename Deep Throat).

Websites with special security features are being developed for people to leak secret and sensitive documents from governments and organizations without getting caught. Some conspiracy theorists, however, think the sites could actually be fronts for government intelligence agencies.

Off-the-record

When politicians tell journalists something "off-the-record", they do not want to be quoted. Sometimes the politicians are simply being friendly. More often, the idea is to influence the way journalists present things without the public knowing they are doing it. Off-the-record briefings happen all the time, but they only come to light when something goes wrong and the politician's name gets out.

Spin

Sometimes information and news stories are released at a particular time or in such a way that they influence the way the public reacts to things. This is called spin. The name comes from how a bowler can give a ball spin so that it curves through the air in a way that confuses the batter. Government press officers are often criticized for using spin, and the most notorious practitioners are called "spin doctors". In some countries, the media is state-controlled and spins the news by reporting only stories that are favourable to the government.

CONFIDENTIAL

Moles

A mole is a spy who "burrows" his or her way into an enemy country's spy network or government to get secrets. A famous case took place at the height of the Cold War (a period during the 20th century when relations between the USA and western Europe and the communist countries of Russia and eastern Europe were particularly frosty). In 1965, Karel Koecher pretended to defect from (leave) communist Czechoslovakia to live in the USA. A few years later he joined the CIA (US foreign intelligence agency) and started feeding back spy secrets to the Russian equivalent, the KGB. Koecher got away with it for almost 20 years until he was found out.

Double agents

Spies who work for one country's secret service while really working for an enemy in secret are known as double agents. In the 1930s, British student Guy Burgess was secretly recruited by the KGB while studying at Cambridge University. He then joined MI5, the British secret service, and passed on secrets to the KGB.

Sleepers

Sleeper agents enter a foreign country and try to blend in as ordinary people. At first they undertake no spying activities, but find jobs that will prove useful to them in the future. When the time is right – sometimes many years later – they are "activated" and begin their espionage activities.

Günter Guillaume was a sleeper agent for communist East Germany during the Cold War. He was sent to West Germany in 1956 where he got a job working for one of the political parties. He eventually became a close aide of the leader of West Germany, Chancellor Willy Brandt, and was able to send back top-secret information to the East German secret service. Guillaume's activities were uncovered in 1974. He was imprisoned, and Chancellor Brandt was forced to resign because of the scandal.

Undercover

Police and intelligence agencies often go undercover to infiltrate criminal gangs. The officers assume new identities, complete with fake ID documents and background stories. To keep their cover, they must sometimes take part in criminal activities themselves.

➔ For other spy stories, go to Everyday surveillance on pp.56–57 and Secret services on pp.64–65.

Some people believe the words, "Novus Ordo Seclorum" ("New Order of the Ages") link the dollar with the Illuminati – a secret cult believed by some to control world events.

The date on the base of the pyramid is 1776 in Roman numerals – that's the year the USA became an independent nation.

There are 13 steps on the pyramid, to represent the 13 original American colonies.

The unfinished pyramid may symbolize that the USA is still far from finished.

The spooky, all-seeing eye on top of the pyramid has inspired all kinds of conspiracy theories, because it looks like a symbol used by the Freemasons Secret Society.

The "$" symbol probably evolved from the letters representing the American nation: US.

An average one-dollar bill is in circulation for about 22 months.

There are 293 coin combinations to change a dollar bill.

The almighty dollar

It may be the most widely circulated currency in the world, but look a little closer… What does all that stuff mean, anyway?

The number 13 pops up all over the place: 13 stars above the eagle, 13 letters in two of the Latin phrases, 13 vertical bars on the shield, 13 stripes at the top of the shield, 13 leaves on the olive branch, 13 olives, and 13 arrows.

Clutched in the eagle's beak is a ribbon that reads, "E Pluribus Unum" ("From many, one").

The shield in front of the eagle is not supported, to represent the idea that the country can stand on its own.

The eagle holds an olive branch and arrows in its claws. Its head points towards the olive branch to show a desire for peace, but if things go wrong, there are always the arrows…

The Latin phrase "Annuit Coeptis" above the pyramid translates as, "God has favoured our undertaking".

How many American icons are hidden on this spoof dollar bill?

For more curious codes, see Bar codes on pp.58–59 and Secret writing on pp.110–111.

FLAG IT UP

Every country has a national flag, each with a unique design. Often, the colours and symbols on a flag are significant. Flag experts, known as vexillologists, research the hidden meanings and stories behind the iconic banners.

Ireland

There is no official story to the meaning of the colours on the Irish flag, but many believe the green stripe symbolizes the Catholics of Ireland and the orange stripe the Protestants who fought for William of Orange in the 1600s. The flag may have been an attempt to reconcile these two sides.

USA

The 50 stars on the flag are for the 50 US states and the 13 stripes are for the 13 colonies that formed the original United States.

India

The saffron (orange) colour on the Indian flag stands for spirituality, white for peace, green for fertility, and the wheel for change.

Australia

The five small stars are the Southern Cross, the brightest constellation visible from Australia. The seven-pointed star is the Federation Star. This has one point for each of the six states, and a seventh for Australia's other territories.

China

When the Communist Party seized control of China in 1949, a competition took place to design a new flag. In the winning design, the red symbolizes the revolution, the large star represents the Communist Party, and the small stars are the Chinese people.

Switzerland

The white cross on the red base of the square-shaped Swiss flag represents Christianity. The Red Cross humanitarian organization reversed the colours to create the Red Cross flag in honour of its Swiss founder, Henri Dunant.

Canada

The red represents the red cross of England's patron saint and the white comes from the French royal emblem, reflecting the country's English and French heritage. In the centre is a leaf of Canada's national tree, the maple.

Spain

The four shields in the centre of the Spanish flag commemorate the four ancient kingdoms of Spain – Castile (the castle), Léon (the lion), Aragon (stripes), and Navarre (chains).

Denmark

According to legend, the Danish flag (the "Dannebrog") fell from the sky during a battle with the Estonian army in 1219, helping the Danes to victory. Vexillologists, however, believe the flag was derived from the battle banners of crusaders (Christian warriors).

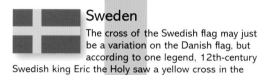

Sweden

The cross of the Swedish flag may just be a variation on the Danish flag, but according to one legend, 12th-century Swedish king Eric the Holy saw a yellow cross in the blue sky and made this the design for his flag.

Japan

The big red circle in the middle represents the rising sun. This is to symbolize the emperors of Japan who were regarded as descendants of the sun goddess Amaterasu.

Rwanda

Rwanda introduced a new flag in 2002. The green symbolizes hopes of prosperity; yellow stands for economic development; blue is for peace; and the sun represents light and enlightenment.

Norway

Norway became an independent nation in 1814. The cross comes from the flags of Sweden and Denmark with which it had been united. The red, white, and blue were inspired by the colours of the French Revolution, and symbolized liberty.

United Kingdom

The UK flag dates from 1606, three years after Scotland and England were united as a single kingdom. The flag combines the red and white cross of England's patron saint, George, and the blue and white cross of Scotland's patron saint, Andrew.

Germany

The black, red, and gold on the German flag can be traced back to the uniform of soldiers in the early 1800s. The soldiers wore black coats with red braid and gold buttons.

Italy

The green in the flag is said to represent the land; the white is the Alps; and the red is blood spilled in Italy's wars.

Greece

Some say the nine stripes on the Greek flag represent the muses (goddesses of art) in Greek mythology. The colour blue may represent the sea.

→ Want to quench your curiosity about countries of the world? Go to Mind the gaffe! on pp.12–13 and Law tour on pp.206–207.

Cheyenne Mountain

Deep inside a mountain in Colorado, USA, in a huge cavern blasted out of solid granite, is a secret military base. On the surface it looks just like any other tree-covered mountain, but get past the security guards and you will find your way into an entire underground city. Although the base is no longer in use, the military personnel once stationed here constantly monitored potential threats to the United States. It was always staffed with five crews of 40 people, but could accommodate 800 people in the event of an attack. Let's take a tour of the base in its heyday.

1. The tunnel entrance is the only sign of what lies hidden underground.

2. Deep into the mountain, a huge pair of 3-ft- (1-m-) thick steel doors protect the complex from a nuclear blast. Each door weighs more than 22 tonnes.

3. The buildings float on 1,319 strong steel springs that can soak up the vibration from a nuclear explosion by squeezing or stretching more than 30 cm (1 ft) in length.

4. The Missile Warning Center (MWC) is at the heart of America's defence against nuclear attack, detecting missiles launched anywhere in the world.

5. The North American Aerospace Defense Command (NORAD) scans the skies night and day for threats, including terrorist planes and spacecraft.

6. The Space Defense Operations Center (SPADOC) keeps tabs on every single one of more than 8,500 objects orbiting the Earth in space, from space stations to loose bolts.

7. The Combined Intelligence Watch Center (CIWC) looks for any potential danger to the United States around the world, from any source.

8. The National Warning Facility monitors the country for signs of civil unrest and protest movements.

9. Metal walls on the chambers and buildings shield the complex from the electromagnetic pulse of a nuclear explosion.

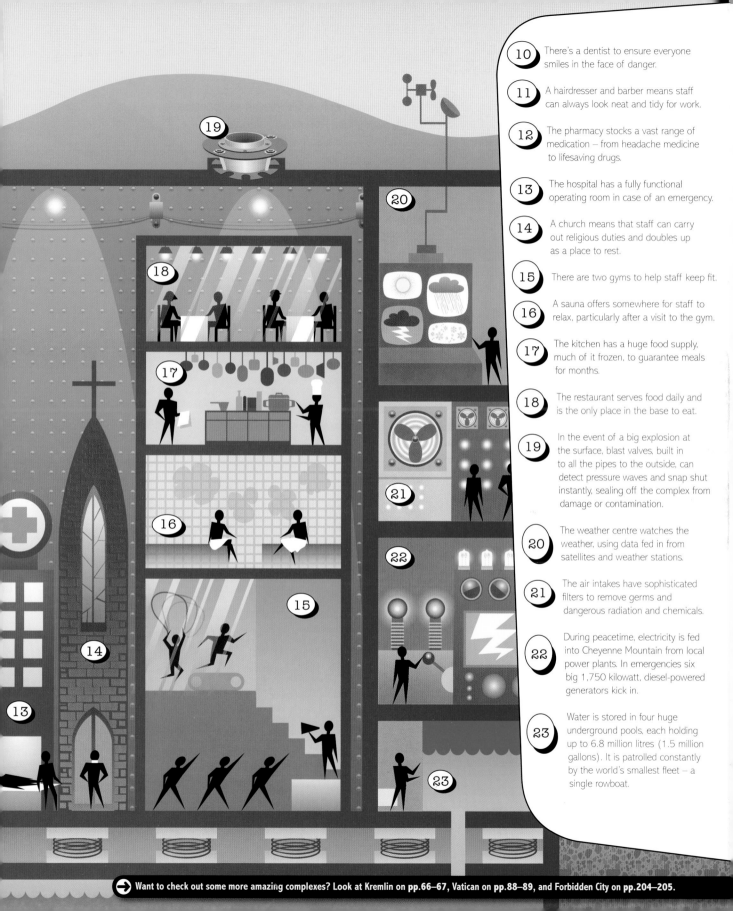

10 There's a dentist to ensure everyone smiles in the face of danger.

11 A hairdresser and barber means staff can always look neat and tidy for work.

12 The pharmacy stocks a vast range of medication – from headache medicine to lifesaving drugs.

13 The hospital has a fully functional operating room in case of an emergency.

14 A church means that staff can carry out religious duties and doubles up as a place to rest.

15 There are two gyms to help staff keep fit.

16 A sauna offers somewhere for staff to relax, particularly after a visit to the gym.

17 The kitchen has a huge food supply, much of it frozen, to guarantee meals for months.

18 The restaurant serves food daily and is the only place in the base to eat.

19 In the event of a big explosion at the surface, blast valves, built in to all the pipes to the outside, can detect pressure waves and snap shut instantly, sealing off the complex from damage or contamination.

20 The weather centre watches the weather, using data fed in from satellites and weather stations.

21 The air intakes have sophisticated filters to remove germs and dangerous radiation and chemicals.

22 During peacetime, electricity is fed into Cheyenne Mountain from local power plants. In emergencies six big 1,750 kilowatt, diesel-powered generators kick in.

23 Water is stored in four huge underground pools, each holding up to 6.8 million litres (1.5 million gallons). It is patrolled constantly by the world's smallest fleet – a single rowboat.

➜ Want to check out some more amazing complexes? Look at Kremlin on pp.66–67, Vatican on pp.88–89, and Forbidden City on pp.204–205.

GLOBAL EAVESDROPPING

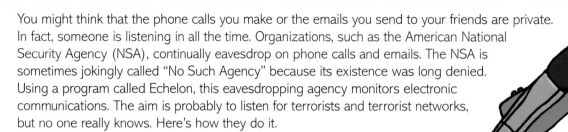

You might think that the phone calls you make or the emails you send to your friends are private. In fact, someone is listening in all the time. Organizations, such as the American National Security Agency (NSA), continually eavesdrop on phone calls and emails. The NSA is sometimes jokingly called "No Such Agency" because its existence was long denied. Using a program called Echelon, this eavesdropping agency monitors electronic communications. The aim is probably to listen for terrorists and terrorist networks, but no one really knows. Here's how they do it.

Email exchanges
When you send an email, the electronic signal carrying the email goes to your Internet Service Provider (ISP). From there it is sent via an Internet Exchange Point (IXP) to your friend's ISP, and then on to your friend. To intercept your email without you knowing, the eavesdropper simply taps into the IXP. The NSA's computers also continually search through every website on the Internet in order to locate anything suspicious.

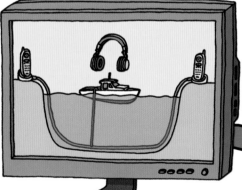

Telephone cables
The cables that carried phone calls under the sea used to be made of copper wires. Eavesdroppers could listen in by sending divers down to wrap electric coils around the wire. This enabled listeners to hear the phone signals which "leaked" out from the copper. Nowadays the cables are fibre optics, which are completely untappable... or are they?

Mobile signals
When you call someone on your mobile, microwave signals travel through the air to an antenna, from where they are relayed through other antennae until they reach the mobile of the person you are calling. All an eavesdropper has to do is intercept the microwave signal as it travels between antennae.

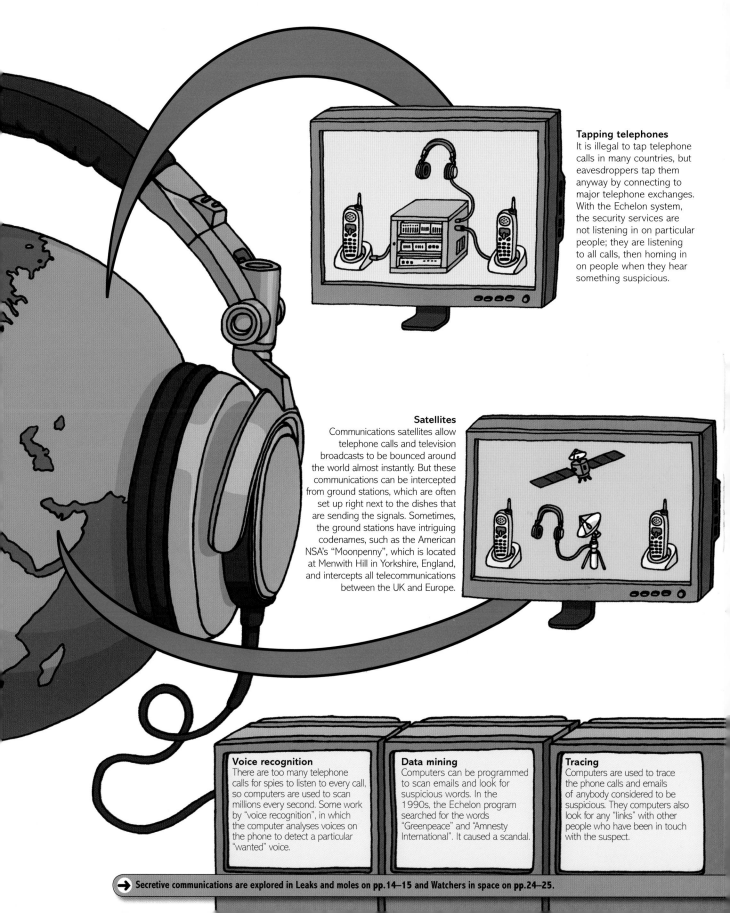

Tapping telephones
It is illegal to tap telephone calls in many countries, but eavesdroppers tap them anyway by connecting to major telephone exchanges. With the Echelon system, the security services are not listening in on particular people; they are listening to all calls, then homing in on people when they hear something suspicious.

Satellites
Communications satellites allow telephone calls and television broadcasts to be bounced around the world almost instantly. But these communications can be intercepted from ground stations, which are often set up right next to the dishes that are sending the signals. Sometimes, the ground stations have intriguing codenames, such as the American NSA's "Moonpenny", which is located at Menwith Hill in Yorkshire, England, and intercepts all telecommunications between the UK and Europe.

Voice recognition
There are too many telephone calls for spies to listen to every call, so computers are used to scan millions every second. Some work by "voice recognition", in which the computer analyses voices on the phone to detect a particular "wanted" voice.

Data mining
Computers can be programmed to scan emails and look for suspicious words. In the 1990s, the Echelon program searched for the words "Greenpeace" and "Amnesty International". It caused a scandal.

Tracing
Computers are used to trace the phone calls and emails of anybody considered to be suspicious. They computers also look for any "links" with other people who have been in touch with the suspect.

Secretive communications are explored in Leaks and moles on pp.14—15 and Watchers in space on pp.24—25.

Watchers in Space

Satellites in space are too small and high for you to see them, but they can see you – and it is amazing what they can reveal. From the invisible movement of disease across a field of crops to your boots being moved to a different place on your doorstep, satellites can spot it.

NASA's Aqua satellite can detect moisture in soil and, as a result, inform farmers when crops need watering or when the soil is ready for planting.

Satellites can track large fires, wildlife tagged with radio transmitters, and glaciers breaking into icebergs, and changes in the size of the hole in the ozone layer.

The TOPEX/Poseidon satellite can measure miniscule variations in the depth of the oceans. This amazing level of accuracy was used to reveal hidden mountains on the sea bed. Using this technology, scientists could create a complete map of the ocean floor.

Soon, spy satellites will be able to continuously track the movement of something as small as a mouse from high up in space.

Spy satellites
The most secret satellites are military surveillance satellites, such as the American Keyhole satellites and Lacrosse/Onyx satellites. These satellites keep track of army movements and terrorist activity. They can receive signals from secret agents' transmitters and even send coded messages.

Early warning satellites use infrared sensors to detect a nuclear missile's hot exhaust just seconds after it is launched.

Satellites can chart the meanderings of the Gulf Stream and other currents affecting the weather and climate.

Earth watch
It's not just spy satellites that reveal extraordinary things. Satellites can identify whether a field is planted with wheat, oats, cotton, or corn by reading each crop's "spectral signature" – the wavelength of light each type of plant reflects back into the atmosphere. Satellites can also warn of the spread of disease or pests attacking the fields.

Satellite images can be used to search for petroleum deposits, to plot ancient stream beds in the desert, to identify earthquake-prone areas, and to search for shipwrecks on the ocean floor.

Listening devices allow satellites to pick up any signal travelling through the air on the ground, such as a radio message or a mobile phone call.

The pull of gravity varies slightly over Earth. The GRACE satellite can detect these variations with astonishing accuracy, revealing a lot about Earth's oceans and hidden interior. For instance, it could track the movement of molten rock far below the water's surface.

The latest US Ikon/Keyhole spy satellites can photograph the smallest area. Some have cameras that can read tiny details, such as a book cover or a car's number plate.

The three US PARCAE satellites can track the position, speed, and direction of any ship anywhere in the world. They do this by picking up on the signals each ship gives off, including radio and navigation signals. Missiles fired from the other side of the world can also be guided to their targets by these satellites.

Satellite pictures help us gauge how human activities are affecting the planet by documenting the destruction of rainforests, monitoring water temperatures in the ocean, and measuring the warming of Earth's atmosphere.

Satellites use a special kind of radar called Synthetic Aperture Radar to enable them to take detailed pictures through clouds and at night.

Thermal imaging cameras on board satellites can detect heat sources — whether it is the warm body of a person hiding inside a hut, or the small amount of heat emanating from a camouflaged target or underground bunker.

Weather satellites record cloud patterns and movements which can help predict storms. They also measure temperature, atmospheric moisture, air pressure, rainfall, and snowfall.

Satellites reveal geology and land forms, as well as where oil or minerals may be. Copper, nickel, zinc, and uranium deposits have been found in the United States in this way. Satellites have also revealed tin in Brazil and copper in Mexico.

American spy satellites are controlled by the ELectronic INTelligence (ELINT) system, which is monitored by a little-known government agency called the NGA (National Geospatial-Intelligence Agency)

Want to know more about who might be watching you? Take a look at Global eavesdropping on pp.22–23 and Everyday surveillance on pp.56–57.

Found!
In 1999, the wreck of a 15th-century Chinese treasure ship carrying porcelain was found just off the coast of Brunei in the South China Sea.

Found!
In 1987, high-tech robots found the wreck of the gold-filled steamer *SS Central America*, which went down in a hurricane off Florida in 1857.

Lost treasures

See if you can discover where they are...

Rumour has it that this notorious criminal buried his treasure on Gardiner's Island, Long Island, near New York, USA.

Found!
In 2005, it was announced that 600 barrels of Spanish gold had been found buried on Robinson Crusoe Island (Juan Fernandez Is) 700 km (435 miles) west of Chile.

Found!
In 2000, the wreck of pirate Black Sam Bellamy's ship, the *Whydah*, was found off Cape Cod, Massachusetts. In 1996, pirate Blackbeard's ship, the *Queen Anne's Revenge*, was found near Beaufort, North Carolina.

William Kidd: Upon hearing that he was about to be brought to trial in 1698, the notorious pirate Captain Kidd is said to have buried the treasure from his greatest prize, the *Quedagh Merchant* ship, which was laden with silks and rubies from India.
From death's cruel head, step 11 squares E, then 10 N

King John: When King John was travelling across England in 1215, his treasure wagons were taken on a short cut across the marshes, but were cut off by the tide, never to be seen again.
Drink a royal health, then go 8 squares NW and 11 SW

Henry Morgan: In 1671, the infamous pirate Henry Morgan attacked Panama City and looted treasure, which he is believed to have hidden in a cave deep underwater, guarded by sharks and barracuda.
A Jamaican spirit will lead you 6 N and 6 E

Moctecuma: Legend has it that when the Spanish conquistadors were driven from the Aztec city of Tenochtitlan in 1520, the Aztec ruler Moctezuma was killed, perhaps by his own people. The Aztecs then gathered all his treasure and hid it safely away.
Fired from the iron-ball spitter 5 S and 4 NW

Yamashita: Japanese General Yamashita looted and stashed away $200-billion worth of jewels and gold from China and southeast Asia during World War II (1939–45). Before he could recover the treasure, he was tried and executed as a war criminal in 1946.
A case of oak takes you 18 squares E

Butch Cassidy and the Sundance Kid: When these infamous robbers raided the bank in Winnemuca, Nevada in 1900, and stole $32,000 worth of gold coins, they vowed it would be their last robbery. Legend has it that they buried the loot before fleeing to South America.
Look sharp and long 3 N and 4 W

Blackbeard: In 1812, British captain Blackbeard (not the pirate) recovered a vast treasure from a Spanish galleon, wrecked near the Bahamas. On the sea he was in danger from both French warships and pirates, so he trekked across land until it all became too much and he buried the treasure.
Hold your ship fast here, then go 12 W and 4 S

→ Like looking for lost things? Then have a look at Lost tribes on pp.36–39 and Bermuda Triangle on pp.40–43.

CHRISTOPHER

Christopher Columbus is a hero in many history books. This explorer extraordinaire is said to have discovered America on 12 October 1492, and many Americans still celebrate this achievement. However, the real truth is something that Columbus would not have wanted anyone to discover...

What they tell you

The Earth is flat!

In Columbus's time, everyone thought that the world was flat. If you sailed west from Europe, for example, it was thought that you would eventually sail off the end of the Earth. Ouch! Only Columbus got his head round the fact that the world was round, and only he had the courage to sail across the Atlantic into the unknown to prove it... or so Washington Irving's 1828 biography of Columbus would have us believe.

Hello! I've arrived!

What they don't tell you

Erm... actually it's round

People had, in fact, known that the Earth was round for thousands of years before Columbus. The Greek scholar Eratosthenes had accurately calculated its size as long ago as 250 BCE. Scholars warned Columbus that the Earth was much bigger than he thought, and that his voyage across the Atlantic would be far too long for him and his crew to survive.

Who *are* these awful people on my beach?

COLUMBUS

Having lived in the Americas for many thousands of years, Native Americans greeted Columbus on his arrival. Far from being an unknown land, the Vikings had reached America at least 500 years before Columbus. Mistakenly believing he was in Asia, Columbus called the Americas "the Indies". He died still believing this.

I saw it first, you fools!

The terrible tyrant
Columbus was a harsh captain who whipped his crew. He even claimed the reward for being the first to spot land, even though it was lookout Juan Bermeo who saw it. Columbus was taken to Spain in chains because his colonies were in chaos and his cruel crimes had been discovered. However, his influence, smooth talking, and gifts of gold ensured his release from prison after six weeks. Columbus died a wealthy man at home in Valladolid, Spain.

The brutal beast
Columbus saw that the New World offered him and his companions the chance to dominate the land. They unleashed a reign of terror on the native people. By the time he left, millions of Native Americans had perished through torture, murder, forced labour, and starvation.

In 1492, Columbus sailed westwards across the Atlantic, with a fleet of three little ships. He was hoping to reach the Indies (India, China, and Indonesia) but instead, he discovered the Americas – a vast, unknown land that became known as the New World. Columbus's amazing achievement is still celebrated every Columbus Day in the United States. Result!

Poor, poor pitiful me

The neglected hero
Columbus was a humane captain driven by a glorious vision. Only the stupidity of the Spanish court led to his being dragged back in chains to Europe where he died a pauper, his great achievements ignored. He bitterly wrote, "Over there I have placed under their sovereignty more land than there is in Africa and Europe… I, by the divine will, made that conquest". Sour grapes, anyone?

Come to Sunday school!

The missionary man
Columbus believed he had a divine mission to bring Christianity to the ignorant people of the New World. He built many churches and helped spread the word of God among the native peoples. His religious zeal and saintly manner proved a model for all settlers.

→ Find out the truth about other historical stories, including Anastasia: the lost princess on pp.138–139 and Knights Templar on pp.210–211.

WHO CROSSED THE
Atlantic first?

Most people think that Christopher Columbus was first to cross the Atlantic, reaching America in 1492. However, Vikings made the crossing 500 years before Columbus, and some historians think other brave sailors did, too. Most of these early contestants in the transatlantic race sailed further north than Columbus. The weather is colder and stormier here, but the journey is shorter, and they could stop off at islands, such as Iceland and Greenland on the way.

FINISH

Kennewick Man
The bones of a man who lived 9,000 years ago were unearthed in Kennewick, Washington, on the banks of the Columbia River. No-one knows where Kennewick Man came from, but a reconstruction of his face revealed that he looked more like modern-day Europeans than Native Americans. Was he the first to cross the Atlantic Ocean?

Racing line-up:
Here are the contestants in the transatlantic race, set out in the order they are thought to have arrived in. While there is decisive evidence that the Vikings, for instance, did cross the Atlantic, some stories are probably little more than myths.

1. Prehistoric French
Similarities in stone tools and DNA suggest that French cavemen crossed the Atlantic more than 15,000 years ago. They may have travelled in canoes along the edge of the Arctic ice sheet.

2. Ancient Jews
A 2,000-year-old stone dug up at Bat Creek, Tennessee, USA, has writing on it that could be Hebrew. Some say this shows Jews reached North America thousands of years ago. Unlikely.

3. Ancient Romans
A Roman ceramic was found near Mexico City, Mexico, and Roman coins have been unearthed in Indiana and Ohio, USA. The artefacts were most likely brought to America long after Ancient Roman times.

4. Irish saint
Documents from the 9th century claim that Irish saint Brendon crossed the Atlantic in the 5th century in a leather boat. A replica boat built in 1977 proved it was possible.

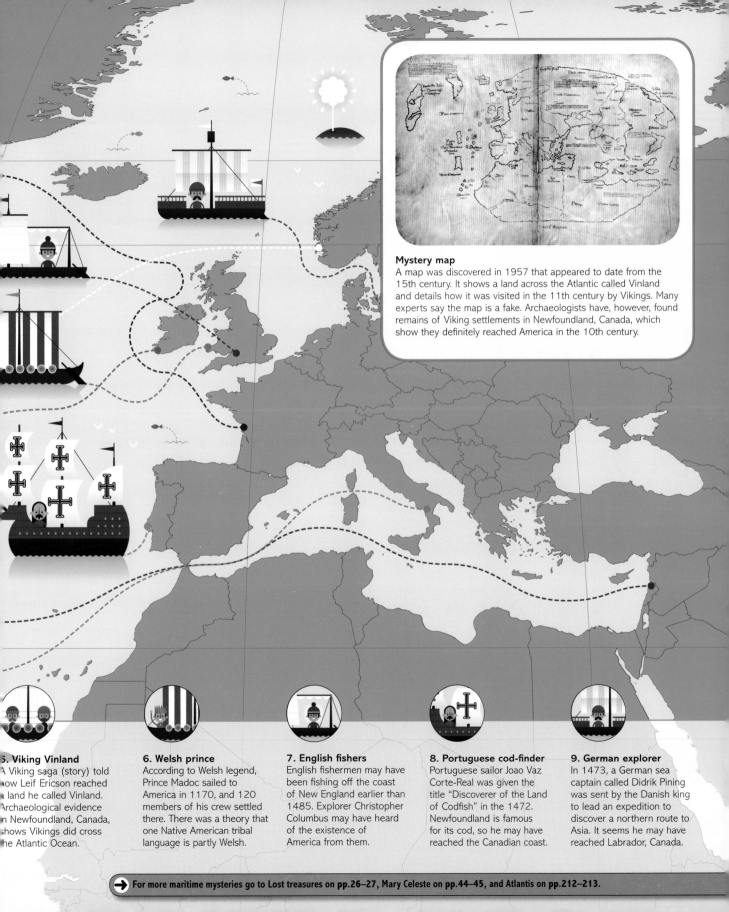

Mystery map

A map was discovered in 1957 that appeared to date from the 15th century. It shows a land across the Atlantic called Vinland and details how it was visited in the 11th century by Vikings. Many experts say the map is a fake. Archaeologists have, however, found remains of Viking settlements in Newfoundland, Canada, which show they definitely reached America in the 10th century.

5. Viking Vinland
A Viking saga (story) told how Leif Ericson reached a land he called Vinland. Archaeological evidence in Newfoundland, Canada, shows Vikings did cross the Atlantic Ocean.

6. Welsh prince
According to Welsh legend, Prince Madoc sailed to America in 1170, and 120 members of his crew settled there. There was a theory that one Native American tribal language is partly Welsh.

7. English fishers
English fishermen may have been fishing off the coast of New England earlier than 1485. Explorer Christopher Columbus may have heard of the existence of America from them.

8. Portuguese cod-finder
Portuguese sailor Joao Vaz Corte-Real was given the title "Discoverer of the Land of Codfish" in the 1472. Newfoundland is famous for its cod, so he may have reached the Canadian coast.

9. German explorer
In 1473, a German sea captain called Didrik Pining was sent by the Danish king to lead an expedition to discover a northern route to Asia. It seems he may have reached Labrador, Canada.

→ For more maritime mysteries go to Lost treasures on pp.26–27, Mary Celeste on pp.44–45, and Atlantis on pp.212–213.

NAZCA LINES

Stretching across Peru's Nazca desert are gigantic drawings, or geoglyphs, only visible from the sky. Known as the "Nazca Lines", they were rediscovered in the 1920s when aircraft flew over the area. We now know that they were created by the ancient Nazca people, between 200 BCE and 700 CE, by taking away strips of the dark oxide-coated pebbles that litter the desert to reveal the light earth beneath. The mystery is, why did they do it?

Runway

Length 55 m (180 ft)

Long bands like this fan out across the desert in a pattern that looks like the runways of a modern airport. Hardly surprising, then, that some people came up with the theory that aliens visited the area long ago, and built these long strips as landing areas for their spaceships!

Monkey

Length 55 m (180 ft)

The Nazca people didn't worry about accuracy in their drawings of animals. The Monkey has three toes on each foot, four fingers on one hand, and five on the other. As a result, some historians wonder whether the numbers had a special meaning.

Spaceman
Length 32 m (105 ft)

The Nazca geoglyphs include humanoid figures. The most famous is the one shown here, nicknamed the Spaceman, discovered in 1982. Others include ET, the Man with the Hat, and the Executioner.

THEORIES

No-one really knows why the Nazca people made these lines. Some believe that they acted like a giant map to locate underground water sources, and that the pictures were figures of gods, or names given to the water sources. Many experts believe that they were actually walking temples – lines along which the Nazca walked, led by a priest-like figure, in a pattern dedicated to a particular god. There is also the theory that the lines are simply pictures intended for the gods to look down on. Or they could point to places on the horizon where the sun and stars rise and set. Perhaps the Nazca actually flew up in primitive hot-air balloons to see their pictures. Maybe the truth is up there …

Pelican
Length 285 m (935 ft)

The Pelican is the largest of the geoglyphs created by the Nazca people. At first, people could not believe that the Nazca could draw a picture so big, but, in the 1980s, archaeologists showed it was possible with a small team and simple surveying equipment.

LOST CITY

Archaeologists started excavating a buried city in the 1980s at Cahuachi, just south of the Nazca Lines. Along with mummified remains of the Nazca people, pottery has been unearthed that has patterns painted on it, identical to the Nazca Lines themselves. Signs of an ancient weaving technique for making such patterns were also discovered, which could have been used to plan the Nazca Lines.

For more tales of lost cultures, visit Lost tribes on pp.36–39 and Ancient pyramids on pp.118–119.

HIDDEN GOLD

NEW YORK'S GOLDEN SECRET

More than a quarter of the world's gold is stashed away in just a single bank vault 24 m (80 ft) below the streets of New York City, USA, inside the Federal Reserve Bank of New York (FRBNY) Countries buy and sell billions of dollars worth of gold in secret, simply by shifting it around the vault.

The Federal Reserve Bank of New York contains more than 7,250 tonnes of gold. The exact amount is not known because some countries do not release details of how much gold they have.

Most of the gold in the FRBNY is in the form of brick-like bars. Each is worth at least US$160,000, weighing 400 troy ounces (12.4 kg/27 lb). A troy ounce is a unit of weight used for measuring precious metals.

As well as the bricks, there are tiny bars of gold made from the left-overs from each casting. These are nicknamed "Hershey bars" because they look like the bars of chocolate produced by US confectioner Hershey.

The gold in the FRBNY is owned by 122 countries. Each country has its own gold store in the vault, in which bars of gold are piled up in overlapping layers like brick walls.

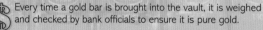

Countries put their gold in the FRBNY because it allows them to trade gold very easily – without the risk of transporting it across the world.

When one country wants to sell its gold to another country, it simply asks the FRBNY to shift the right number of gold bricks from its store to the store of the other country. That way no-one has to worry about moving gold around the world. It's simply shuffled around the FRBNY vault.

Every time a gold bar is brought into the vault, it is weighed and checked by bank officials to ensure it is pure gold.

The largest single compartment in the bank contains 107,000 gold bars. You can't tell which country it belongs to, since every country's vault is identified only by a secret code number.

Bank officials enter the vault through a door in a narrow passage in a giant 90-tonne steel cylinder, which rotates to block off the passage and seal the vault.

No *one* person knows all the combinations for the eight bolts that secure the cylinder. Eight people have to be present to add the code they know in order to open it.

NOTEWORTHY CHANGE

In the past, gold was widely used as money. Over time, people began to put their gold in banks for safekeeping. In return, the bank gave them paper receipts that said the bank "promise to pay" back their gold should they ever want it. Soon people began to buy things with these receipts, instead of actual gold, and they became the first bank notes. Even today, since bank notes are actually worthless paper, they are simply a "promise to pay".

MONEY MAKING

As bank notes were just receipts for gold in the bank, the value of notes in circulation matched the amount of gold in the banks. For economies to grow, more money needs to be in circulation. So banks simply print more bank notes – regardless how much gold they actually have in reserve. This is called "fractional reserve banking", because the gold reserve is just a fraction of the value of the notes in circulation. It's a neat way for banks to literally make money. Minted!

BREAKING THE BANK

Fractional reserve banking works fine as long as all the people with bank notes don't actually ask for their gold. But in troubled times, such as war, they sometimes did. Then the bank would go bust because it didn't have enough gold to pay everyone. To stop people losing out when banks collapsed, governments set up central banks. The central bank holds most of the country's reserves of gold, and issues bank notes. The US Federal Reserve Bank and the Bank of England are central banks like these.

THE GOLD STANDARD

When banks print money regardless of how much money they have in reserve, you can't be sure how much gold the notes actually buy. This is a problem when you want to pay for things in another country where they have different notes. So, in the 1800s, governments in countries such as Britain and the USA set up a "gold standard". This ensured a pound or a dollar would always be worth a particular amount of gold.

SPEND, SPEND, SPEND

In the last century, economic depression and world wars encouraged governments to print more money to spend their way out of trouble. It seemed to work, regardless of how much gold they actually had in reserve. So in 1971 the world's governments decided to get rid of the gold standard. Now governments can print as much money as they want. They still keep some gold in reserve, but it's only a small proportion of the amount of money in circulation.

A MATTER OF INTEREST

The amount of money in circulation today depends not on gold reserves, but entirely on the heads of each country's central bank, who meet regularly in secret. They decide how much money is worth in their country by setting the percentage of interest to be paid on bank loans. In this way, they have a profound effect on how well-off we all are.

Want to know more about what's going on underground? Go to Cheyenne Mountain on pp.20–21 and Paris underground on pp.208–209.

LOST tribes: how many live in the rainforests?

Lost tribes

Hidden away in dense tropical rainforests in the Amazon and Indonesia live a handful of small tribes, mostly untouched by the modern world. These tribes exist in exactly the same way as they have done for tens of thousands of years.

Threats

The modern world poses many dangers for the people living in the rainforests. The threats take many forms — some attack the tribes' forest homes, and others affect the tribes directly.

➤ **Bulldozers, fire, and chainsaws:** These are the weapons of the developers who strip away the forest to make way for farmland, towns, and roads.

➤ **Ranchers:** Sometimes ranchers take over tribes' hunting lands to grow soya beans and raise cattle.

➤ **Loggers:** These are the men who cut down the forest trees for their wood.

➤ **Gold hunters:** The discovery of gold in some forest areas has attracted gold seekers, who chop down large areas of forest to make way for mines. Mercury, used to retrieve the gold, is flushed into the river and poisons fish — a source of food for the tribes.

➤ **Oil companies:** These companies are starting to move in on many forest areas to get at oil deposits.

➤ **Guerillas:** In politically unstable parts of the world, guerilla warfare has disrupted the peace of the forest.

➤ **Genocide:** Tribal people have been killed by those who simply want them out of the way.

➤ **Diseases:** Tribal people have never built up any immunity to diseases such as measles and the flu, so even fleeting contact with infected outsiders can be devastating.

The **Awa Guaja** live on the remote sierra of northeast Brazil, where the men hunt using bows and arrows, and the women harvest bananas and wild berries. They are always naked, and are known for smiling a lot!

The **Naua** people of northwest Brazil's rainforests were thought to have died out in the 1920s, but they were just living in secret. In 2000, about 250 Naua people were spotted. Some were working as rubber tappers, gathering latex from rubber trees.

The **Zo'e** or **People of the Moon** live in unexplored rainforests in northern Brazil, where they hunt monkeys. Their bottom lips are pierced by a wooden plug called a poturu, and they smear their bodies in the red dye of the urucum fruit.

The **Yanomami** are found on the border between Brazil and Venezuela. They live together in huge round huts called yanos, and grow plants for food and medicine in "gardens" in the forest. They hold huge tug-of-war games that last for hours.

The **Huaorani** of Ecuador have a deep knowledge of plants. From one specific vine they extract the paralyzing poison, curare, which they then use on the darts of blowpipes to hunt howler monkeys. They honour trees and worship jaguars.

The **Nukak** of Colombia build makeshift houses of leaves, but soon move on to hunt monkeys with blowpipes. They dip rattan vine roots in streams to release a drug that stuns fish. The fish can then be hunted with bows and arrows.

The **Mashco Piro** live in the far west of the Amazon jungle in Peru, in swampy river regions where they fish for food. They were given the name "mashco", which means "nakeds", by rubber barons, who tried to enslave them before they escaped into the jungle.

The **Yora** live in the rainforest of southeast Peru. During the dry season, they live by rivers to make fishing easier, and to pick up turtles' eggs on the rivers' beaches. In the wet season, they retreat into the forest to hunt, and collect fruits and nuts.

The **Korubo** or **Dslala** live in Brazil's Javari Valley. They use clubs and poisoned arrows to kill fish and spider monkeys. They are sometimes known as "the head-bashers" because of a mistranslation of the word for "clubbers".

The **Korowai** of New Guinea live among forest treetops. Their skins are marked by scars, their noses skewered with pointed bones, birds' ribs curve upwards from their nostrils. It is thought that they are cannibals (eat other humans).

The **Una** people of New Guinea make axes from basalt stone. Great skill is needed to shape the stone. This talent is so highly valued that stone-cutters in the tribe are considered to be magicians.

The **Agta** of the Philippines are one of the few lost tribes living by the sea. They live on fish, shellfish, honey, and wild fruit. The Agta believe that when any living thing dies – be it animal or plant – its soul goes to Anito, the world of the dead.

For other mysterious peoples, go to Nazca Lines on **pp.32–33**, Rosetta Stone on **pp.116–117**, and Ancient technology on **pp.128–129**.

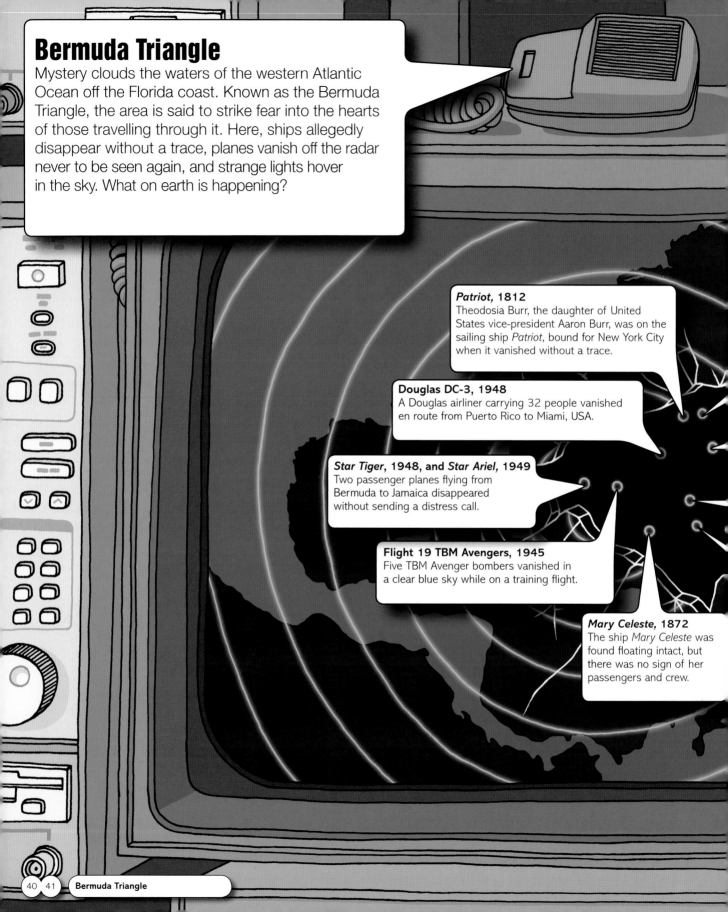

Bermuda Triangle

Mystery clouds the waters of the western Atlantic Ocean off the Florida coast. Known as the Bermuda Triangle, the area is said to strike fear into the hearts of those travelling through it. Here, ships allegedly disappear without a trace, planes vanish off the radar never to be seen again, and strange lights hover in the sky. What on earth is happening?

Patriot, 1812
Theodosia Burr, the daughter of United States vice-president Aaron Burr, was on the sailing ship *Patriot*, bound for New York City when it vanished without a trace.

Douglas DC-3, 1948
A Douglas airliner carrying 32 people vanished en route from Puerto Rico to Miami, USA.

Star Tiger, 1948, and Star Ariel, 1949
Two passenger planes flying from Bermuda to Jamaica disappeared without sending a distress call.

Flight 19 TBM Avengers, 1945
Five TBM Avenger bombers vanished in a clear blue sky while on a training flight.

Mary Celeste, 1872
The ship *Mary Celeste* was found floating intact, but there was no sign of her passengers and crew.

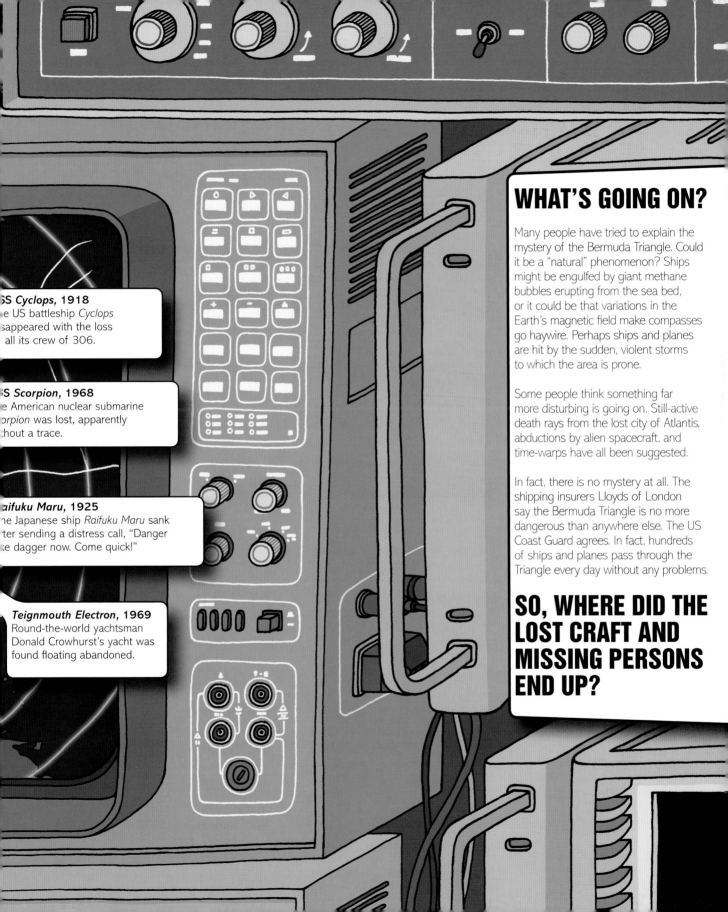

SS Cyclops, 1918
The US battleship *Cyclops* disappeared with the loss of all its crew of 306.

SS Scorpion, 1968
The American nuclear submarine *Scorpion* was lost, apparently without a trace.

Raifuku Maru, 1925
The Japanese ship *Raifuku Maru* sank after sending a distress call, "Danger like dagger now. Come quick!"

Teignmouth Electron, 1969
Round-the-world yachtsman Donald Crowhurst's yacht was found floating abandoned.

WHAT'S GOING ON?

Many people have tried to explain the mystery of the Bermuda Triangle. Could it be a "natural" phenomenon? Ships might be engulfed by giant methane bubbles erupting from the sea bed, or it could be that variations in the Earth's magnetic field make compasses go haywire. Perhaps ships and planes are hit by the sudden, violent storms to which the area is prone.

Some people think something far more disturbing is going on. Still-active death rays from the lost city of Atlantis, abductions by alien spacecraft, and time-warps have all been suggested.

In fact, there is no mystery at all. The shipping insurers Lloyds of London say the Bermuda Triangle is no more dangerous than anywhere else. The US Coast Guard agrees. In fact, hundreds of ships and planes pass through the Triangle every day without any problems.

SO, WHERE DID THE LOST CRAFT AND MISSING PERSONS END UP?

Flight 19 TBM Avenger
05.12.1945
Piecing together various of evidence reveals that group of aircraft got lost cloud and was blown by much further out over the Atlantic than they realize The probable explanation is that they ran out of fu

Teignmouth Electron
10.07.1969
Donald Crowhurst's logbooks, recovered from *Teignmouth Electron*, reveal that he was in a very disturbed state of mind. He falsified his position in the round-the-world yacht race, so he wasn't even in the Bermuda Triangle. He may have jumped overboard.

Raifuku Maru
21.04.1925
There was nothing mysterious about the disappearance of the *Raifuku Maru*. It was caught in a severe storm some distance outside the Bermuda Triangle. Another ship, *Homeric*, witnessed the *Raifuku Maru* sinking and made an unsuccessful rescue attempt.

Douglas DC 3
28.12.1948
Documents at the time show the aircraft's batteries were not fully charged before the flight, but the pilot insisted on taking off. However, there is no way of knowing if this had any effect on the plane, which was powered by gas engines.

Mary Celeste
05.12.1872
The *Mary Celeste* was actually found off the coast of Portugal, thousands of kilometres across the Atlantic, and not in the Bermuda Triangle at all. However, another ship, called the *Mari Celeste*, did sink near Bermuda in 1864 – hence the mix-up.

USS _Cyclops_
14.03.1918
Although there were no signs
of a battle, _Cyclops_ was lost
at the height of World War I –
so enemy action cannot be
ruled out. In 1975, there was
a sighting of the ship's wreck
on the ocean bed off Virginia,
USA, where a powerful storm
had occurred back in 1918.

Patriot
30.12.1812
Pirates were very active in the
area at this time, so _Patriot_ may
have come under attack. Or, the
ship may have been a casualty
of the war of 1812 between
the US and UK. No one knows
what happened to the vice-
president's daughter.

USS _Scorpion_
26.05.1968
The _Scorpion_ did not
disappear in the Bermuda
Triangle at all, but near the
Azores, far to the east. The
navy bathyscaphe _Trieste_
later took pictures of the
wreck. A court inquiry
concluded that the USS
Scorpion was destroyed
by one of her own
malfunctioning torpedoes.

Star Tiger and _Star Ariel_,
1948 and 1949 respectively
These were not the only Avro Tudor IV planes to
disappear. In 1947, _Star Dust_ also vanished – over
the Andes Mountains. The wreckage was found in
1998, and the evidence suggests the cause was
pilot error or instrument failure.

LOST PROPERTY OFFICE

➜ Want to know about other mysterious disappearances? Go to The mystery of the Mary Celeste on **pp.44–47** and Lord Lucan on **pp.142–143.**

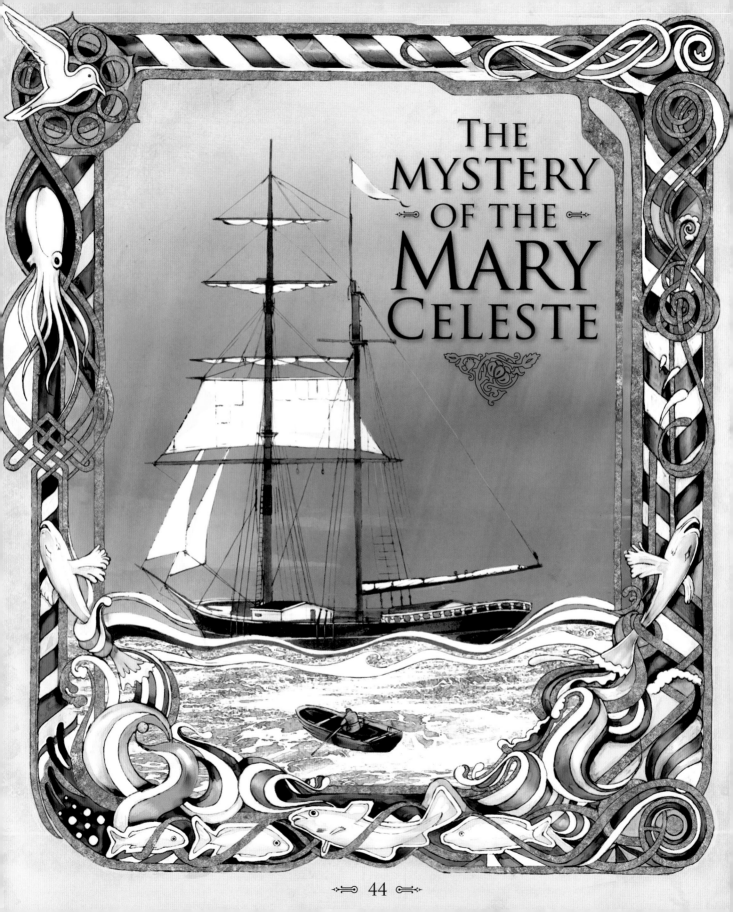

THE MYSTERY OF THE MARY CELESTE

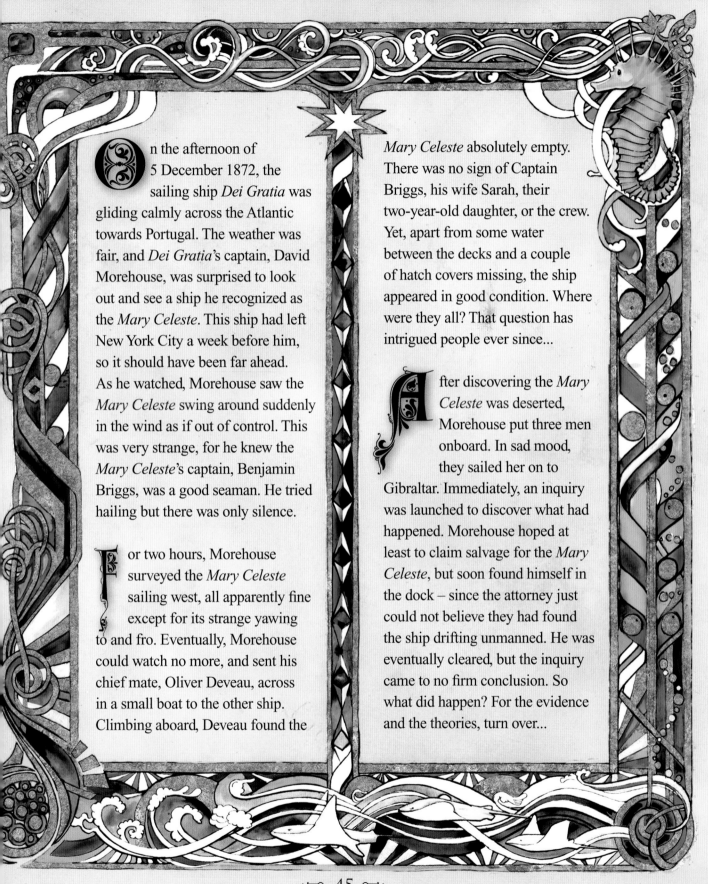

On the afternoon of 5 December 1872, the sailing ship *Dei Gratia* was gliding calmly across the Atlantic towards Portugal. The weather was fair, and *Dei Gratia*'s captain, David Morehouse, was surprised to look out and see a ship he recognized as the *Mary Celeste*. This ship had left New York City a week before him, so it should have been far ahead. As he watched, Morehouse saw the *Mary Celeste* swing around suddenly in the wind as if out of control. This was very strange, for he knew the *Mary Celeste*'s captain, Benjamin Briggs, was a good seaman. He tried hailing but there was only silence.

For two hours, Morehouse surveyed the *Mary Celeste* sailing west, all apparently fine except for its strange yawing to and fro. Eventually, Morehouse could watch no more, and sent his chief mate, Oliver Deveau, across in a small boat to the other ship. Climbing aboard, Deveau found the *Mary Celeste* absolutely empty. There was no sign of Captain Briggs, his wife Sarah, their two-year-old daughter, or the crew. Yet, apart from some water between the decks and a couple of hatch covers missing, the ship appeared in good condition. Where were they all? That question has intrigued people ever since...

After discovering the *Mary Celeste* was deserted, Morehouse put three men onboard. In sad mood, they sailed her on to Gibraltar. Immediately, an inquiry was launched to discover what had happened. Morehouse hoped at least to claim salvage for the *Mary Celeste*, but soon found himself in the dock – since the attorney just could not believe they had found the ship drifting unmanned. He was eventually cleared, but the inquiry came to no firm conclusion. So what did happen? For the evidence and the theories, turn over...

The Mystery of the Mary Celeste

The evidence

❈ Two hatches were open.

❈ The ship's clock was upside down and had stopped.

❈ The sextant (instrument for celestial navigation) and chronometer (shipping timepiece) were missing.

❈ The Captain's bed was sodden and there was water between the decks.

❈ Under the bed was the Captain's sword, with red stains.

❈ The lifeboat was missing, leaving a frayed rope.

❈ The cargo of 1,700 barrels of pure alcohol was intact, except for nine empty barrels.

❈ On board, there was food to last six months.

❈ The last entry in the ship's log was about a week old.

The theories

Mutiny!

Theory: The crew became angry with Briggs' leadership and murdered him and his family, then escaped in the lifeboat.
Evidence: The red-stained sword, the missing lifeboat, and the deserted ship.
Problems: Briggs was renowned for being a good and fair captain. The stain on the sword turned out to be rust and not blood. Even if there was a mutiny, this does not explain why the crew would jump into a lifeboat in the middle of the Atlantic Ocean.

Drunken sailors

Theory: The crew murdered the captain and his family to get at the alcohol in the cargo, then escaped in the lifeboat.
Evidence: The stained sword and the nine empty barrels, which had contained alcohol.
Problems: The cargo of alcohol was undrinkable and, like the captain, the crew had an admirable reputation. As we know, the stain on the sword was rust, and the crew would have faced great danger on a small lifeboat in the turbulent Atlantic.

Rogue wave

Theory: The entire crew were swept overboard by a giant wave.
Evidence: The water between the decks.
Problems: It seems highly unlikely that a single wave would have caught everyone. Even if it had, you would expect a lot more items to be missing than just the sextant and the compass.

Sinking

Theory: The crew thought the ship was sinking, so took to the lifeboat to escape. This was the theory decided by the court hearing at the time.
Evidence: Water in the hold.
Problems: The ship's pump was working well enough for the sailors from the *Dei Gratia* to pump out the water and take the *Mary Celeste* safelyback to port.

Insurance scam

Theory: Briggs and Morehouse conspired in a scam to get the insurance money.
Evidence: None.
Problems: The ship and its cargo would have to be lost for there to be an insurance claim. Instead, everybody on board was missing but the cargo remained largely intact. So who was supposed to claim the insurance, and for what?

Poisoning

Theory: They got ergot (a fungus) poisoning from the rye bread they were eating. This turned them mad and they left in the lifeboat.
Evidence: The bread on the *Mary Celeste* was rye, and is poisonous if made from ergot-infected grain.
Problems: All the bread found by the *Dei Gratia* crew was fine. Even if they did go mad, why would they want to flee together in the lifeboat?

The Bermuda Triangle

Theory: The crew were abducted by aliens in the Bermuda Triangle.
Evidence: None.
Problems: The ship was sighted near Portugal and so was nowhere near the Bermuda Triangle.

Explosion

Theory: Alcohol leaking from some of the barrels exploded, frightening Briggs and his crew into abandoning the ship temporarily. The lifeboat then separated from the *Mary Celeste* during a heavy storm.
Evidence: The nine barrels may have exploded, blowing off the hatch covers. The missing sextant and chronometer would have been helpful in the lifeboat. The frayed rope that trailed the *Mary Celeste* could have been used to tie the lifeboat to the ship. The water on board could be evidence of bad weather. Recent scientific tests have shown that alcohol can explode without a fire.
Problems: There was little evidence of an explosion anywhere on the ship.

You've seen the evidence and you've read the theories, so what do you think happened on board the mysterious *Mary Celeste*?

For more mysteries at sea, see Who crossed the Atlantic first? on **pp.30–31**, Bermuda Triangle on **pp.40–41**, and Atlantis on **pp.212–213**.

WHO ARE THE MEN IN BLACK?

An alien encounter is a freaky experience, but what happens after can be just as unsettling. Some witnesses describe visits from shadowy characters dressed in sharp black suits, who demand they zip their lips.

Target 1

One night in 1953, Albert Bender, a leading researcher in flying saucers and other UFOs (unidentified flying objects), was visited by three men wearing dark suits. They scared him so much he gave up all his work on UFOs.

Join the Men in Black
Your mission is to keep the lid on alien sightings. Whenever someone claims to have seen an alien or a UFO, you must move in swiftly to keep them quiet. The truth must not get out! **First choose your character and select your super-slick vehicle.**

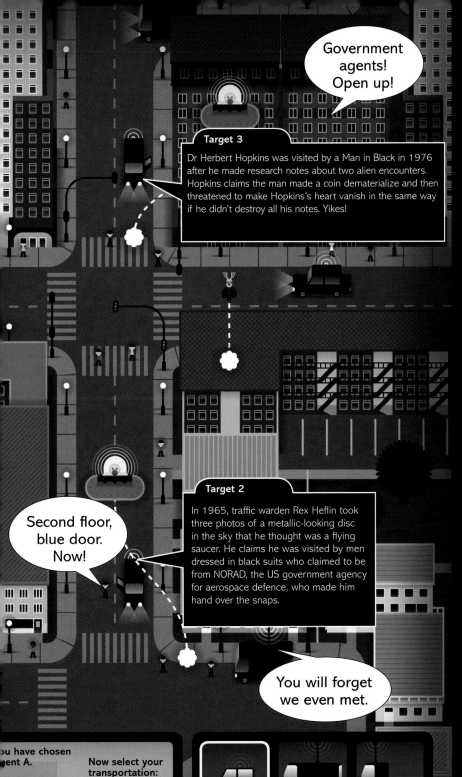

THE THEORIES

Aliens in disguise?
Some people say the Men in Black are aliens who disguise themselves as human beings. The makeover isn't always that convincing. Herbert Hopkins described the Man in Black who visited him as having very pale skin, lacking eyelashes and eyebrows, and wearing bright red lipstick!

Government agents?
A popular theory is that the Men in Black are really government agents. The reason they target alien watchers is uncertain. Does the US government want to keep people in the dark about aliens? Or are they simply concerned that the public will discover military secrets?

All in your head?
The Men in Black could just be figments of people's imaginations, created when in a dreamy state of mind, or when under extreme stress. It could be that the alien witnesses are undergoing some sort of mental upheaval at the time of the encounter and are more prone to fantasy.

Fictional fakes
The idea of Men in Black may be an elaborate hoax by an American UFO researcher. Gray Barker published books about alien encounters and often included stories about Men in Black. However, one of his colleagues claims that Barker often presented fictional tales as factual accounts. Did he make up the Men in Black tales?

Mothman
In 1966 and 1967, several people in West Virginia, USA, claimed they saw a strange creature the size of a man with eyes in its chest and moth wings. Since mysterious men dressed in black had also been seen in the area, some people speculated that they were linked.

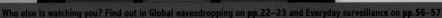

Who else is watching you? Find out in Global eavesdropping on pp.22–23 and Everyday surveillance on pp.56–57.

TIME TRAVEL

Could we ever travel through time? Is it possible to go back to Roman times and watch a chariot race, or drop in on the prehistoric era and come face to face with a dinosaur? How about zooming forwards in time to see what wonders the future holds? People have always travelled through time in their imaginations, but, in 1895, H G Wells wrote a story called *The Time Machine* about an amazing vehicle that could physically carry people through time. Could such machines ever become a reality? Time to find out...

IS TIME TRAVEL POSSIBLE?

If humans were to invent a time machine in the future, why have they never travelled back in time to visit us? As far as we know, there are no records...

The most famous argument against time travel asks what would happen if you travelled back in time and killed your grandparents before your parents were born. Then you could not have been born. So, either way, it would not be possible for you to kill your grandparents – a relief to grandparents everywhere.

Some scientists have come up with an ingenious solution to this paradox. They say that, if you did go back in time, it would be impossible to change anything that would affect things in the time you have come from. So, maybe the gun jams, or the shot misses. They call this idea "self-consistency".

Another answer to the grandparent paradox can be found in quantum physics (the study of subatomic particles). Simply put, it says that a new world opens up for every possible choice. So, if you did choose to kill your grandparents, then you would find yourself living in a parallel world to your own. But in a next-door world, granny and grandad are alive and well. Phew!

Physicist Albert Einstein was a great thinker about space and time. His famous "theory of relativity" shows that time is not fixed. For example, if you were to travel into space at a speed close to the speed of light, and then return to Earth, people on Earth would have aged more than you have. Einstein demonstated this with some very clever maths, but his maths also showed it was impossible to travel faster than the speed of light. Einstein believed that you needed to travel faster than light to travel through time. So, a no-go.

TOP TIPS FOR BREAKING THE TIME BARRIER

Even though Einstein thought time travel was impossible, other scientists have used his ideas to theorize how it might be done. Amazingly, they have discovered that there is nothing in the laws of physics to forbid it. Here are two of the time-travel options.

BLACK HOLES, WHITE HOLES, AND WORMHOLES

Time travel could be achieved using black holes – areas in space where gravity is so powerful that they suck in everything, including light. Black holes could provide the entrance to wormholes – shortcuts through space and time. Wormholes can tunnel through space and time like a worm through an apple, and emerge at the other end through reverse black holes, called white holes. There are a lot of holes in this theory.

ROLLING UP TIME

US astronomer Frank Tipler believes it is possible to build a time machine with a piece of incredibly dense material – say ten times as dense as the Sun. Simply roll it into a cylinder shape a few billion kilometres long, then set it spinning. Once it's spinning fast enough, space and time will bend around it. A spaceship sent on a precisely plotted spiral course around it should emerge almost instantly in a different galaxy and time. So, make sure you are up to date with your travel jabs.

Of course, there are no materials available today that could withstand the massive forces encountered on these "trips". But scientists are working on that.

So, watch this space...

➜ For a look at what else is happening in the skies, see Air Force One on **pp.10–11** and Watchers in space on **pp.24–25**.

Piri Reis map

In 1929, as builders worked on the crumbling Topkapi Palace in Istanbul, Turkey, one of them spotted something poking out of the rubble. It turned out to be an ancient map drawn on gazelle skin showing the Atlantic Ocean and the lands around. The map was drawn in 1513 by Piri Reis, an admiral in the Turkish navy. As scholars studied it, some began to wonder if it was much, much more than just a very old map. Could it be hiding an astounding story about ancient civilizations?

Amazing claim 1
According to fans of the map, it is so accurate that it could only have been made with knowledge centuries ahead of its time. Claimants say that although it doesn't look like a standard map, it matches astonishingly well with a kind of modern map called an azimuthal projection, which offers a similar view to that from a space satellite. So, they claim, Piri Reis could have borrowed from maps drawn by ancient space travellers.

Amazing claim 2
The second claim is that the map shows the coast of Antarctica accurately. This is amazing not just because no-one had explored it at that time, but because the land was under thick ice – as it is today and has been for the last 6,000 years! So, the belief is that some remarkable explorers from an advanced ancient civilization could have got to Antarctica even before the ice froze.

What does it show?
Piri Reis's map shows the Atlantic Ocean, with the coast of the Americas on the left and the coasts of Europe and Africa on the right. In South America, Piri Reis identifies the Orinoco River and the Rio de la Plata. Across the bottom is the coastline of a land some identify as Antarctica.

Was it really accurate ahead of its time?
The map was certainly bang up-to-date, and Piri Reis even acknowledges his debt to Columbus, who made his voyage across the Atlantic just 20 years earlier. However, the coastline of South America is accurate only as far south as the Rio de la Plata, which the explorer Amerigo Vespucci had sailed along just 10 years before. Elsewhere the map is very fuzzy...

Did he really draw Antarctica under the ice?
Any resemblance between the outline on Piri Reis's map and the coastline of Antarctica under the ice is pure chance. He didn't even know Antarctica existed. Piri Reis probably just drew where he guessed the coastline of South America might continue past the bit he knew.

North America
Piri Reis says this country is inhabited, but the natives go naked.

Spain

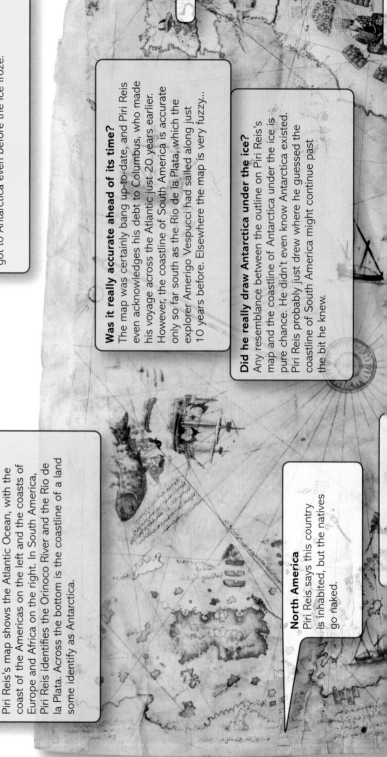

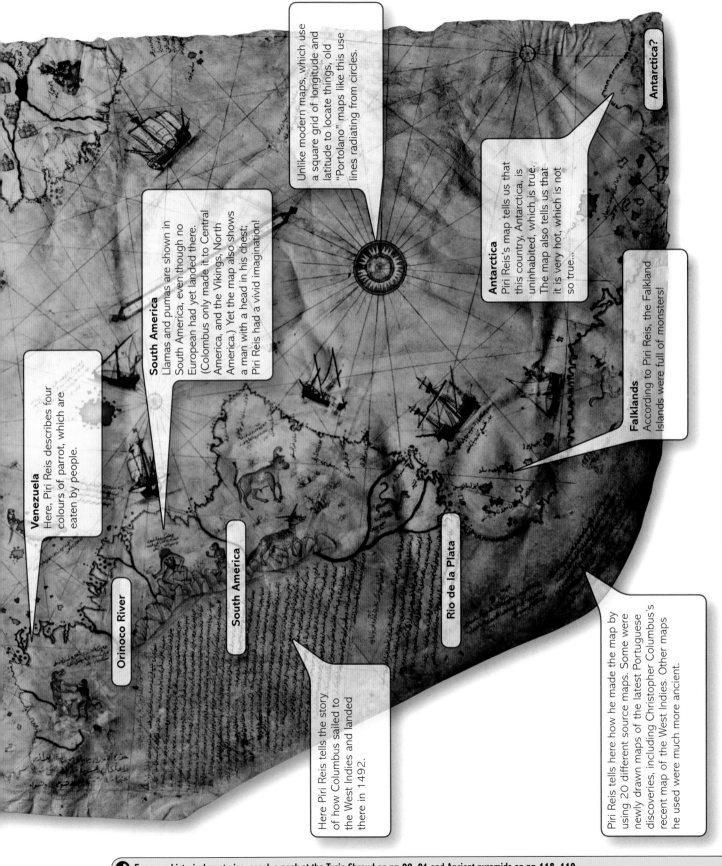

Venezuela
Here, Piri Reis describes four colours of parrot, which are eaten by people.

South America
Llamas and pumas are shown in South America, even though no European had yet landed there. (Colombus only made it to Central America, and the Vikings, North America.) Yet the map also shows a man with a head in his chest; Piri Reis had a vivid imagination!

Unlike modern maps, which use a square grid of longitude and latitude to locate things, old "Portolano" maps like this use lines radiating from circles.

Antarctica
Piri Reis's map tells us that this country, Antarctica, is uninhabited, which is true. The map also tells us that it is very hot, which is not so true...

Falklands
According to Piri Reis, the Falkland Islands were full of monsters!

Antarctica?

Orinoco River

South America

Rio de la Plata

Here Piri Reis tells the story of how Columbus sailed to the West Indies and landed there in 1492.

Piri Reis tells here how he made the map by using 20 different source maps. Some were newly drawn maps of the latest Portuguese discoveries, including Christopher Columbus's recent map of the West Indies. Other maps he used were much more ancient.

For more historical mysteries, sneak a peak at the Turin Shroud on **pp.90–91** and Ancient pyramids on **pp.118–119**.

Create your own state

Have you ever wanted to see your own head on a coin, or fancied yourself as a world leader? Have you ever wondered what life would be like without this law or that rule, or had a notion to make up your own? If so, then hesitate not and set up your very own nation.

Micronations

Can you really set up a brand new country? In theory, yes! However, a new nation, no matter if it is lawfully created, is unlikely to be recognized by other established nations, so don't expect to be on the prime minister's christmas card list, nor expect any invites to important diplomatic events. Most new countries that are set up are referred to as "micronations". One such micronation is the Principality of Sealand, which was founded in 1967 on an artificial island in the North Sea. It has its own currency, citizens have Principality of Sealand passports, and there is an absolute monarch who rules the island.

So how is it done?

First of all, you need to think of a name for your new nation. The following are ideas of how you might rule your nation along with some pointers for legitimizing it in the eyes of the world community.

Choose a location

With a shortage of unclaimed land space, an artificial floating city could be your best bet, or perhaps yours could be the first self-supporting micronation on the Moon. Of course, you could always simply exist just on the Internet, as a virtual nation.

Appoint a leader

What would you prefer? A presidential-style government, or an absolute monarch? Would you appoint yourself as leader, or somebody else? Either way, a good leader should have such qualities as charisma, noble values, and a sense of responsibility.

Design a flag

Flags are the accepted representations of a person or nation, and have been employed throughout history as such. Each element of a flag symbolizes part of its country's history or make-up.

Impose a set of laws

It is important to have laws to maintain order in the world. Most countries constantly review their laws to ensure the preservation of fairness and equality for all. You might want to have some sort of police force to enforce your laws.

Create a currency

Money makes the world go round, so why not have your own coins and notes made? You could include a bust of Your (highness) self on the coins, and perhaps other people, or items, that have inspired your new nation on the notes.

Decide on a language

Either choose a language from the array of already exisiting ones, or make up your own! It is worth noting that Chinese and English are the most widely spoken languages, and so would help your nation in communicating with others.

Compose a national anthem

A national anthem is a way for citizens to display their sense of belonging to their nation. Most national anthems are a mixture of words and music in order to effectively evoke the history and traditions of the nation's people.

Enrol some citizens

With your nation set up and ready to roll, it's time to request allegiance from people who you are happy to grant the honour of citizenship. Ensure you choose your citizens carefully, though, as you don't want any traitors!

→ For more fascinating facts on notable nations, go to Flag it up on pp.18–19 and Law tour on pp.206–207.

Everyday surveillance

You may think what you do is your own business, but you're mistaken. From a trip to the shops to logging on to a computer, there are people watching your every move... Say cheese!

Caught on camera
Closed-circuit televisions (CCTVs) are positioned in almost every public place to survey people's movements. In the UK, for example, there are five million CCTVs, and the average Londoner is filmed 300 times a day. Many are high-quality cameras that can zoom in to film you in detail, so stop picking your nose!

Mobile giveaway
Your mobile phone gives away more personal information than you might think. Mobile phone companies are obliged to provide security services with details of who you called, the time and duration of the call, and even where you called from. The latest phones have technology that allows your exact location to be pinpointed at any time.

Web watch

When anyone makes an online purchase, the seller keeps a record. By tracking the products you buy, sellers can build personal profiles and target you with offers. Security services access purchasing information to build profiles of people they are suspicious of. They also want the right to access everyone's web searches.

Car spotting

Speed cameras can automatically record a vehicle's registration details and link up to national computers to reveal if the vehicle is stolen. In future, all cars are likely to be tracked everywhere they go, using a satellite link-up called Global Positioning Systems (GPS). This information can help track suspects and ensure driving tolls are paid in certain areas.

On the cards

When a person makes a purchase with an electronic card, such as a debit or credit card, their bank knows what has been bought. Every time money is withdrawn from a cash dispenser, details are recorded, so there is a trail of where the person has been and how much they have spent. Police find this helpful when tracking criminals or missing people.

 For more undercover investigations, sneak a peak at Secret services on pp.64–65 and Private eye on pp.106–107.

BAR CODES

When you go to pay for something in a shop, the assistant scans the bar code. As the laser scans the black and white stripes, it picks up a pattern. Instantly, the shop's computer knows what you're buying and tells the till how much you've got to pay. So what's the bar code saying?

Reading bar codes

Along the bottom of a bar code are numbers that you can read. The stripes give the same numbers in a form that only a computer can read. There are many different types of bar code that all work slightly differently, but they all use this basic convention.

The code for 8 starts with a space 1 unit wide...

...next is a bar 2 units wide...

...followed by a space 1 unit wide...

...and it ends with a bar 3 units wide.

8002

The two bars and a space at the beginning tell the computer that the code has begun.

The first part of the code indicates the country and/or manufacturer the product has come from.

The two bars and three spaces in the middle separate the two halves of the bar code.

What the stripes mean

The stripes are a code that represents numbers in the form of bars and spaces. Each number is shown by a set of two bars and two spaces. The bars and spaces can be one, two, three, or four units wide. The number the scanner reads depends on the combination of different widths in each set of four bars and spaces.

How the numbers add up

Below are the numbers 0 to 9 in their bar code form. For each number there are two versions – the first one is used in the first half of the bar code and the second version is used in the second half. The second version is the same as the first, but substitutes bars for spaces, and vice versa. Representing the numbers in the two halves in a different way like this means that the bar code can be scanned in any direction and the computer can still figure out which bit of information is which.

Pattern as it would be in the first half of the bar code

Pattern as it would be in the second half of the bar code

0	3-2-1-1	5	1-2-3-1
1	2-2-2-1	6	1-1-1-4
2	2-1-2-2	7	1-3-1-2
3	1-4-1-1	8	1-2-1-3
4	1-1-3-2	9	3-1-1-2

The second part of the code identifies exactly what the product is.

The last number is a "checksum" – a digit worked out using the seven previous numbers.

The last two bars and one space tell the computer that the code has finished.

For more code-cracking, go to Secret writing on **pp.110–111** and Enigma Code on **pp.132–133**.

HACKERS

Computers connected via the Internet are vulnerable to hackers, who can use cunning tricks to gain access to them… or even take them over.

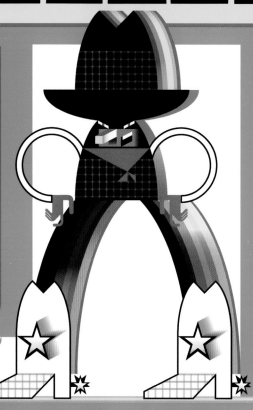

FAMOUS HACKERS

■ In 1992, Argentinian student Julio Ardita hacked into the computer systems of Harvard University and the US Naval command. He was finally caught by police in 1997.

■ Young British hackers Richard Pryce and Matthew Bevan (nicknamed Datastream Cowboy and Kuji) broke into US military computers in 1994.

■ In 2002, Gary McKinnon (known as Solo) hacked into NASA and US military computers from a room in London, UK. He claimed to have been looking for evidence of UFOs.

▲ PASSWORD CRACKING

People help hackers by using obvious passwords, like their names or birthdays. Serious hackers use password-cracker software that runs through all the possible combinations of numbers and letters until it finds the right one.

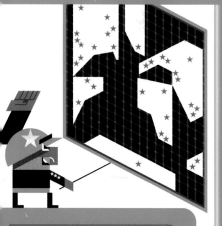

▲ GETTING A NUMBER

"War dialer" programs identify the phone numbers organizations use to connect to the Internet. By finding these, hackers can bypass security systems.

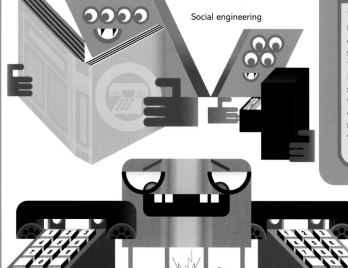

Social engineering

Phreaking

Phishing

▼ TRICKS AND TACTICS

Using data from phone books or company files to access someone's computer is called "social engineering". "Phreaking" involves hacking into telephone systems to get free calls. Another tactic is "phishing" – sending emails pretending to be from a recognized organization so the victim emails back their details.

▼ GETTING INSIDE YOUR COMPUTER

Serious hackers don't just want to eavesdrop on your computer's links to the outside world, they want to get inside your computer and take it over. These are some of the tools they use:

① A Trojan Horse is a file that looks harmless until opened, but once open it installs a rogue program that takes control of the computer.

② Keylogging is a method of linking up to someone else's computer and monitoring every key that is pressed – useful for gaining passwords or other security information.

③ Backdoor programs allow hackers to access your computer without a password.

④ Programs designed to scan for weaknesses in a computer's "firewall" (protection) systems are called vulnerability scanners.

⑤ Sniffers monitor information travelling to and from a computer system, in order to capture all the passwords and user IDs of anyone using it.

⑥ Computer worms infect networks by sending copies of themselves to all the machines in the system. Unlike viruses, they don't have to attach themselves to a program – this makes them harder to stop.

⑦ A virus is a computer program that infects a host program and alters the way it works.

▲ HIDDEN IDENTITY

Hackers can use "IP spoofing" software to conceal their true identity online. Information is sent over the Internet in packets of data. Each packet contains information about the computer it has come from, but IP spoofers change this information so that it seems as if the packet has come from somewhere else. Hackers use this software to get through security systems, or when they want to attack a network by flooding it with data.

① Trojan Horse
② Keylogging
③ Backdoor
④ Vulnerability scanner
⑤ Sniffers
⑥ Computer worm
⑦ Virus

⊙ To find out about other types of technological trickery, go to Everyday surveillance on pp.56–57 and Iris recognition on pp.62–63.

In the future, we may all be identified by our eyes.

The pattern of marks in the iris of our eyes is as unique as a fingerprint.

The iris in one eye has a different pattern to the iris in the other eye. Each iris is truly original!

Your iris stays the same all through your life.

Iris recognition systems use small cameras to take an instant photograph of your eye.

Iris photographs can be translated into a digital form called a biometric code.

A computer scans its memory to find a match for the biometric code.

IRIS RECOGNITION

Iris recognition could be used for cash machines and credit cards instead of using a private Personal Identification Number (PIN).

Iris recognition will soon be used to check people in at the airport, instead of a passport.

Iris recognition can work through glasses and contact lenses.

Your computer could be personalized to work only with your iris pattern.

Identification by iris recognition can take just seconds.

Blink, and you'll miss it.

Want to know more body secrets? Take a look at Human genome on pp.152–153 and Unconscious mind on pp.180–181.

Secret services

Whatever agency they belong to and wherever in the world they go to sneak and snoop, the modern spy can choose from a wealth of gadgets and gizmos to make sure they get that mission accomplished.

Binoculars

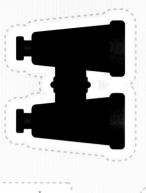

Handgun

Earpiece

Camera pen

Night vision goggles

Button camera

The spy files

CIA

The Central Intelligence Agency (CIA) is the secret service for the United States. Its spies gather information about governments, corporations, and terrorist groups in other countries. Some CIA agents go undercover to infiltrate the target organizations abroad.

FSB

Formed from the KGB (the intelligence agency and secret police of the communist Soviet Union from 1954 to 1991), the **Federalnaya Sluzhba Bezopasnosti (FSB – "Russian Federal Security Service")** employs more than half a million agents. The agency targets criminals, drug smugglers, and terrorists, although critics claim it targets anybody who disagrees with the Russian government.

DGSE

La Direction Générale de la Sécurité Extérieure (General Directorate of External Security) is France's secret service. The DGSE's most secret branch is the Action Division. Apart from undercover operations abroad, the Action Division looks after the security of France's nuclear installations. In 1985, it notoriously sank the Greenpeace ship *Rainbow Warrior* to stop the charity protesting against France's nuclear tests in the Pacific.

SIS

In the UK, the **SIS (Secret Intelligence Service)** – also known as MI6 – sends out secret agents to track down terrorists,

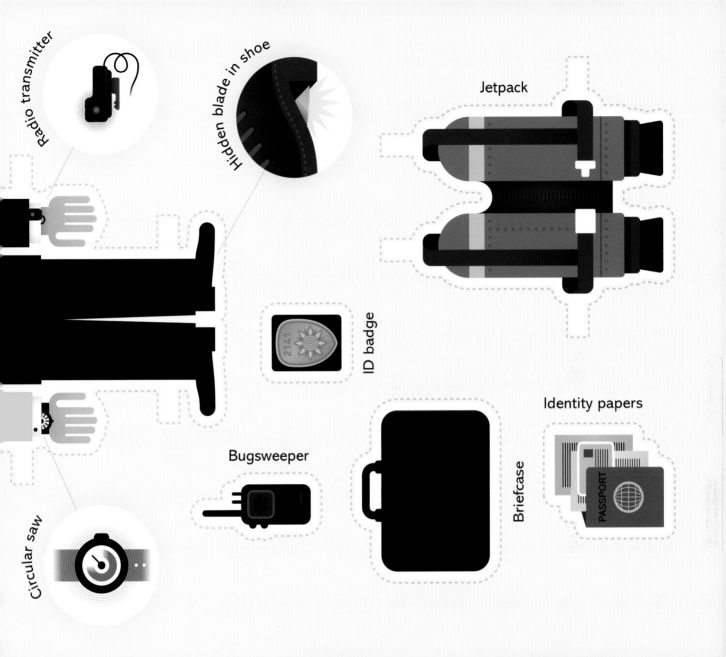

Radio transmitter

Hidden blade in shoe

Jetpack

Circular saw

ID badge

Bugsweeper

Briefcase

Identity papers

PASSPORT

2141

major international crime rings. James Bond is a fictional agent for MI6.

Mossad

Mossad is the Hebrew word for **"The Institute"** (short for The Institute of Intelligence and Special Operations) and is Israel's secret service. Mossad's most secret division is that of Special Operations, or Metsada, which seeks out and neutralizes enemies of Israel, as well as conducting raids on terrorist bases.

MOIS

Iran's secret service is **MOIS (The Ministry of Intelligence and Security)**. Its main task is to track and gather information about any opponents of Iran's government at home and abroad. Iran is an Islamic country and by law the head of MOIS must be a religious cleric who reports directly to the country's supreme religious leader, Ayatollah Ali Khamenei.

ASIS

ASIS, the **Australian Secret Intelligence Service**, protects Australia's interests by gathering intelligence in foreign countries. A news report broadcast in the 1990s, claimed the ASIS gathered intelligence on Australians, too, but the government denied it. The ASIS often works with the CIA and SIS.

To uncover more spy secrets, go to Leaks and moles on **pp.14–15**, Global eavesdropping on **pp.22–23**, and Private eye on **pp.106–107**.

КРЕМЛЬ

The Moscow Kremlin is the formidable fort that has been at the heart of Russian power for five centuries. From inside its towering red walls, tsars, such as Ivan the Terrible, and communist leaders, such as Stalin, ruled over their vast empires. Even today, it is the home of the Russian president and a powerful symbol of Russian power.

Arsenal

Nuclear suitcases
The State Kremlin Palace was built in 1961 by the Soviet government after some historic buildings were demolished to clear a space. Amazingly, half the building – at least five storeys – is underground! Inside the concrete and glass State Kremlin Palace is one of three nuclear suitcases containing the controls for responding to a nuclear attack.

State Kremlin Palace

What a blast!
The Tsar Cannon is a real monster at 5 m (16 ft) long. It dates back to 1586 and can take cannon balls as big as barrels, but it has never actually been fired.

Gem gallery
Housing a collection of gems from the reign of Emperor Peter I of Russia, and all succeeding monarchs, the Diamond Treasury is a true treasure trove. Among its delights is the infamous Orlov Diamond. One legend that accompanies this 190-carat rock claims that it was stolen from the eye of a statue of a Hindu god in southern India by a French soldier.

Cathedral of the Dormition

Deposition of the Virgin's Robe

Palace of Facets

Biggest bell
At 6 m (20 ft) tall with a diameter of 6.5 m (21 ft), the Tsar Bell is the largest ever made. It has never been rung due to a crack down its side that occurred during casting.

Grand Kremlin Palace

The Armoury
This is home to the most fabulous silver collection in the world!

Robe remnants
One of the churches in Cathedral Square is called "Deposition of the Virgin's Robe". This rather strange name does not refer to a stain on the Virgin Mary's clothing, but is, in fact, a reference to a religious relic that many Christians believe was a remnant of her robe.

Private line
A secret extension of the Moscow Metro links the Kremlin to the Moscow underground. It was built by Stalin – presumably so that Kremlin officials didn't get caught in rush-hour traffic!

Murder most foul?
The Palace of Facets is so named because of the weird ridges on its walls. It is where the cruel tsar, Ivan the Terrible, died while playing chess in 1584. When his tomb was opened in the 1960s, his remains were found to contain a lot of mercury, which means he was probably poisoned.

Blind faith
According to legend, somewhere in the underground labyrinths of the Kremlin lies the medieval library of Ivan the Terrible, said to contain a priceless collection of ancient manuscripts. Even Stalin's finest spies couldn't locate the goods. In 1997, 87-year-old Apalos Ivanov claimed to know where it was. People believed him because the legend states that anyone finding it goes blind, and Ivanov was blind. The library is still in a blind spot though.

➔ **Want to know more about centres of power?** Go to Air Force One on pp.10–11, Cheyenne Mountain on pp.20–21, and Forbidden City on pp.204–205.

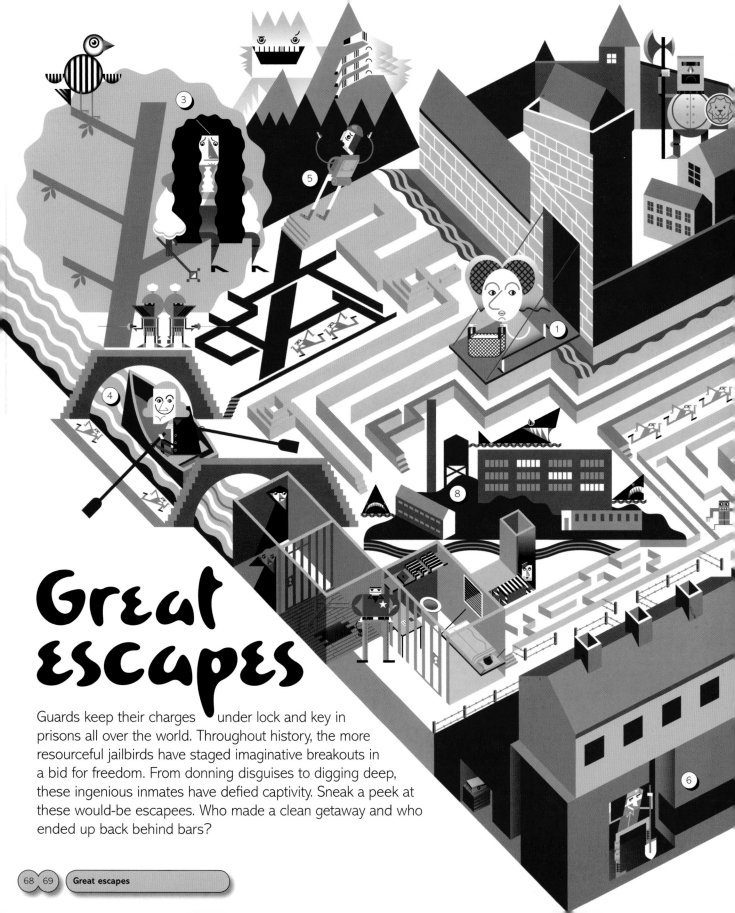

Great
ESCAPES

Guards keep their charges under lock and key in prisons all over the world. Throughout history, the more resourceful jailbirds have staged imaginative breakouts in a bid for freedom. From donning disguises to digging deep, these ingenious inmates have defied captivity. Sneak a peek at these would-be escapees. Who made a clean getaway and who ended up back behind bars?

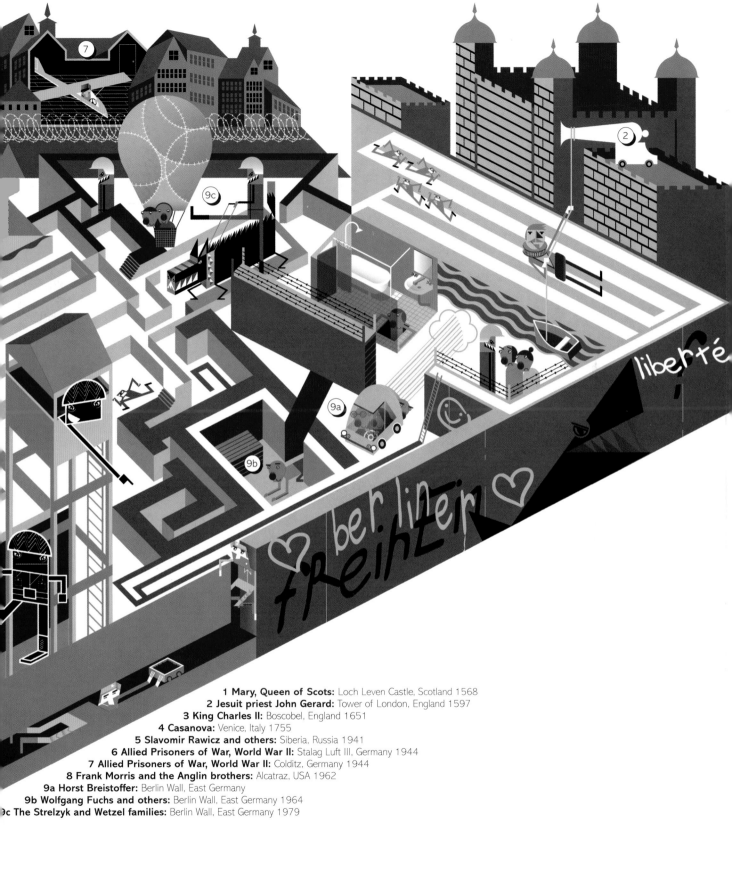

1 **Mary, Queen of Scots:** Loch Leven Castle, Scotland 1568
2 **Jesuit priest John Gerard:** Tower of London, England 1597
3 **King Charles II:** Boscobel, England 1651
4 **Casanova:** Venice, Italy 1755
5 **Slavomir Rawicz and others:** Siberia, Russia 1941
6 **Allied Prisoners of War, World War II:** Stalag Luft III, Germany 1944
7 **Allied Prisoners of War, World War II:** Colditz, Germany 1944
8 **Frank Morris and the Anglin brothers:** Alcatraz, USA 1962
9a **Horst Breistoffer:** Berlin Wall, East Germany
9b **Wolfgang Fuchs and others:** Berlin Wall, East Germany 1964
9c **The Strelzyk and Wetzel families:** Berlin Wall, East Germany 1979

who got away?

1568

Mary, Queen of Scots

In 1567, young Mary, Queen of Scots, was imprisoned by rebel Scottish earls in a castle on an island in the middle of the bleak Loch Leven. Determined to escape, Mary enlisted the help of the castle owner's brother, George Douglas, and his young orphaned cousin, Willy. First, she had to get out of the castle. Attempting to leap the wall would be too dangerous, but could a disguise work? On 2 May 1568, Willy stole the castle keys and let Mary slip out of the side gate dressed as a common country woman. But they still had to cross the water. As Mary hid in the bottom of a boat, Willy rowed to the loch's shore, where George met them with a fast horse, stolen from his brother's stables. Mary and wily little Willy rode off into the night.

1597

John Gerard

For nearly nine centuries, the terrifying Tower of London was the forbidding prison where political prisoners in England were sent. One of the few who escaped was the resourceful Catholic priest and spy John Gerard. Corresponding with helpers outside through letters written in diluted orange juice – which acts as invisible ink – John Gerard hatched a convincing and daring escape plan. On the night of 4 October 1597, he and another prisoner, John Arden, broke out of their cells and made for the Tower walls. They threw a thin thread across the moat to their accomplices, who attached a rope, which the two prisoners hauled back and tied to a cannon. Gerard was weak from torture, but managed to inch his way along the rope with Arden and made it to the riverside, where a boat took the two men to freedom.

1651

King Charles II

As a 21-year-old king, Charles II was defeated in Worcester, England, by the rebel Oliver Cromwell's Commonwealth Army in 1651. With only a few supporters remaining, his plight was desperate, and his only hope – escape to France – seemed impossible, as Cromwell's troops were scouring the countryside. Disguised as a woodsman, Charles made it to Boscobel House in Shropshire, the day after the battle, where he hid in an oak tree (later called the Royal Oak) while the troops searched the house and surrounding fields. That night, Charles hid in one of the house's secret priest holes and in the morning, disguised himself as a lady's servant. He made it to the coast and escaped across the English Channel to France. You go, girl... or guy.

1755

Casanova

Famous for his affairs with women, Giacomo Casanova was imprisoned for allegedly practising witchcraft in 1755. He was sent to the notorious Leads prison in Venice, from which no one had escaped for centuries. Nevertheless Casanova was determined to get out. Using a piece of iron he found in the prison yard, Casanova dug a tunnel beneath the floor of his cell. But, to his frustration, he was moved to another cell before the tunnel was complete. His sturdy piece of iron still with him, Casanova managed to persuade prisoner Balbi, in the end cell next to his, to dig two tunnels: one linking their cells, and another through to the outside. Both prisoners made their getaway, using the iron bar one last time to break through a set of gates on their way to freedom. Ciao.

Houdini believed the milk churn escape to be his best, as the trick heavily relied on his presentation. After being handcuffed and locked in a water-filled churn, which was then placed in a cabinet, Houdini would emerge minutes later dripping and breathless. The audience didn't know that the rivets around the neck of the churn were fakes, which allowed Houdini to simply lift the lid.

ESCAPOLOGY

THE MYSTERIOUS ART OF BREAKING FREE

An escape artist's job is to get out of seemingly impossible situations. Being manacled with handcuffs, belted into straightjackets, and padlocked into trunks are all everyday acts for the escapologist. Some escapes are simply tricks, but others are tremendous feats of flexibility, strength, and daring. Showcasing these feats with elements of danger and surprise excites and thrills any audience.

HOUDINI
HARRY

Master of escape

Few performers have captured the public imagination quite like Harry Houdini. He was not just a brilliant escape artist, he was also a terrific showman who knew how to make all of his acts spectacular and exciting to watch. He thrilled his audiences time and again with daring escape acts, leaving them gasping with relief and exhilarated.

Many of his acts were mere illusion and trickery, some of which he revealed in books and articles. But others were astonishing physical achievements, accomplishable only by someone like Houdini who had trained his body and was much stronger than his small frame suggested.

Houdini's real name was Ehrich Weiss, and he was born in Budapest, Hungary, in 1874. When he was four years old, his parents moved to the United States. Like many immigrants, growing up in a strange land gave him a burning determination to succeed.

Houdini began performing magic tricks in circuses at the age of 17, and his break came eight years later, in 1899, when theatre manager Martin Beck invited him to perform an entire act of escapology in his music hall theatres. Within a year Houdini had astounded the USA with his fantastical feats and the following year he conquered Europe. Constantly creating new acts, such as breaking out from a water-filled milk churn and escaping unscathed from hanging bags suspended high in the air, Houdini's feats soon became legendary across the globe.

Devastation struck though in 1926 when a young man thumped Houdini in the stomach on-stage. Houdini often invited his audience members to test his strength in this way, but this time it injured his appendix. Houdini would only consent to be operated upon once he had completed his tour – but by then the infection had gone too far. The great Houdini died of appendicitis on 31 October 1926.

The most marvellous feat ever attempted in this or any other age.

DO NOT TRY THIS AT HOME

1941

Slavomir Rawicz

During Stalin's dictatorship of the Soviet Union (communist Russia), Polish soldier Slavomir Rawicz was just one of hundreds of thousands of people who were imprisoned in terrible conditions in Siberia. Slavomir was first sent to Moscow's notorious Lubyanka prison in 1939, allegedly for spying. From there he was sent to Siberia, where he and other prisoners were forced to walk hundreds of kilometres chained together in subzero temperatures, and then build their own prison camp. In 1941, Slavomir and six others escaped from Camp 303 in a blizzard. They trekked 6,400 km (4,000 miles) south through the terrible cold of Siberia, the scorching Gobi Desert, and the heights of the Himalayan Mountains to reach India. It took them a year, and three of the seven died on the way.

1944

Allied Prisoners of War: Stalag Luft III

During World War II, German guards at Stalag Luft III were so determined to stop prisoners from tunnelling their way to freedom that they raised prison cells on stilts and installed seismographs to detect sounds of digging. But that didn't stop prisoners led by South African airman Roger Bushell from digging three tunnels, which they nicknamed Tom, Dick, and Harry. The tunnels were so deep – 9 m (30 ft) beneath the ground – that the digging couldn't be picked up by the seismographs. As they dug, the prisoners hid the dirt in their trousers and then discarded it around the prison grounds. On 24 March 1944, 76 men escaped through tunnel Harry, but only 3 got safely away; 23 were recaptured and brought back to prison, while the other 50 were shot on orders from the German dictator, Hitler.

1944

Allied Prisoners of War: Colditz

The Germans' most escape-proof prison was Colditz Castle, with more guards than prisoners. It was where prisoners were sent after escaping from other prisons. Yet, during World War II, 130 prisoners managed to break out of Colditz, and 30 managed to get away for good. The variety of ways they tried to escape was astonishing. They fled through holes cut in floors, along tunnels, and down ropes made of bedsheets. Prisoners also tried disguising themselves as women, or hid in mattresses and garbage bags. Perhaps the most ambitious plan was the building of a glider by British prisoners, from mattress covers and wooden shutters. The war ended before it could be used, but reconstructions suggest it probably would have worked.

1962

Frank Morris and the Anglin brothers

The notorious Alcatraz Island in San Francisco Bay was the United States's most secure prison. Even if prisoners got past its electric wires, hidden microphones, gun towers, and watchful guards, they then had to cross the dangerous waters that surrounded the island. That didn't stop some prisoners from trying to escape. In 1962, Frank Morris and brothers Clarence and John Anglin began to chip away at the concrete around a ventilation shaft, using nail clippers, some spoons, and a drill made from a fan. Every night, they hid the hole with some paste made from wet newspaper. After six months, they were able to slide out of the prison through the ventilation system and board a raft made from barrels, wire, and raincoats. But did they sink or swim? Who knows – they were never heard from again.

1961–1989

East Berliners

In the 28 years between 1961 and 1989 that the Berlin Wall divided East and West Berlin, many thousands of people risked their lives trying to escape to the West, or help others to do so. Horst Breistoffer, for example, bought an Italian Isetta – a "bubble car" so small that he thought guards wouldn't check it. He was right! He made nine trips across the border with one person at a time hidden inside a special compartment within the car. He was caught on his tenth trip. Another group of people, led by Wolfgang Fuchs, dug a 128-m (420-ft) tunnel from a bathroom in East Berlin to a basement in the West, allowing more than 100 people to pass through it. But perhaps the most daring were the Strelzyk and Wetzel families, who made it over the Wall in 1979 in a hot-air balloon made from curtains and bedsheets.

→ Ever been in a tight spot? Learn some tricks of the trade in Escapology on pp.72–77 and from Lord Lucan on pp.142–143.

MAGIC TRICKS REVEALED

3

This impressive trick relies on a trapdoor in the stage. Positioning himself on a particular part of the stage, the magician waves his wand, signalling for a stage technician to let the trapdoor beneath him open. The magician drops through the trapdoor, while a flash and a puff of smoke distract the amazed audience and prevent them from seeing what is really happening.

2

Despite the magician's assurances that the box has no hidden compartments, it does! As the girl gets into the box, she curls up her legs in one half, letting only her head show, while fake feet poke out of the other end. In some versions of the trick, the feet belong to another girl, curled up and hidden in the other half before the show. This trick is called Goldin's Illusion, after the magician Horace Goldin who perfected it in the 1920s. He didn't do things by halves.

1

Just before the show, the magician puts a rabbit on a black cloth with curtain rings at each corner. He picks up the cloth by the corners and hangs it on the back of his stage table. During the show, he places his hat brim down on the table. Then, he turns it over, hooking his thumb into the rings and lifting the bag. He waves his wand to distract the audience, and as the hat is turned upside down, the rabbit swings into it. The magician puts the hat down, taps the brim with his wand, and out pops the bunny!

→ For more tricks of the trade, check out Escapology on **pp.72–77** and Advertising tricks on **pp.160–161**.

Painted in oil on oak wood, The Ambassadors is 207 cm x 209 cm (81 in x 82 in), and is currently on display in the National Gallery, London.

HOLBEIN'S
THE AMBASSADORS

If a picture paints a thousand words, then German painter Hans Holbein's masterpiece could say a million. Few paintings are as rich in secrets as *The Ambassadors*. The double portrait shows two Frenchmen who visited London in 1533. Jean de Dinteville, on the left, was an ambassador to the court of King Henry VIII. On the right is his friend, clergyman Georges de Selve. The painting is choc-a-block with hidden messages and meanings.

◄ Secret skull The most dramatic hidden message lies in the middle of the painting. Viewed straight on it is hard to work out what the object is, but when viewed from the side – where the green dot is on the opposite page – a large skull becomes clear (as shown here). This type of distortion is called anamorphism. The skull was a symbolic reminder that everyone eventually dies. Cheerful!

► Jean de Dinteville Fine clothes emphasise the ambassador's wealth. Black dye was expensive and only worn by the rich. The colour was also used by artists to symbolize intellect. A Latin inscription on his dagger reveals he was 29 years old.

► Hidden cross Barely visible in a gap in the curtains is a crucifix (a representation of the cross on which Jesus died). This is a symbol of the hope of life after death in Christianity. It contrasts with the skull, which symbolizes death.

◄ Georges de Selve More modest clothing indicates that Georges was a cleric in the Catholic Church. He also worked as an ambassador for the pope. A Latin inscription on the book under his arm reveals he was 24 years old in 1533.

▼ Sundial The date on the portable sundial reads 11 April. In 1533, this date was Good Friday – the day in the Christian calander that marks the crucifixion of Jesus – so the sundial is a symbol of the sacrifice of Christ on the cross.

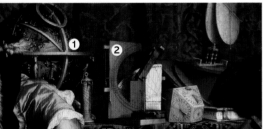

◄ Upper shelf The discovery of new lands in the 16th century was transforming peoples' vision of the world. The upper shelf has instruments used by explorers to navigate the oceans, including a torquetum (1), used to measure the distance of the stars, and a quadrant (2) for measuring longitude (distance east or west from an imaginary line on Earth).

▲ Lower shelf The globe (3) is upside down, symbolizing the way religious reforms were turning the world on its head. The lute (4) has a broken string and a flute is missing from the musical set (5). Both represent religious discord. At the time, the writings of German religious reformer Martin Luther were dividing the Catholic Church in Europe.

→ For more artistic enigmas go to Arnolfini Marriage on pp.84–85 and Magic Eye on pp.220–221.

ARNOLFINI MARRIAGE

At first sight, the painting called the *Arnolfini Marriage* looks quite ordinary. Painted in Bruges, Belgium, in 1434, by Dutch artist Johannes van Eyck, it appears to be just a realistic portrait of a well-to-do 15th-century couple. But the more closely you look into the painting, the more mysteries it seems to contain.

Who are they?

For years, experts believed the picture showed merchant Giovanni di Arrigo Arnolfini with his bride Giovanna Cenami. Recently, a document was discovered indicating that Arnolfini and Giovanna did not marry until 14 years after the picture was painted. So just who does the painting show? Some say it could be Giovanni's cousin and his wife, but no one really knows for sure.

Hidden meanings

We know exactly when the picture was painted and by whom because the artist wrote, "Johannes van Eyck was here, 1434" above the mirror. So that's sorted, then. But many of the other things in the painting are more mysterious. Here are just some of the hidden meanings behind the objects depicted in the painting.

1 The man stands nearer to the window than the woman, symbolizing his closer relationship to the outside world in his role as provider.

2 The single candle in the chandelier may represent Giovanni Arnolfini, whose first wife died, leaving him a widower.

3 Van Eyck's signature above the mirror has led some experts to believe that the painting was a legal marriage document.

4 The two figures reflected in the mirror may be the marriage witnesses – one of them may even be van Eyck himself.

5 The medallions around the mirror show scenes from the Christian story of Jesus's crucifixion.

6 The colour red stands for physical love.

7 On the bedpost is a statue of St Margaret, the patron saint of childbirth.

8 The brushes hanging from the bedpost near the woman symbolize her role as homemaker.

9 The mirror might be a symbol of the eye of God, suggesting the religious aspect of marriage.

10 The lady's bump was probably a fashionable style of dress, not a sign of pregnancy.

11 The contrast between the red and green fabrics suggests a coming together of opposites – the different roles of husband and wife.

12 The dog is a symbol of loyalty, suggesting that the couple would remain faithful to each other.

13 Clogs were a gift traditionally presented to a bride by her husband.

14 The oranges on the chest are a sign of wealth since oranges were very expensive in Belgium at the time.

The photographic eye

In 2001, artist David Hockney and physicist Charles Falco suggested that van Eyck might have had a device called a camera obscura to help him paint accurately. A camera obscura is a box, or even a darkened room. Light shines into the room through a small hole. Curved mirrors focus the light to project an image of the world onto the artist's table. Van Eyck may have made his first sketch simply by tracing over this image.

➡ For other hidden meanings, go to The almighty dollar on pp.16–17 and Body language on pp.186–187.

0, 1, 1, 2, 3, 5, 8, 13, 21, 34,

Back in the 12th century, an Italian mathematician named Fibonacci (c. 1170–1250) discovered an extraordinary sequence of numbers. Each number in the sequence is found by simply adding together the previous two. Here's how it goes: 0, 1, 1, 2, 3, 5, 8, 13, 21, 34, and so on. What's amazing is just how often this sequence of numbers, called the Fibonacci Numbers, applies to the world around us. Check out these magic numbers.

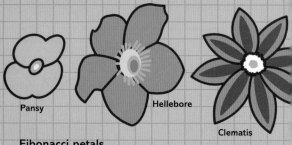

Pansy

Hellebore

Clematis

Fibonacci petals
The Fibonacci Numbers seem to play a part in the number of petals most flowers have. Not all flowers work like these, but here are some that do.

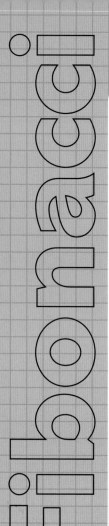

MCMXXVIII
(1928)

Fibonacci and numerals
Fibonacci's real name was Leonardo of Pisa. He introduced Europe to the Arabic numerals we use today – that is 1, 2, 3, and so on. Beforehand, Europeans used cumbersome Roman numerals.

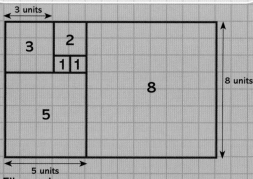

3 units

3

2

1 1

8

8 units

5

5 units

Fibonacci squares
Using Fibonacci Numbers for the lengths of the sides of a square, you can build up a sequence of ever bigger touching squares. Each new square's sides are as long as the previous two put together.

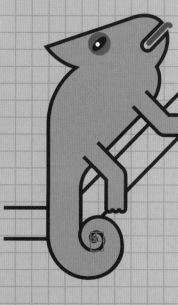

Chameleon's tail
You can drop the Fibonacci square sequence over the ta[il] of a chameleon to show tha[t] it has the same spiral shape

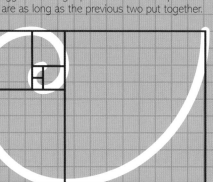

Fibonacci spiral
By drawing a quarter circle between the corners of the sequence of Fibonacci squares, you can create a spiral. This particular spiral shape frequently crops up in nature.

Nautilus shell
The shell of the nautilus (a type of squid) also grows in a spiral that fits the Fibonacci square sequence. As it grows, it keeps to the sequence, adding new, bigger parts to the parts that are already there.

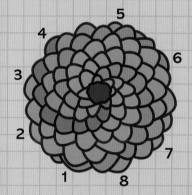

Golden Ratio

Long before Fibonacci's time, the Ancient Greeks discovered a special ratio that works in a similar way to the Fibonacci Numbers. They called this the Golden Ratio, and worked it out to be 1:1.618. This is the same ratio you get if you divide any number in the Fibonacci sequence by the number that precedes it. The Ancient Greeks liked it so much that their temples, such as the Parthenon, were often based on Golden Rectangles – rectangular shapes with side lengths in the ratio 1:1.618.

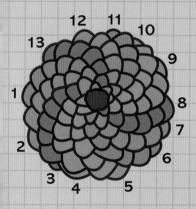

5
4
3
6
2
1
7
8

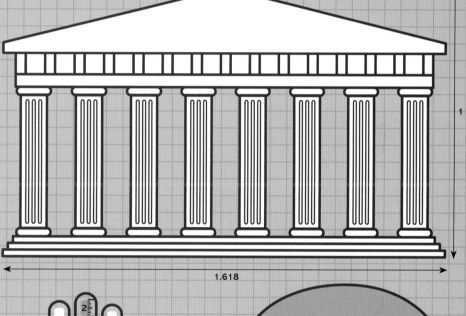

1

1.618

12 11
13 10
9
1
8
2 7
6
3
4 5

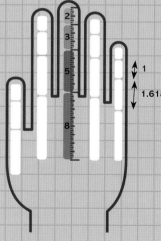

2
3
5
8

1
1.618

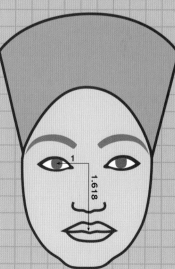

1
1.618

Fibonacci cones

If you look at a pinecone closely, you will see that its scales are arranged in spirals – some clockwise, and some anticlockwise. Their shapes look very much like the Fibonacci spiral, and the number of spirals in each direction are usually Fibonacci Numbers. The two examples numbered above show 8 spirals going clockwise and 13 going anticlockwise.

Golden fingers

Even the lengths of the different parts of your hand and fingers can be in Golden Ratio proportions, which also work as Fibonacci Numbers, as shown here.

Golden face

Some people say that the human face has Golden Number proportions – for example, the position and length of the eyes and mouth in relation to each other.

➜ **For more number-crunching, check out Numbers on pp.112–113 and Fractals on pp.226–227.**

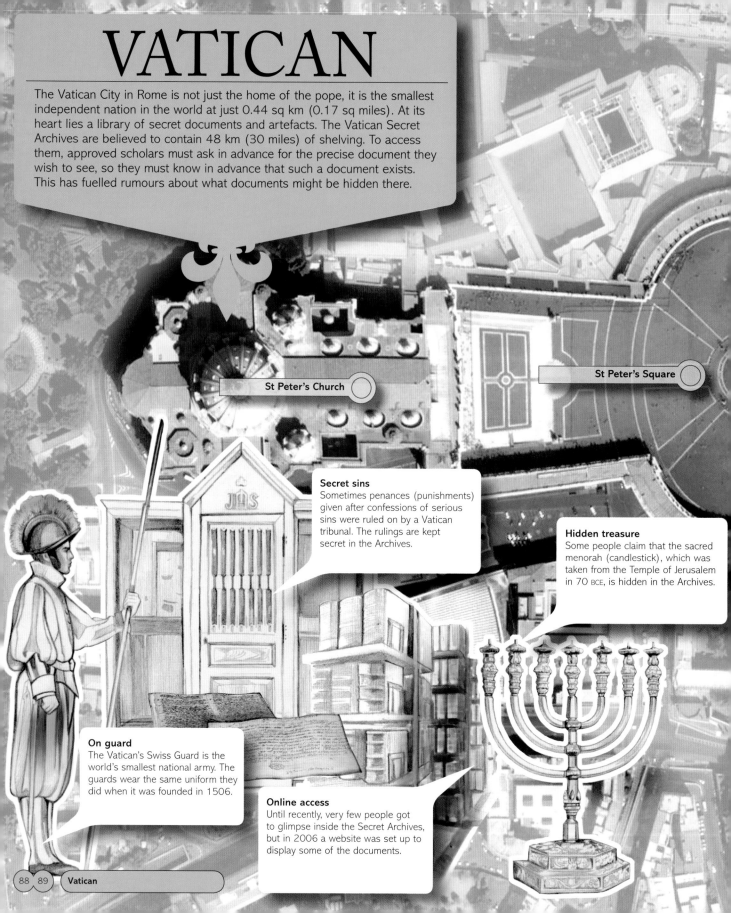

VATICAN

The Vatican City in Rome is not just the home of the pope, it is the smallest independent nation in the world at just 0.44 sq km (0.17 sq miles). At its heart lies a library of secret documents and artefacts. The Vatican Secret Archives are believed to contain 48 km (30 miles) of shelving. To access them, approved scholars must ask in advance for the precise document they wish to see, so they must know in advance that such a document exists. This has fuelled rumours about what documents might be hidden there.

St Peter's Church

St Peter's Square

Secret sins
Sometimes penances (punishments) given after confessions of serious sins were ruled on by a Vatican tribunal. The rulings are kept secret in the Archives.

Hidden treasure
Some people claim that the sacred menorah (candlestick), which was taken from the Temple of Jerusalem in 70 BCE, is hidden in the Archives.

On guard
The Vatican's Swiss Guard is the world's smallest national army. The guards wear the same uniform they did when it was founded in 1506.

Online access
Until recently, very few people got to glimpse inside the Secret Archives, but in 2006 a website was set up to display some of the documents.

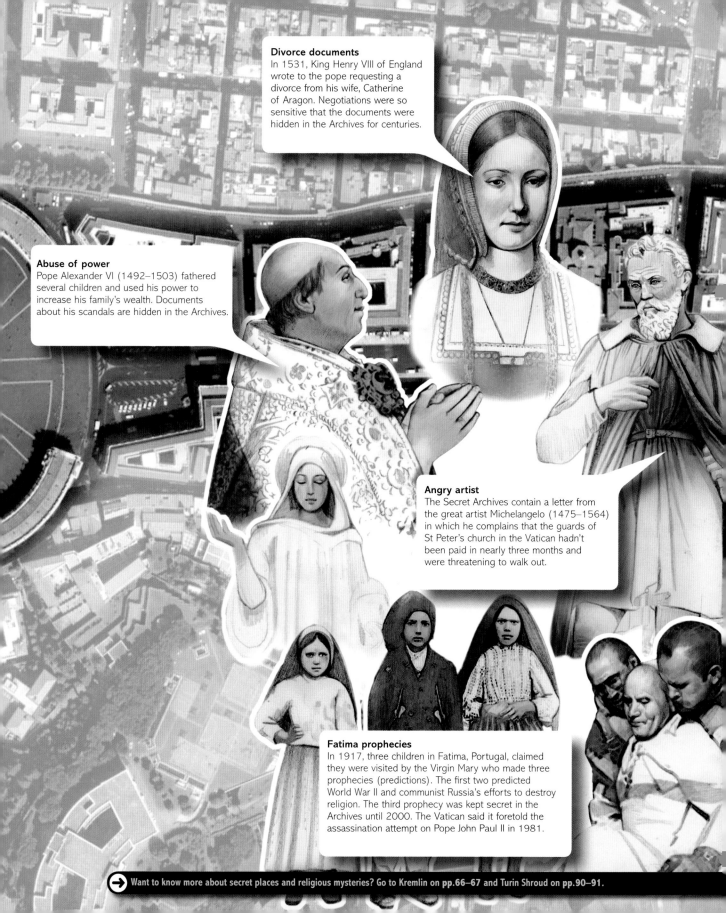

Divorce documents
In 1531, King Henry VIII of England wrote to the pope requesting a divorce from his wife, Catherine of Aragon. Negotiations were so sensitive that the documents were hidden in the Archives for centuries.

Abuse of power
Pope Alexander VI (1492–1503) fathered several children and used his power to increase his family's wealth. Documents about his scandals are hidden in the Archives.

Angry artist
The Secret Archives contain a letter from the great artist Michelangelo (1475–1564) in which he complains that the guards of St Peter's church in the Vatican hadn't been paid in nearly three months and were threatening to walk out.

Fatima prophecies
In 1917, three children in Fatima, Portugal, claimed they were visited by the Virgin Mary who made three prophecies (predictions). The first two predicted World War II and communist Russia's efforts to destroy religion. The third prophecy was kept secret in the Archives until 2000. The Vatican said it foretold the assassination attempt on Pope John Paul II in 1981.

➜ **Want to know more about secret places and religious mysteries? Go to Kremlin on pp.66–67 and Turin Shroud on pp.90–91.**

TURIN SHROUD

The world's most famous piece of linen cloth shows a faint, dark image of a bearded man bearing the same wounds as a person who has been crucified (nailed to a wooden cross and left to die). Some say it was the actual cloth that covered Jesus following his crucifixion, others claim it is just a medieval hoax. But no one knows how the image was made. What is most remarkable is that when the cloth is looked at as a photographic negative, as shown here, the image shows up even more clearly. The Turin Shroud has been kept in the Cathedral of St John in Turin, Italy, since 1578 and has been shrouded in mystery ever since.

Where did the Shroud come from?

The exact origins of the Shroud remain unknown. Its first certain appearance was in 1357, when the widow of the Templar knight Geoffroy de Charnay displayed it in a church in France. Some people believe the image dates from this time and shows the Templar knight himself. There are legends of an image of Jesus on a cloth in places such as Constantinople (now Istanbul, Turkey) long before, but they are unproven. In the 6th century, a similar image was described in Edessa (now part of Turkey), but it showed only a face.

How was the image made?

This is one of the Shroud's great mysteries. The image is strange because it looks like a black (or rather brown) and white photograph, yet it was made long before photography was invented. Computer reconstruction reveals that the marks on the cloth make up a three-dimensional image, as if they were made while the cloth was resting on a real body, not drawn on flat cloth. A high-powered microscope shows the image is not paint or dye, but a microscopic layer of caramelized sugar. To this day, no one really understands how the image was produced.

How old is the Shroud?

In 1988, the pope let scientists take a fragment of the Shroud for radiocarbon dating. The scientists agreed that the Shroud dated from 1260–1390. If so, the cloth could not possibly be the burial shroud of Jesus. However, US professor Raymond Rogers showed that the sample material used came from a piece of the cloth that was likely to be a medieval patch different from the rest. Microchemical tests showed traces of a natural substance called vanillin in the sample patch, but not in the rest of the Shroud. Vanillin decomposes with time, and is found in medieval materials, but not older ones. As a result, the main Shroud could be much older.

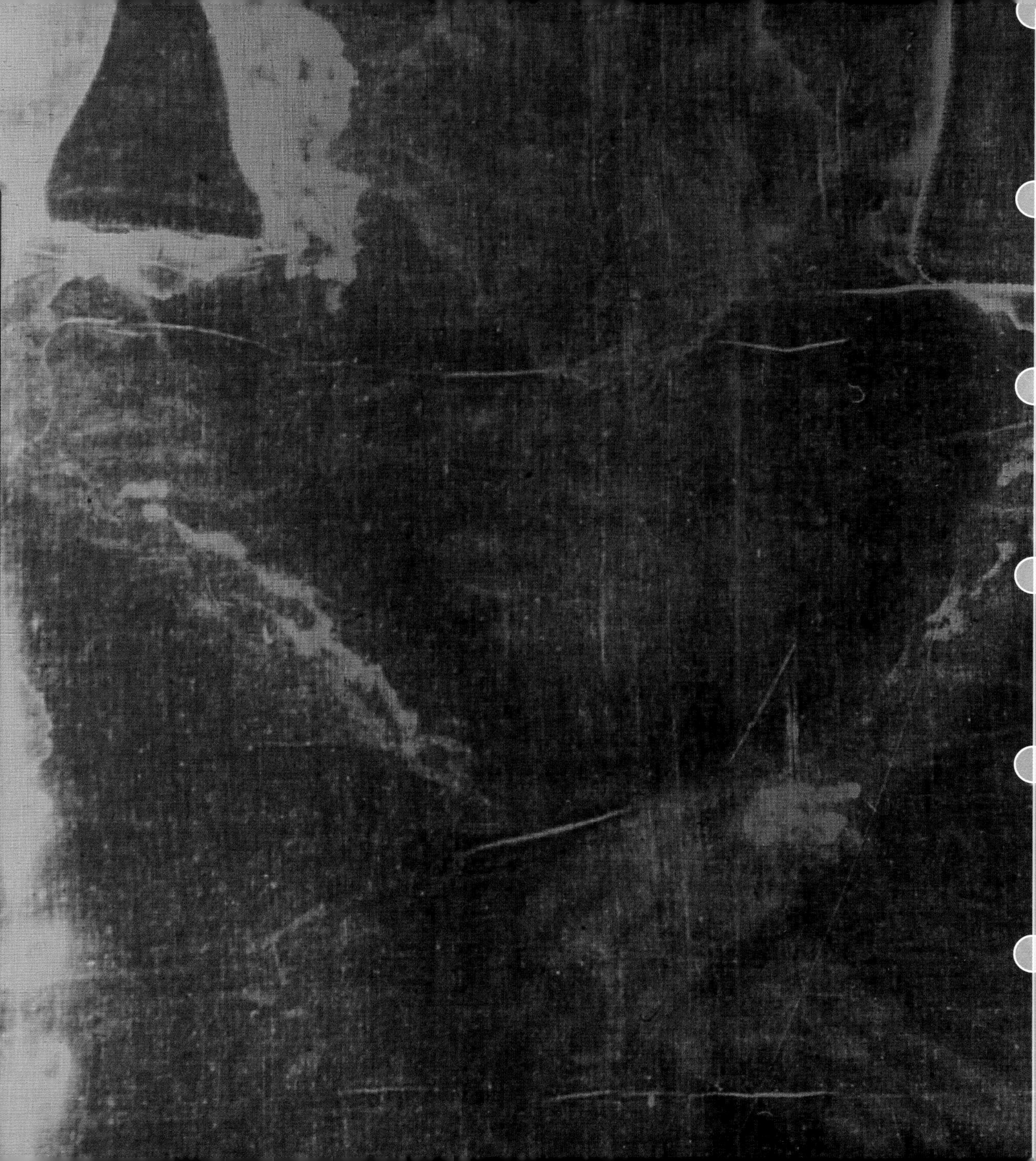

1354

The first historical mention of the Shroud, when it is recorded as being in the hands of Geoffroy de Charnay. After his death three years later, Geoffroy's widow displays the cloth for all to see in Lirey, France.

1389

The image on the Shroud is denounced as a fraud by Bishop Pierre d'Arcis in a letter to the pope. The bishop claims a painter admitted to making the Shroud, but he does not name the artist.

1453

Geoffroy's granddaughter, who has inherited the Shroud, sells it to Louis of Savoy, who displays it in many cities all around Europe.

1532

Unfortunately, the Shroud is burned in a fire at the house of Savoy. A group of nuns tries to repair the damage to the cloth and use patches to rectify some parts.

1578

The Shroud is moved to Turin Cathedral, where it has stayed to this day. In 1978, to commemorate the 400th anniversary of its move to Turin, the Shroud is put on display for the public to see.

2002

During restoration work, a mysterious second image of a face is discovered on the back of the cloth. Are there yet more mysteries to the Turin Shroud?

The photographic negative shown here has been tinted to enhance the image.

For more religious mysteries, go to Vatican on pp.88–89, and Knights Templar on pp.210–211.

THE CODE THAT TRAPPED
MARY QUEEN OF SCOTS

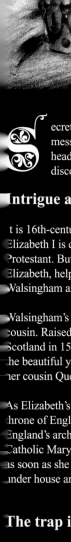

Secret codes are great for getting private messages to people, but they can also get your head chopped off, as Mary Queen of Scots discovered first-hand...

Intrigue and plot

It is 16th-century England, intrigue and espionage are rife. Elizabeth I is queen, and the country's official religion is Protestant. But Catholics are plotting against her. Luckily for Elizabeth, help is at hand from brilliant spymaster Sir Francis Walsingham and Thomas Phellipes, a master codebreaker.

Walsingham's biggest headache is Mary, Elizabeth's Catholic cousin. Raised in France, Mary took her place as queen of Scotland in 1542, aged just 19. But things went wrong for the beautiful young queen, and she fled to England to ask her cousin Queen Elizabeth for help.

As Elizabeth's cousin, Mary also has a claim to the throne of England. Catholics in England as well as Spain, England's arch enemy, would be only too happy to see the Catholic Mary replace Elizabeth on the throne. This is why, as soon as she arrived in England in 1568, Mary was put under house arrest – and was never allowed out again.

The trap is set

After almost 20 years of incarceration, and with the terms of her imprisonment increasingly strict, Mary is determined to escape. Legally, Walsingham can do nothing to harm her, but if he can catch Mary plotting against Elizabeth, she will be tried and executed. So, the cunning Walsingham lays a trap...

The bait is Gilbert Gifford, one of Mary's former supporters who is now a double-agent. On Walsingham's instructions, Gifford becomes Mary's middleman – smuggling letters between the Scots queen and her supporters. Gifford bribes a brewer to take the letters in and out of the castle where Mary is imprisoned, hidden inside the stoppers of beer barrels. In case anyone discovers the letters, they are always written in code. But Gifford passes on a copy of every letter to Phellipes, who is able to crack the code and decipher the letters very quickly.

Tipped off by Walsingham, Gifford gets his claws into a young Catholic named Anthony Babington who is touched by Mary's fate and longs to free her. He soon devises a plot to put her on the throne of England. Helped by Gifford, Babington sends a letter to Mary to tell her of the plot. Walsingham knows that if Mary writes back giving her consent, she will be guilty of treason.

Mary's fate is sealed

After reading the letter, Mary hesitates. Who is this young man? Can she trust him? But she is so utterly miserable in prison that she takes a risk. She writes back giving him the go-ahead.

Walsingham now has the evidence he needs. But he also knows his case would be stronger if he can prove that Mary intends to assassinate Elizabeth. So, before sending the letter on to Mary's supporters, he asks Phellipes to add a postscript, in the correct code, enquiring about the would-be assassins.

The arrest and execution of Babington and his conspirators follows swiftly. When Mary stands trial at Fotheringay Castle, the letter is damning evidence against her. The jury has no hesitiation in finding Mary guilty. Elizabeth signs her cousin's death warrant, and Mary loses her head.

The code and the cracker:
Mary's code used symbols substituted for letters. To crack it, Phellipes used a system of code-breaking devised by the Arab mathematician Al-Kindi, which depends on the frequency that letters appear. In English, "e" is the most frequently used letter, so the most frequent letter in a coded message must also be "e".

For more secret messages, visit Secret writing on pp.110–111, Enigma code on pp.132–133, and Magic Eye on pp.220–221.

HAUNTED PLACES

Army of ghosts
More than 1,000 years ago, Emperor Charlemagne smashed a pagan altar stone at the sacred site of Osnabrück-Haste, Germany, to show the triumph of Christianity. Ever since, people have seen balls of light, bloodstains, and a ghostly army led by Charlemagne.

Murder mystery
The 19th-century country retreat of Monte Cristo is said to be Australia's most haunted house, with reports of ghostly voices, phantom footsteps, and floating heads. Psychics say a young girl was murdered here long ago and that they can sense her body being carried across the paddock, dripping blood. Creepy!

Come in, I've been expecting you...

The world's most scary sites are usually ancient buildings, steeped in turbulent history. From headless horsemen to wailing women, the ghosts of the past are restless, tortured by traumatic events and untimely endings. There are countless reports of hauntings through the ages, but these are some of the most chilling. Enter at your peril...

Headless hauntings
The Tower of London, England, dates from the 11th century. Many poor souls have been beheaded here over the years, including Anne Boleyn, wife of King Henry VIII, and the explorer Sir Walter Raleigh. The towers are teeming with headless spirits, if reports are to be believed!

Castle chills
Dark and ancient vaults lie inside the rock on which Scotland's Edinburgh Castle stands. Some parts of the vaults are more than 900 years old, and many visitors sense unexplained chills or see a phantom presence. So much paranormal activity has been reported that scientists are conducting tests to see if there is any explanation.

Impaled prisoners
The cruel Vlad Dracula lived in Hunedora Castle in Wallachia, Romania, during the 15th century. The ghosts of prisoners he impaled have been seen here. During renovations in 1995, builders reported that objects began flying around.

Ghostly guide
In 1901, two ladies were walking in the gardens of Versailles by a cottage kept by French queen Marie Antoinette. They talked to a man in 18th century attire about the house and only later found out that the door he had emerged from had been bricked up more than a century before.

Smelly spectres
Odd odours, floating bricks, the sound of galloping horses, and the face of a ghostly nun have all been reported at Borley Rectory, England. Built in the 1800s for the Reverend Henry Bull, it is said to be one of England's most haunted houses.

➡ For more spine-tingling stories, see Spooky! on pp.96–97, UFO on pp.200–201, and Vampires versus werewolves on pp.240–241.

spooky!

Vortex

Often felt in cold places, vortexes are green or white swirling funnels of air. They are usually seen in graveyards or old buildings. Paranormal believers suggest this is because vortexes are the spirits of the visiting dead, either returning to where they are buried or where they once lived. Sceptics say such images are either faulty camera film or deliberately faked.

Telekinesis

In a seance, a psychic tries to contact the dead. Participants often claim to see objects moving for no apparent reason, such as tables tipping up or scissors flying around. This is called telekinesis. Psychics believe this is the energy of dead spirits, but sceptics blame electric and magnetic energy fields, or, in the case of table-tipping, wobbly knees!

Poltergeists

Tapping, knocking, bumping, banging... this type of spirit makes its presence felt by moving or affecting objects. In 1977, the world's most famous case of poltergeist activity occurred in London, U Flying furniture, sudden fires, and even possession by evil spirits were reported. The children living there later admitted the had faked at least some of the phenomen Naughty nippers.

Any phenomenon that cannot be explained by experience or science is classed as paranormal. From ghostly figures and flashing lights, to strange mists and moving objects, people report a range of supernatural encounters, yet cynics dismiss them, offering more scientific explanations. So, are you spooked or sceptical?

Ghosts

Seeing a spirit and capturing it on camera is extremely rare. This ghost, filmed in 2003 by closed circuit television at haunted Hampton Court Palace in London, UK, is unusual in its clarity. Sceptics say it is time to give up the ghosts because images are either too blurred to analyse or it is simply a person dressed up as a spook!

Orbs

These balls of light have been seen in many photographs. They usually occur around inhabited buildings, especially those where there are children. The real enthusiasts claim to see the faces of dead people in the orbs! Needless to say, sceptics explain orbs as just pollen, dust, drops of water, or smears on the camera lens. Granny or just grimy: you decide.

Ectoplasm

Some ghost hunters believe that, in death, the spirit becomes a vapour. Known as ectoplasm, this white mist is said to ooze from psychics when they make contact with the dead during seances. Fake mediums have been known to regurgitate chewed fabric to fool clients. In the dark, this fabric can resemble ectoplasm.

Religious phenomena

Reports of crying or bleeding statues and paintings are well-known in many religious communities. People of faith regard these happenings as miracles and worship the religious icons. Non-believers and scientists see them as staged, fake events, using liquid released from porous materials.

➜ If your skin is crawling and your hairs are standing on end, visit Haunted places on pp.94–95 and Vampires versus werewolves on pp.240–241.

At the theatre

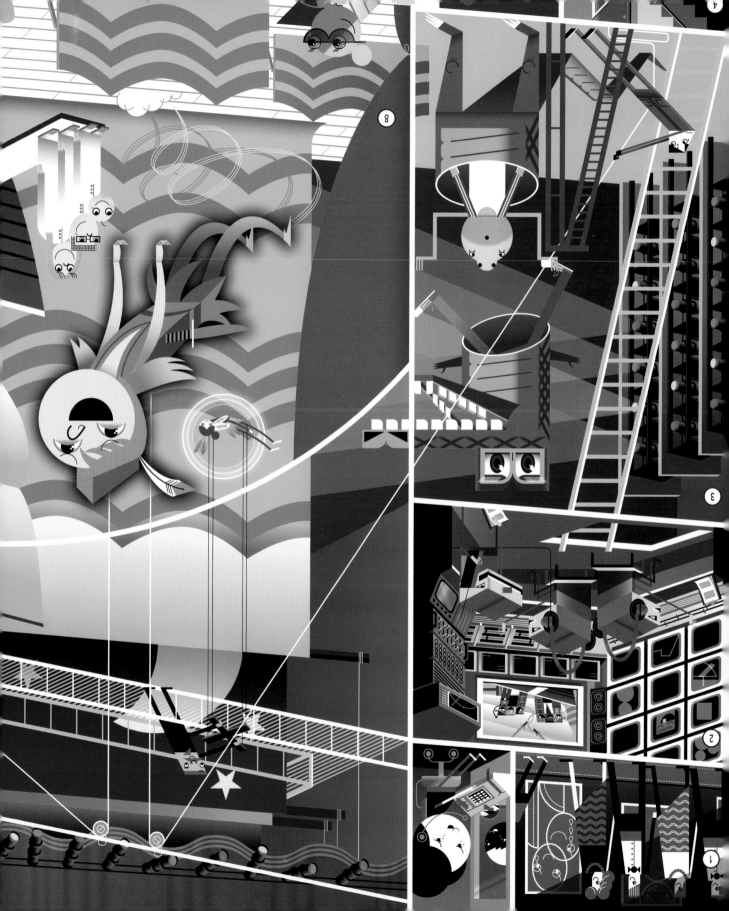

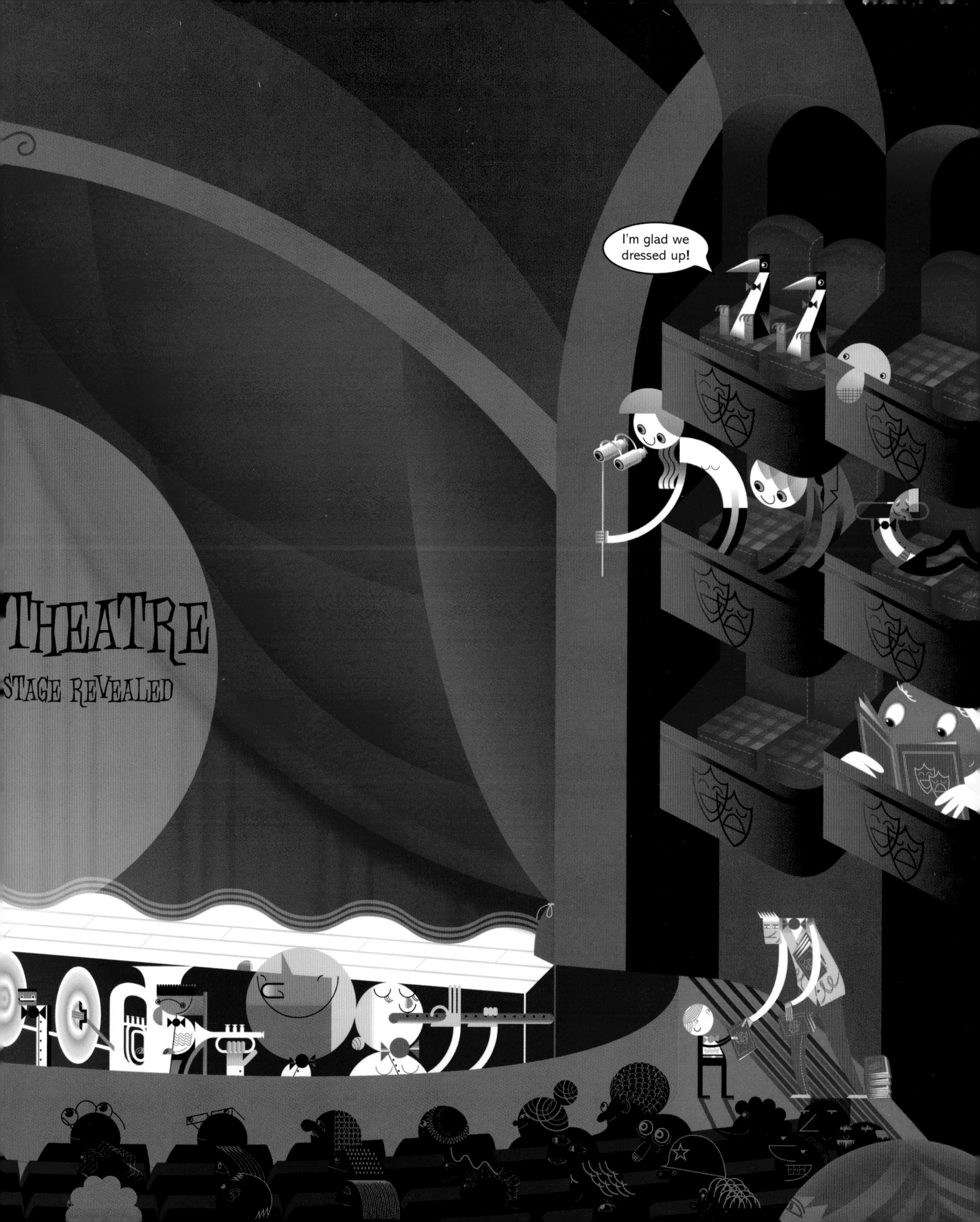
THEATRE
STAGE REVEALED
I'm glad we dressed up!

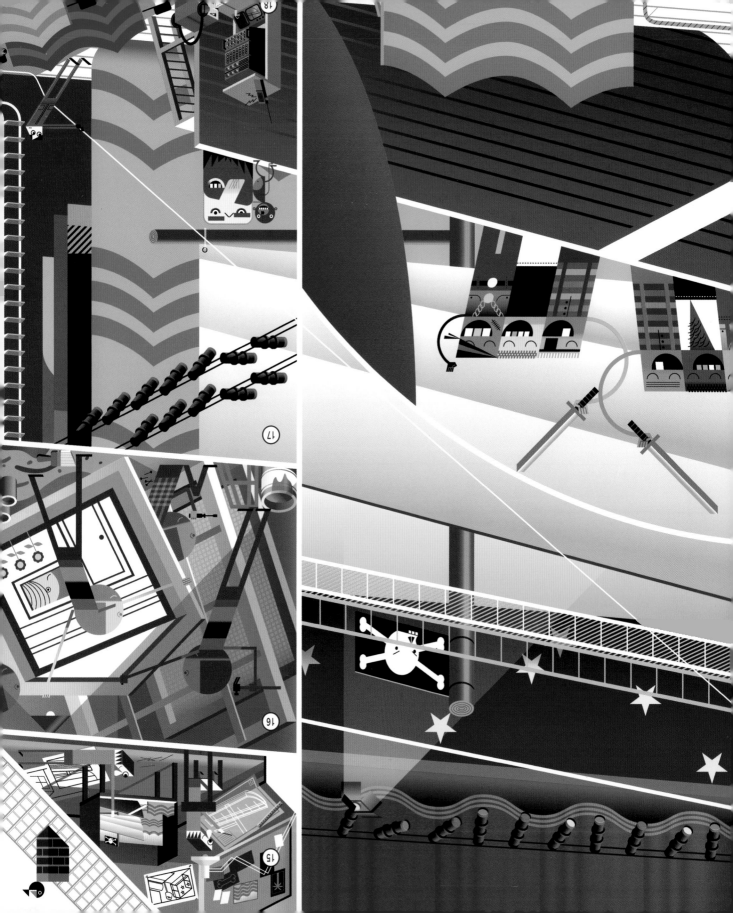

What's happening behind the scenes?

1 Box office The excitement begins at the box office, where people buy tickets for the show.

2 Sound Music and sound effects are programmed into a computer in the correct order to make the show's unique soundtrack. An operator starts each sound when instructed by the stage manager.

3 Backstage The areas that the audience can't see are known as backstage. Behind, above, and below the stage as well as in the wings (the sides of the stage), the stage crew scurry to and fro during the show. They must make sure all the lighting, sounds, props, and set changes happen at the right time. The stage manager coordinates the crew so that everything runs smoothly from start to finish.

4 Stairs A maze of stairs and corridors connects areas backstage.

5 Ushers Staff called ushers show audience members to their seats before the show. The ushers have their own dressing room where they change into uniform before the audience arrives.

6 Dressing rooms Here, the actors change into costume and wait for their cue to go on stage. The stars of the show have private dressing rooms.

7 Hat room Big theatres have rooms just for storing hats and headpieces.

8 Stage The stage looks flat, but actually it slopes forward slightly so the audience can see actors at the back of the stage. For this reason the back of the stage is called upstage, while the front is called downstage. High above the stage, out of sight of the audience, is an elaborate grid of metal walkways and bars. These hold all the stage lights and tabs (curtains), and allow parts of the set or even the actors themselves to "fly" using hoists, ropes, and pulleys.

9 Orchestra pit In big theatres, the musicians sit in a pit in front of the stage. Every musician has a little glowing light so they can read the music in the dark of the auditorium. The conductor leading the orchestra stands on a podium. In the orchestra pit there is a special hatch onto the stage. Inside the hatch a person called a prompt sits, invisible to the audience but seen by the performers on stage. The prompt follows a script ready to "prompt" (remind) the actors of their lines in case any of them forget their words.

10 Storage space Underneath the orchestra pit is a large storage area, with enough space to fit three grand pianos.

11 Winches A system of winches moves bits of the stage.

12 Hydraulics Parts of the set and stage can be moved during the performance using a system of hydraulics – pipes filled with pressurized liquid.

13 Wardrobe department Costumes for the show are designed well in advance. Once made, the costumes are looked after by the wardrobe department. Actors often need to change quickly during the show, so costumes rarely have zips and buttons. Instead, they use hooks, magnetic fastenings, and velcro that are quicker to do up and less likely to snag. Sometimes entire costumes may be sewn together in a single piece, allowing the actor to slip in and out instantly through a slit fastened with velcro.

14 Make-up To stop their faces looking washed out in the bright stage lights, actors always wear make-up that would look far too strong in daylight. Make-up can help to create character – for example, wrinkles can be added to make someone look older. A prosthetic (false) nose, chin, or ears built out of wax or latex can change the shape of an actor's face.

15 Graphics Computer visuals are projected onto the set to create elaborate moving scenery.

16 Set design The design of the sets is crucial to the look of a show. Designers spend months working with the show's director, often building complete models of the set to show how they will look.

17 The set Between shows, the stage is just an empty space. Often a single show needs many different sets. Complete sets are assembled offstage then moved quickly on stage when needed on movable platforms or hydraulic hoists.

18 Cues The deputy stage manager coordinates the stage crew guided by the "book", a script marked with numbered "cues" or points in the show where certain things are to happen.

19 Green room Before and after the show, performers relax in the green room. During the show, performers use the green room as a waiting area.

20 Prop room Everything the actor uses on stage is called a prop (short for property). The stage crew ensures each prop is in exactly the right place. In between performances, props are kept in the prop room backstage.

21 Wigs Elaborate hairstyles are created using wigs, built up on nets that can be glued to the actors' heads.

Want to know more about what happens behind the scenes? Go to Magic tricks on **pp.78–81** and Movie studios on **pp.214–219**.

PRIVATE EYE

Private investigators (PIs) are employed to do a whole range of tasks – from checking up on cheating spouses and looking for missing persons, to tracking down debtors, and finding evidence of fraud.

KEEPING WATCH

Active surveillance
This means following a target to see where they go and who they meet. This can be done on foot or in a car. Tailing by car usually requires a team in two cars to avoid arousing suspicion. One car parks outside the target's house and the other stays out of sight around the corner. When the target leaves the house, the person watching from the car outside tells the driver waiting round the corner which way to go. PIs watching a house or office might secretly film the target. If the target is on the move, you might shoot the action on a mobile phone while pretending to make a call.

Tracking from a distance
You don't have to follow someone in order to keep tabs on them. Mobile phone tracking uses phone signals to find a phone's location. Magnetic trackers can be attached to a vehicle, using Global Positioning System (GPS) satellites to give the car's position to within a few metres. Even using public transport, a target can be located if he or she is using an electronic travel card, as every time such a card is used the journey is recorded.

INFORMATION GATHERING

Backgrounding
A lot of PI work is basic research, called backgrounding. Using Internet search engine online public records, and social sites like Facebook and MySpace can reveal huge amounts of information. Local newspapers hold useful snippets in their archives and the are even special websites for PIs.

Interrogation
Simple face-to-face interviews with friends a neighbours are often the best technique for finding details about someone.

"Some people call me a private eye – or worse. Me, I call myself a private investigator. My job is to get the lowdown on someone who has gone missing or is acting strangely. People come to me when there's trouble – a worried wife who wants to check up on her husband, or a company wanting to find a customer who's run off without paying. The work is mostly dull, footslogging research – but every now and then it gets exciting…"

Checking contacts

You can find out a lot about what people are up to by checking who they contact. An investigator with access to a suspect's computer can install a keylogger that monitors every keystroke they make. Computer records obtained from a computer hard drive or an Internet service provider will provide details of every message and Internet search done from a particular computer. And mobile phones can be set up to reveal all text messages sent to – even after they have been deleted.

ILLEGAL METHODS

Wire tapping

There are ways some PIs bend the law to nail their suspect. It's usually illegal to listen in on phone calls, but wire-tapping equipment that lets you do just that is easy enough to get hold of.

Bugs

Bugging rooms with hidden microphones and cameras is another illegal tool in the PI's arsenal.

Pretexting

The term "pretexting" is investigators' jargon for lying in order to get information.

COUNTERMEASURES

Industrial espionage

Sometimes, a PI might be employed to turn the tables on someone who is doing a little spying themselves. A PI might be hired to find a spy inside a company. If secrets are being leaked to a company's competitors, the first step would be to make checks on all the staff. If secrets are still getting out, a PI would look for hidden cameras, phone taps, and evidence of computer hacking.

 To find out more about the murky world of espionage go to Leaks and moles on **pp.14–15** and Global eavesdropping on **pp.22–23**.

Strange vibrations

To communicate with another person we use our senses; we talk, we listen, we touch. But many people believe there is another way to share thoughts and feelings – through telepathy, or reading the minds of others. British scientist Rupert Sheldrake has developed a mindboggling theory about telepathic connections called "morphic resonance". He reckons that our minds send out vibrations others may pick up on subconsciously. I know what you're thinking. It's mindblowing stuff.

The natural world

In the 1920s, blue tits in one area of the UK learned to tear the foil tops off milk bottles to get at the cream. The habit spread far and wide so quickly that no one could explain it. Perhaps the "resonance" of one bird's action spread from its mind to the other blue tits.

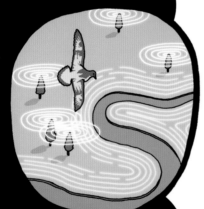

Pigeons and other creatures are remarkably good at finding their way. Scientists usually suggest they navigate by following Earth's magnetic field. Yet could the animals be guided by a mental map created by patterns of resonance?

Mindreading If you think of a shoe, for example, a telepathically connected person would think of the same shoe. Despite many scientific tests, telepathic communication has never been proved – or disproved. No-one really knows what's afoot.

According to morphic resonance theory, every time a shape is made, it leaves a resonance behind. The more times a shape is made, the stronger the resonance becomes. They believe that these resonances help living things, such as plants, grow into the same form over again.

On call Do you ever know who is ringing before you answer the phone? Research shows that this happens so often it may be more than coincidence. Perhaps, when someone is thinking about phoning you it sets up a resonance that you detect.

Stop staring! Ever had the feeling you are being watched, then looked around to find you are? It may be that you become aware of the morphic resonance set off by the person staring at you.

Spooky space Many people can detect a special atmosphere in historic houses. But where does it come from? It could be linked to the resonances of objects and people from long ago.

Psychic pups Dogs seem to know when their owners are on the way home. Is it just their routine or are they picking up on the morphic resonance of their owner?

→ Want to know more about your brain? Go to Brainwashing on **pp.158–159**, Memory tricks on **pp.176–179**, and Unconscious mind on **pp.180–181**.

Got a message that only one person must see? Need to pass along a secret that must not, at any cost, fall into the wrong hands? Over the centuries, people have developed many ways to keep writing secret. Cryptography involves changing letters and words to a code or cipher. With steganography, you hide the message altogether.

SECRET WRITING

CODES AND CIPHERS

In everyday speech, code and cipher are often used to mean the same thing, but, to the cryptographer, these two terms have different meanings. A code is the substitution of one word for another. So, if you were talking about oranges, you could call them elephants. Armies and police often use codes – giving operations particular codenames. A cipher is when you substitute letters in the original text with other letters, numbers, or symbols.

ALBERTI DISC

The great 15th-century mathematician Leon Alberti invented a cipher system called the Alberti disc. The disc consisted of two rings of letters. To encode a letter you find it on the outer ring, turn the inner ring a fixed number of places, and read off the adjacent number on that ring. To make the code harder to break, you can vary how many places you turn the ring in a sequence agreed in advance with the person who is receiving your message.

CAESAR'S CIPHER

One of the simplest ciphers is that used by Roman general Julius Caesar when sending secret messages to his troops. He simply replaced each letter in the message with another a fixed number of positions further on in the alphabet.

ABCDEFGH...
ABCDEFGH...

This famous cipher is called the Caesar Shift. It is easy to crack – you simply experiment with all the possible shifts until you hit on a sensible message.

SCYTALE

THE ANCIENT GREEK INSTRUMENT CALLED A SCYTALE USED A LONG STRIP OF LEATHER ROLLED AROUND A ROD. THE STRIP HAD AN UNBROKEN SERIES OF LETTERS ON IT, SO THE HIDDEN MESSAGE COULD ONLY BE READ WHEN WRAPPED AROUND A ROD OF THE SAME SIZE.

MODERN CIPHERS

Today, powerful computers are used to create complicated ciphers which are very hard to break – but, of course, computer hackers also have powerful machines to help them break these codes.

HIDDEN HANDWRITING

The simplest way to keep a message secret – with or without putting it in code – is to hide it. The science of hiding messages is called steganography.

WAX WARNING

In 480 BCE, Greek general Demaratus sent a hidden warning to Greece that the king of Persia was about to invade. At the time, messages were written on wax tablets with wooden bases. Demaratus simply scratched his message onto the wood and set fresh wax on top with a false message written on it. To see the real message, the recipient simply had to melt the wax.

DARK SECRETS

Alchemists often wrote their research in code. In 1499, German alchemist Trithemius wrote a book about steganography, but in a code that made it look like a book on black magic.

HAIR PIECE

In the 5th century BCE, Greek general Histiaeus tattooed his battle plans onto a slave's shaven head. He waited until the slave's hair had grown back before sending him off with the message – which the recipient could reveal by a haircut.

INVISIBLE INK

An easy way to hide a message is to write in invisible ink – or ink that only becomes visible when you know how to reveal it.

There are lots of different kinds of invisible ink, but the simplest ones can be found in a kitchen cupboard. Milk, lemon juice, sugar or honey dissolved in water, and vinegar or wine can all be used to make hidden messages. When applied to white paper and left to dry, they will all be invisible, but the message will show up brown when the paper is heated against a radiator or under a cool iron.

Many other foods can also be used as invisible ink and are revealed using a chemical reaction. A mesage written in vinegar, for example, becomes visible when red cabbage water is painted over the top, and messages written with starch will turn blue in iodine.

Some special pens use ink that is only visible under ultraviolet (UV) light. Security marker pens, used to mark people's possessions in case of theft, work like this.

➡ Want to know more cool stuff about codes? Go to Hackers on pp.60–61 and Mary Queen of Scots on pp.92–93.

NUMBERS

If you ask your friends and family, you will no doubt find that some of them have a lucky number. They might use this number in all kinds of ways, from playing the lottery to planning an event on a lucky date. Some cultures view certain numbers as lucky or unlucky. The reasons can range from religious significance to the way a number is pronounced. If your lucky number is 112, this is the page for you.

13

Jews and Sikhs consider 13 a lucky number because it is associated with the worship of God. However, to many it is unlucky. Christians feel it is linked to Judas, who was the 13th apostle at the Last Supper and betrayed Jesus. When the 13th of the month falls on a Friday it is especially feared. Some believe Jesus was crucified on Friday 13th. The Ancient Romans felt the number 13 was a sign of destruction.

9

In Thai, the word for nine is the same as the word "progress". In neighbouring Japan, though, the number sounds like the word for "pain" or "torture" and so is dreadfully unlucky.

4,233

This was an unlucky number in Ancient Egyptian culture. The hieroglyphs (pictures) that represented 4,233 can also look like they are showing a young pharaoh being murdered.

33

In Spain, the phrase "trienta y tres" is said to make people smile when they are having their picture taken.

7

In Irish folklore, a seventh son of a seventh son is believed to have magic powers, but in Portuguese legends he is a werewolf. In Iran, a cat is said to have seven lives, not nine. The number symbolizes perfection and God in the Jewish and Christian faiths.

40

Some Russians believe that a dead person wanders the earth for 40 days after they die. During this period they cover all the mirrors in the dead person's house so the person is free to go to heaven. Some Russians also believe that you will be forgiven 40 sins for every spider you kill. Unlucky for spiders.

328

Three digit numbers are very popular in China, as the number three stands for liveliness. The number 328 sounds like "business will prosper" when spoken, and business owners will happily pay extra to have these digits in their phone number.

18

The Hebrew word for life has a numerical value of 18. In Jewish culture, it is common to give gifts and donations in multiples of 18 in hope for the blessing of a long life.

14

In South America, 14 is a very lucky number as it is two times the lucky number seven. If you go to China, however, 14 is considered one of the scariest numbers is as it sounds like "want to die" when said.

5

In the Islamic faith, five is a sacred number. There are five major parts to the faith, called the Pillars of Islam. Followers of the faith pray five times a day, and there are five types of Islamic law and five law-giving prophets.

666

Many Christians believe the number 666 to signify evil as it is recorded in the Bible as being the number of the devil. But, in China, it is one of the luckiest numbers as the word for six sounds like the word for "smooth" or "flowing" so saying "666" is like saying "everything flowing smoothly".

4

The fear of the number four in many Asian countries is comparable to the fear of 13 in the West. In China, Korea, and Japan, the word for four sounds like "death". Companies like Nokia have avoided the number in naming their products so they won't lose sales in their Asian markets.

17

In Italy, 17 is considered a very unlucky number. In Roman numerals it is written as XVII, but if you juggle the letters around you get VIXI, which means "my life is over" in Latin. Some Italian airlines skip row 17 on their planes, and Renault sold their "R17" car in Italy as "R177".

888

In Greek, every letter has a corresponding number, and words have a number that is the sum of all its letters. In this system, the number 888 was an early Christian number that represented Jesus, and was often used as a special code. In China, as eight is a lucky number, 888 is extra lucky and indicates prosperity and wealth three times over.

42

In Japanese, when 4 and 2 are pronounced together it sounds like "going to death", and so the number is avoided at all costs.

3

In Russia, the number three is very lucky. It represents the Holy Christian Trinity - God the Father, the Son, and the Holy Spirit. People in Russia kiss each other three times when they meet, and give each other three flowers if they're being extra friendly.

Want to know more about numbers? Go to Fibonacci on pp.86–87 and Fractals on pp.226–227.

NOSTRADAMUS

Back in 1555, French scientist Nostradamus published a book of verses called *The Prophecies*. These were his predictions for the future. Ever since, events have turned out uncannily like his predictions. Most experts think his verses are so vague that they can be twisted to foretell any event, but some people view Nostradamus as a genius who could predict the future. Wonder if he saw controversy coming?

The fortress near the Thames
Will fall when the king is locked up within:
Near the bridge in his shirt will be seen
One confronting the death, then barred in the fort.

According to some people, this verse foretells the beheading of King Charles I of England in 1649. But is such a prediction, without naming names, really so amazing? The Tower of London – "the fortress near the Thames" – had long been the place where royals were imprisoned. Also, we need to question the validity of the phrase "near the bridge", as only one bridge – London Bridge – had been built in the area in 1649, which was far from "near" where Charles was executed.

By night shall come through the forest of Reines
A couple to the cross-road by the white stone of Herne.
The dark monk in grey within Varennes:
Elected head causes tempest, fire, blood, slice.

These lines, from one of Nostradamus's verses, are said to foretell the time in 1791 when King Louis XIV of France and Queen Marie Antoinette fled from the French Revolution – only to be spotted at Varennes and brought back to Paris to be guillotined. Nostradamus's association of "a couple", coming "by night" to "Varennes", with the words "blood" and "slice" (which suggest the guillotine) does seem remarkable. But, in Nostradamus's original French version, he uses the word "tranché" for slice, which actually just means "broken into pieces". Nothing lost in translation, then!

Beasts ferocious with hunger will cross the rivers,
The greater part of the battlefield will be against Hister
Into a cage of iron will the great one be drawn,
When the child of Germany observes nothing.

These lines are said to predict the rise of the German dictator, Adolf Hitler, and how Germany took on the rest of the world in battle. Hitler himself also claimed that the verses were about him. But, by using the name Hister, Nostradamus may actually have been referring to the River Danube in Germany, which was once known as the Ister. If so, then the prediction "There's going to be a big battle down by the Danube" at some point was a pretty safe bet.

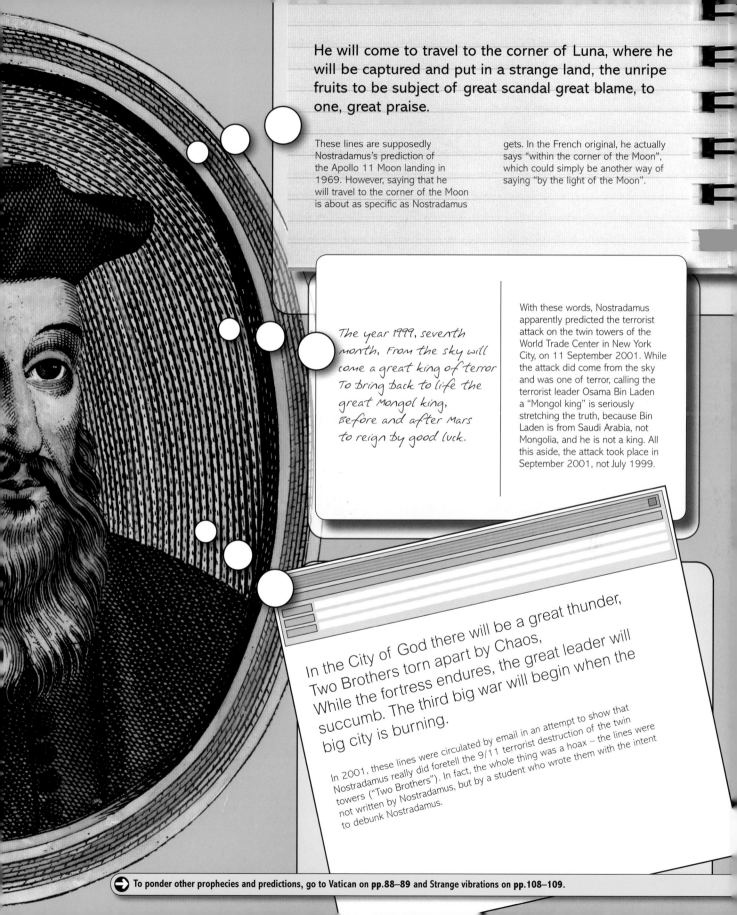

He will come to travel to the corner of Luna, where he will be captured and put in a strange land, the unripe fruits to be subject of great scandal great blame, to one, great praise.

These lines are supposedly Nostradamus's prediction of the Apollo 11 Moon landing in 1969. However, saying that he will travel to the corner of the Moon is about as specific as Nostradamus gets. In the French original, he actually says "within the corner of the Moon", which could simply be another way of saying "by the light of the Moon".

The year 1999, seventh month, From the sky will come a great king of terror To bring back to life the great Mongol king, Before and after Mars to reign by good luck.

With these words, Nostradamus apparently predicted the terrorist attack on the twin towers of the World Trade Center in New York City, on 11 September 2001. While the attack did come from the sky and was one of terror, calling the terrorist leader Osama Bin Laden a "Mongol king" is seriously stretching the truth, because Bin Laden is from Saudi Arabia, not Mongolia, and he is not a king. All this aside, the attack took place in September 2001, not July 1999.

In the City of God there will be a great thunder, Two Brothers torn apart by Chaos, While the fortress endures, the great leader will succumb. The third big war will begin when the big city is burning.

In 2001, these lines were circulated by email in an attempt to show that Nostradamus really did foretell the 9/11 terrorist destruction of the twin towers ("Two Brothers"). In fact, the whole thing was a hoax – the lines were not written by Nostradamus, but by a student who wrote them with the intent to debunk Nostradamus.

To ponder other prophecies and predictions, go to Vatican on pp.88–89 and Strange vibrations on pp.108–109.

ROSETTA STONE

For more than a thousand years, the pictorial language of Ancient Egyptian hieroglyphs was forgotten and no one could translate it. The breakthrough came in 1799, when Napoleon's army took a stone from Egypt back to France. Called the Rosetta Stone, it dated from 196 BCE. The same text was inscribed on it in three ancient scripts – hieroglyphs, demotic (everyday) Egyptian, and Ancient Greek. By comparing passages of the scripts, French scholar Jean-François Champollion decoded the hieroglyphs and unlocked the secrets of the pharaohs' tombs.

Although the hieroglyphs on the Rosetta Stone look baffling, the key to deciphering them is the oval nameplates, called cartouches, that contain a royal name. As Champollion had got the royal name from other scripts, he was able to work out what the hieroglyphs in the cartouches stood for. This meant he could gradually decipher the surrounding hieroglyphs.

As only pharaohs and priests could write in hieroglyphs, there was a demotic writing for the ordinary Egyptians. Though no one could read demotic, Champollion guessed it was similar to Coptic – a language spoken later in Egypt. Using Coptic and the Greek version of the stone's text, Champollion deciphered the demotic version.

The third script was in an Ancient Greek language. Luckily, it was a well-known form of the language, so Champollion could use it to guide him when working out the demotic and hieroglyph versions. There are two older forms of Greek written more than 3,000 years ago — Linear B was only deciphered in 1953, while Linear A remains a mystery.

Rongorongo In the 19th century, wooden tablets covered in a picture script were found on Easter Island in the Pacific Ocean. The script was engraved using shark teeth or volcanic rock, but its meaning is still uncertain.

Phaistos disk This stone disk was found in the Ancient Minoan Palace of Phaistos in 1908, and is thought to date from about 3,600 years ago. It is covered in a strange script. Some people claim to have cracked the code, but scholars are unconvinced.

SECRET STONES

Etruscan Some languages remain a mystery. The Etruscans were people who lived in Italy long before the Ancient Romans. They left many temples, statues, and other artefacts. Many examples of Etruscan writing have been found, but to date, no one has been able to decipher it.

For other crazy code revelations, check out Secret writing on pp.110–111 and Enigma code on pp.132–133.

ANCIENT PYRAMIDS

The great pyramids at Giza are one of the world's architectural wonders, but Egypt is not the only country to have such buildings. Remarkably, ancient pyramids have been discovered as far apart as Mexico and China. What is fascinating is that, although many ancient cultures had little or no contact with each other, they all decided to build the pyramid shape. What was the point? Some were built as elaborate tombs, others as centres of worship.

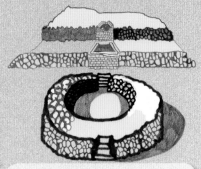

Caral, Peru The pyramid at Caral was built around 4,500 years ago. This makes it about the same age as the pyramids in Egypt, and the oldest one in the Americas.

Huaca del Sol, Peru About 1,500 years ago, the Moche people made Huaca del Sol from 100 million mud bricks. It is now the biggest mud brick building in the Americas.

Altun Ha, Belize On this site is a vast pyramid built by the Mayan civilization about 2,000 years ago. It is thought to be a temple, with an altar for worship on top.

Copan, Honduras In this ruined city stands a pyramid and tombs, crafted 1,300 years ago by the Maya. Portraits of their rulers are carved into the stairway.

Cholula, Mexico Standing 66 m (216 ft) high, Cholula's pyramid is the largest in the world by volume. It took 1,800 years to complete, and was dedicated to the Aztec god Quetzalcoatl.

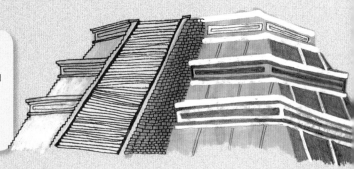

Teotihuacán, Mexico The Pyramid of the Sun is the third largest pyramid ever built. It was constructed by the Aztecs 1,800 years ago as part of their city.

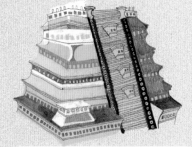

Tenochtitlán, Mexico The Great Temple was the centre of the Aztec world, and the site of blood and sacrifice. Dead bodies were thrown down the 114 stone steps.

Cahokia, USA Named Monks Mound, this pyramid was made of soil about 800 years ago. It was North America's biggest building until the Pentagon was constructed in 1943.

Tenerife, Canary Islands In 1998, six pyramids were discovered on the island of Tenerife. No one knows who built them, but they are said to be about 1,600 years old.

Sakkara, Egypt Thought to be the world's oldest large stone structure, the 4,700-year-old stepped pyramid of Pharaoh Djoser was the first built in Ancient Egypt.

Giza, Egypt Of the three famous pyramids at Giza, the 4,000 year-old pyramid of Pharaoh Khufu is the largest in Egypt and the most perfectly shaped pyramid of all.

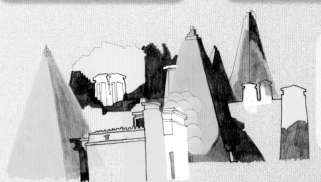

Meroe, Sudan At least 220 small, steep, and beautifully formed pyramids were built by the Nubian kings about 2,000 years ago. It is thought that these are the ruins of a royal cemetery.

MYSTERY PYRAMIDS

Whether it is sightings on the seabed or high up in the air, pyramids are still being discovered by people around the world. Despite further investigation, some of these sites have thrown up more questions than answers...

Great White Pyramid, China During World War II, an American pilot glimpsed a gigantic, glistening white pyramid from the air, yet no one has ever found it on the ground.

Helleniko, Greece There are three small pyramids in Greece, and some scholars think the one at Helleniko may be even older than Djoser's step pyramid.

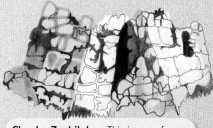

Chogha Zanbil, Iran This is one of many ziggurats (pyramid-shaped temples) found in the Middle East. It was built by the Elamites about 3,250 years ago.

Xi'an, China About 100 small pyramids were built 2,200 years ago, in the time of the Emperor Qin Shi Huang. Many of the pyramids were used as burial sites.

Yonaguni, Japan In 1985, a diver spotted some strange stone structures on the seabed off Japan. Some say they are constructed by humans and are at least 8,000 years old.

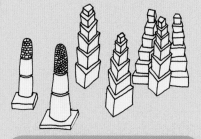

Gympie, Australia These terraced pyramids are said to have been built long before the Europeans reached Australia. Others say they are the remains of a 19th-century mine spoil heap.

➜ For other stony secrets, go to Rosetta Stone on pp.116–117 and Standing stones on pp.230–231.

GIZA SECRETS

Towering above the desert sands at Giza, just outside Cairo in Egypt, is the Great Pyramid. It was built using more than 2.3 million gigantic stone blocks as a tomb for the Ancient Egyptian pharaoh Khufu. It is more than 4,500 years old, yet despite the determined efforts of countless experts to unlock its secrets, many of its mysteries remain unanswered.

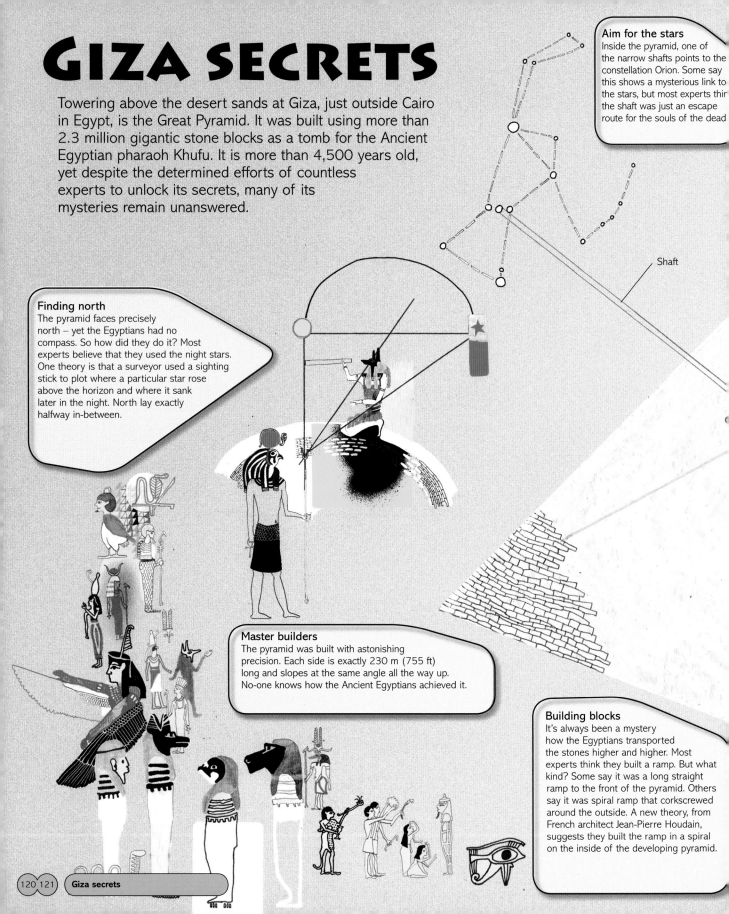

Aim for the stars
Inside the pyramid, one of the narrow shafts points to the constellation Orion. Some say this shows a mysterious link to the stars, but most experts think the shaft was just an escape route for the souls of the dead

Shaft

Finding north
The pyramid faces precisely north – yet the Egyptians had no compass. So how did they do it? Most experts believe that they used the night stars. One theory is that a surveyor used a sighting stick to plot where a particular star rose above the horizon and where it sank later in the night. North lay exactly halfway in-between.

Master builders
The pyramid was built with astonishing precision. Each side is exactly 230 m (755 ft) long and slopes at the same angle all the way up. No-one knows how the Ancient Egyptians achieved it.

Building blocks
It's always been a mystery how the Egyptians transported the stones higher and higher. Most experts think they built a ramp. But what kind? Some say it was a long straight ramp to the front of the pyramid. Others say it was spiral ramp that corkscrewed around the outside. A new theory, from French architect Jean-Pierre Houdain, suggests they built the ramp in a spiral on the inside of the developing pyramid.

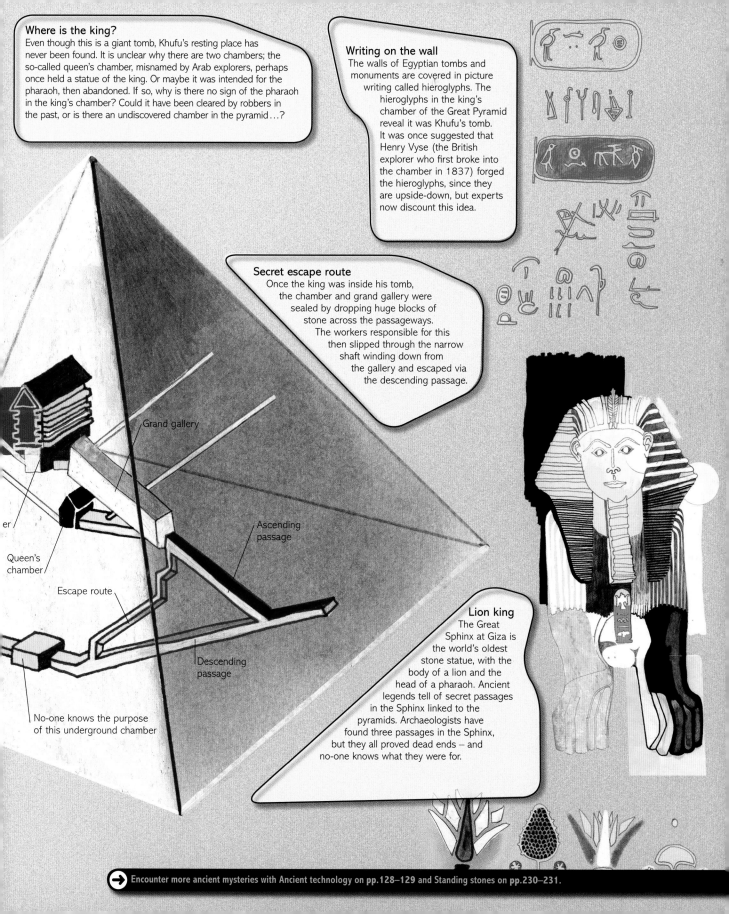

Where is the king?
Even though this is a giant tomb, Khufu's resting place has never been found. It is unclear why there are two chambers; the so-called queen's chamber, misnamed by Arab explorers, perhaps once held a statue of the king. Or maybe it was intended for the pharaoh, then abandoned. If so, why is there no sign of the pharaoh in the king's chamber? Could it have been cleared by robbers in the past, or is there an undiscovered chamber in the pyramid...?

Writing on the wall
The walls of Egyptian tombs and monuments are covered in picture writing called hieroglyphs. The hieroglyphs in the king's chamber of the Great Pyramid reveal it was Khufu's tomb. It was once suggested that Henry Vyse (the British explorer who first broke into the chamber in 1837) forged the hieroglyphs, since they are upside-down, but experts now discount this idea.

Secret escape route
Once the king was inside his tomb, the chamber and grand gallery were sealed by dropping huge blocks of stone across the passageways. The workers responsible for this then slipped through the narrow shaft winding down from the gallery and escaped via the descending passage.

Grand gallery

er

Queen's chamber

Escape route

Ascending passage

Descending passage

No-one knows the purpose of this underground chamber

Lion king
The Great Sphinx at Giza is the world's oldest stone statue, with the body of a lion and the head of a pharaoh. Ancient legends tell of secret passages in the Sphinx linked to the pyramids. Archaeologists have found three passages in the Sphinx, but they all proved dead ends – and no-one knows what they were for.

Encounter more ancient mysteries with Ancient technology on pp.128–129 and Standing stones on pp.230–231.

THE CURSE OF TUTANKHAMUN

Dateline: 3 November 1922, in the Valley of the Kings, Egypt. For years Howard Carter has searched in vain for the tomb of Pharaoh Tutankhamun. It is Carter's last chance to find a king's treasures untouched by greedy graverobbers.

I'LL FIND THAT TOMB IF IT'S THE LAST THING I DO!

In the Valley of the Kings, Carter's team are busy digging away at the suspected tomb site.

As Carter sketches the site, the workers dig deeper and deeper in the debris. The sound of the spades is only broken by Carter's pet canary shrieking as it flies overhead.

MR CARTER! LOOK! COME QUICK!

Suddenly, an excited voice alerts Carter.

One of the workers has spotted a gap in the debris, with a step cut into the rock.

COME ON, HELP ME CLEAR THIS!

Finally, they break through...

They descend 15 steps before reaching a stone door. Carter starts to examine it...

THE SEALS ARE TUTANKHAMUN'S! WE'VE FOUND IT!

BUT WAIT! WE CAN'T OPEN IT UNTIL THE BOSS GETS HERE.

...er sends an urgent telegram to Lord ...arvon, who is paying for the dig.

TUT'S TOMB FOUND. STOP.
COME AT ONCE. STOP. CARTER

Back above ground, a deadly cobra has Carter's canary in its sights.

➜ **Want to know more about the mysteries of Egypt? Visit Rosetta Stone on pp.116–117 and Giza secrets on pp.120–121.**

THE PHARAOH'S SNAKE ATE THE BIRD BECAUSE WE FOUND HIS TOMB — BEWARE!

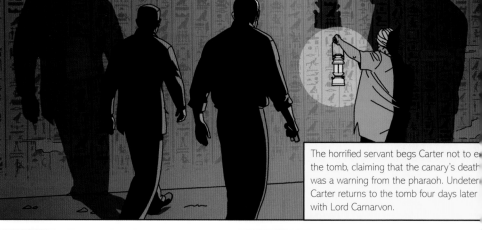

The horrified servant begs Carter not to e[nter] the tomb, claiming that the canary's death was a warning from the pharaoh. Undeter[red] Carter returns to the tomb four days later with Lord Carnarvon.

CAN YOU SEE ANYTHING?

YES, WONDERFU[L] THINGS!

Carter lights a candle and peers through the hole he has made.

Inside, the team are dazzled by the brilliance of the glittering treasures. Carter is nervous as he heads over to Tutankhamun's tomb...

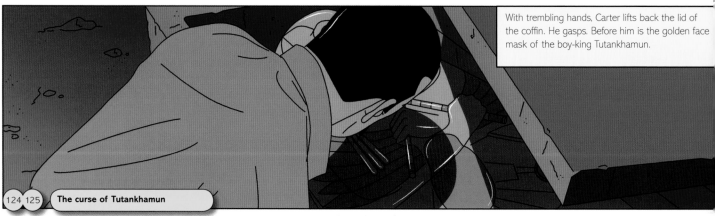

With trembling hands, Carter lifts back the lid of the coffin. He gasps. Before him is the golden face mask of the boy-king Tutankhamun.

world wakes to a media frenzy – long-lost tomb has been unearthed.

TIMES

Egyptian wonders!
Pharaoh's gold discovered

nkhamun's **UMMY EARTHED**

Greatest ever archaeological find

TELL ME CARTER, WHAT DO THESE HIEROGLYPHS SAY?

Reporters want more detail about the historic find.

"I PROTECT THE SACRED TOMB."

HMM, SOUNDS A BIT WEAK. I'LL PUT "THE SWIFT WINGS OF DEATH SHALL VISIT HE WHO ENTERS THIS SACRED TOMB" INSTEAD.

To everyone's horror, Lord Carnarvon falls gravely ill from the mosquito bite. The newspapers are full of speculation. Has the curse of Tutankhamun struck down Lord Carnarvon? Then... disaster! The mosquito bite proves deadly...

n the tomb, a mosquito lands on ord Carnarvon's neck.

For more glittering gems, go to Lost treasures on pp.26–27 and Hidden gold on pp.34–35.

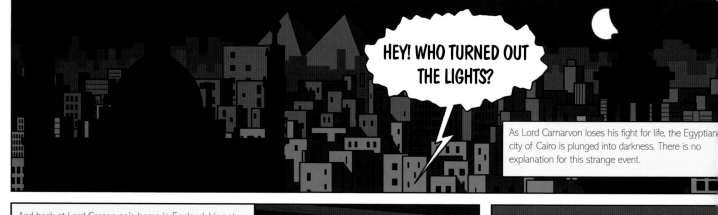

HEY! WHO TURNED OUT THE LIGHTS?

As Lord Carnarvon loses his fight for life, the Egyptian city of Cairo is plunged into darkness. There is no explanation for this strange event.

And back at Lord Carnarvon's home in England, his pet dog, Susie, starts howling and drops down dead.

OWOWOWOWHHH!

Meanwhile, back at the tomb, Carter is unwinding the bandages covering the mummy. He pulls back a bandage and discovers a strange insect bite underneath…

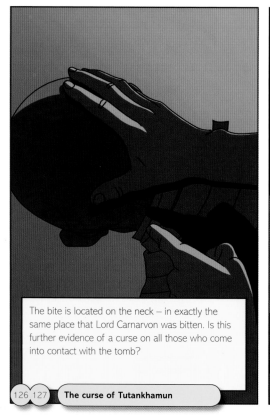

The bite is located on the neck – in exactly the same place that Lord Carnarvon was bitten. Is this further evidence of a curse on all those who come into contact with the tomb?

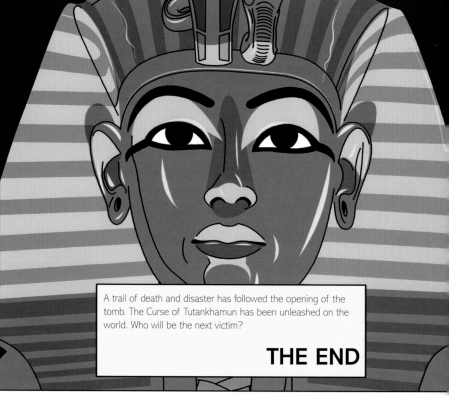

A trail of death and disaster has followed the opening of the tomb. The Curse of Tutankhamun has been unleashed on the world. Who will be the next victim?

THE END

AND NOW THE TRUTH...

In the 1820s, when a mania for all things Ancient Egyptian began, novelist Jane Loudon Webb wrote *The Mummy*, a book about a mummy who came back to life and threatened the hero. In the years that followed, many authors wrote about vengeful mummies. When Carter discovered Tutankhamun's tomb, the idea of "The Mummy's Curse" was firmly planted in the public's imagination.

Shortly after the discovery, novelist Mari Corelli wrote that there would be terrible consequences for anyone who entered the tomb. So, when Lord Carnarvon died a month later, the media went wild with speculation about the curse. Even *Sherlock Holmes* author Arthur Conan Doyle announced that Lord Carnarvon's death could have been due to the pharaoh's curse. This idea had credibility because Carter's canary was killed by a cobra on the day the tomb was opened. Cobras were considered the protectors of the pharaoh, and one was featured on the pharaoh's headdress, where it was said to spit fire at his enemies.

Sceptics point out that the press manipulated the wording of the curse to sensationalize the story. However, it is true that many Ancient Egyptian tombs were inscribed with curses that would punish anyone who entered. The claim that in the instant Lord Carnarvon died, his dog in England dropped dead and all the lights in Cairo went out can neither be proved nor disproved, but the sceptics argue that dogs can die from any number of undiagnosed health problems, and the lights in Cairo regularly go out even today.

By 1935, the media had managed to blame the curse for the deaths of 21 people linked to the tomb. The truth is only six of them died within a decade of the tomb's opening. Lord Carnarvon was the first. His death from pneumonia was a direct result of the mosquito bite, but he had suffered ill health for 20 years. Some people insist the curse is still active. There are many stories of tragic events connected with Tutankhamun exhibitions. In the 1970s, when tomb exhibits were being displayed in the US, a policeman guarding Tutankhamun's mask claimed he suffered a stroke because of the curse. A judge dismissed his claims for compensation.

Recent research has revealed that there may be some scientific basis for "The Mummy's Curse". Scientists say explorers who open Ancient Egyptian tombs may suffer illness from dangerous mould spores trapped in the tomb, such as *Aspergillus niger* and *Aspergillus ochraceus*. So, it seems the mummy may have had the last laugh after all...

➡ Want to unravel more mysteries? Go to Bermuda Triangle on pp.40–43 and Lord Lucan on pp.142–143.

Technology online

 Home

HOMEWARE   **COMPUTERS**   **ELECTRICAL GOODS**

BROWSE

You might think all the clever inventions like computers and electric lights belong to our modern age, and that ancient people had to make do with pretty basic tools and machines. But some recent discoveries of ancient objects are forcing archaeologists to think again. Perhaps ancient people had technology far more advanced than we previously imagined.

Matches found in the category you searched

Aeolipile (1)   **Lamp** (2)

> Ancient technology

Aeolipile (1)   *Not in stock*

This recent reconstruction was made from drawings made by Greek thinker Hero of Alexandria in the 1st century CE. Water in the flask is heated by a fire below, creating steam that emerges as jets from the pipes, making the flask spin around. Jet engines on modern airlines use the same principle to propel them through the air. The Ancient Greeks did not realize its full potential, using it only as a plaything.

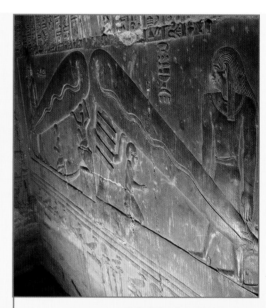

Lamp (2)   *Not in stock*

Is it possible that the Ancient Egyptians used brilliant artificial light to illuminate their dark tombs? In Dendera Temple, near Luxor, Ancient Egyptian reliefs show an object that some people have controversially claimed to be an electric lamp. If the Ancient Egyptians did have electric lights, how did they get their electricity? An ancient <u>battery</u> would have done the trick.

Battery (3) **Antikythera mech**

Antikythera mechanism

In 1901, divers exploring a shipwreck off the Greek island of Antikythera found remnants of a wooden and bronze case containing more than 30 gears. Dating from the 2nd century BCE, this ancient calculating machine had three dials, representing calendars, with hands that indicated the position of the Sun, Moon, planets, and some stars. Experts believe that dates could be entered via a crank and that the machine could then be used to:

See larger image

- track astronomical movements with remarkable precision;

- indicate how the Moon and the Sun move through the sky;

- predict eclipses;

- calculate the irregular orbit of the Moon;

- predict the position of the planets though the year.

Modern reconstruction
In 2006, scientists completed a virtual reconstruction of the Antikythera mechanism. Years of painstaking research have led them to conclude that the machine is an amazing mechanical computer dating back to 150–100 BCE, the earliest known forerunner of the modern computer.

Battery (3) Not in stock

email to a friend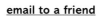

This 2,000-year-old artefact was found near Baghdad, Iraq, in the 1930s. The tiny clay pot containing a copper cylinder and an iron rod is constructed just like a modern torch battery – all you need to do is add acid. In the 1970s, scientists created a replica and filled it with grape juice, a mild acid. It gave an electrical current of one volt. Connected in a series, the batteries could have produced a much bigger current.

➜ For other ancient wonders, see Nazca Lines on **pp.32–33**, Piri Reis map on **pp.52–53**, and Rosetta Stone on **pp.116–117**.

B-2 Spirit

The Northrop B-2 Spirit first flew in 1989, and represented a giant leap forward in stealth technology. It is one of the most expensive planes ever built.

Invisible coating

The B-2 Spirit is coated in Radar Absorbent Material (RAM) – a special coating that allows radar waves to soak into it instead of reflecting them, making the plane "invisible" to radar.

Shield of secrecy

Scientists are now working on a special shield that will make a plane completely invisible by diverting light waves around it.

STEALTH TECHNOLOGY

Normally, an aircraft's presence can be detected through radar, which works by beaming out radio waves. These radio waves then bounce back off any object they come across, revealing the object and its position. To avoid radar detection, stealth technology uses a combination of special materials and multi-angled surfaces to "hide" the aircraft. This can reduce the chances of a radar signal bouncing back off it. Aircraft designers are finding increasingly creative ways to avoid radar detection, while radar designers look for more effective methods to beat those radar-blocking systems.

Silent running

The B-2 has various devices to reduce the sound of its engines, as well as reduce the effect of the sonic boom – the noise it makes when it reaches the speed of sound.

Keeping cool
The exhaust of the B-2 is vented above the wings instead of below the plane, so that it can not be detected by infrared thermal imaging devices on the ground.

Reduced vapour
A trail of vapour from the jet engines makes the presence of a plane obvious, so the B-2's wing tanks incorporate special chemicals that reduce the vapour.

Sky integration
Stealth planes that operate at night are painted black, while the day planes are painted a shimmering grey to blend in with the sky.

Active camouflage
This is a new idea that involves covering the plane with panels or coatings that change its appearance, like a chameleon, so that the plane can blend invisibly into any background.

Airframe
The frames of stealth planes are often made of special materials that make the aircraft undetectable to radar.

Golden cockpit
The cockpit glass is coated with a film of gold thin enough not to obstruct the pilot's view, but thick enough to reflect away radar signals.

Northrop Grumman B-2 Spirit	
Crew: 2	
Length: 21 m (69 ft)	
Wingspan: 52 m (172 ft)	
Wing area: 460 sq m (5,000 sq ft)	
Empty weight: 71,700 kg (158,000 lb)	
Loaded weight: 152,600 kg (336,500 lb)	
PERFORMANCE	
Maximum speed: 850 kph (528 mph)	
Range: 11,113 km (6,905 miles)	
Service ceiling (highest altitude): 15,000 m (50,000 ft)	
ARMAMENT	
227 kg (500 lb) bombs: 80	
340 kg (750 lb) bombs: 36	
907 kg (2,000 lb) missiles: 16	
Nuclear missiles: 16	

 For more action in the skies, see **Air Force One** on **pp.10–11** and **Watchers in space** on **pp.24–25**.

During World War II, machines that sent coded messages were vital for the safe transfer of secret information. "Enigma" was what the British called the Germans' message-coding machine, which the Germans used in co-ordinating U-boat submarine attacks on Allied convoys. The British intelligence service, based at Bletchley Park in England, were desperate to crack the code to save their ships.

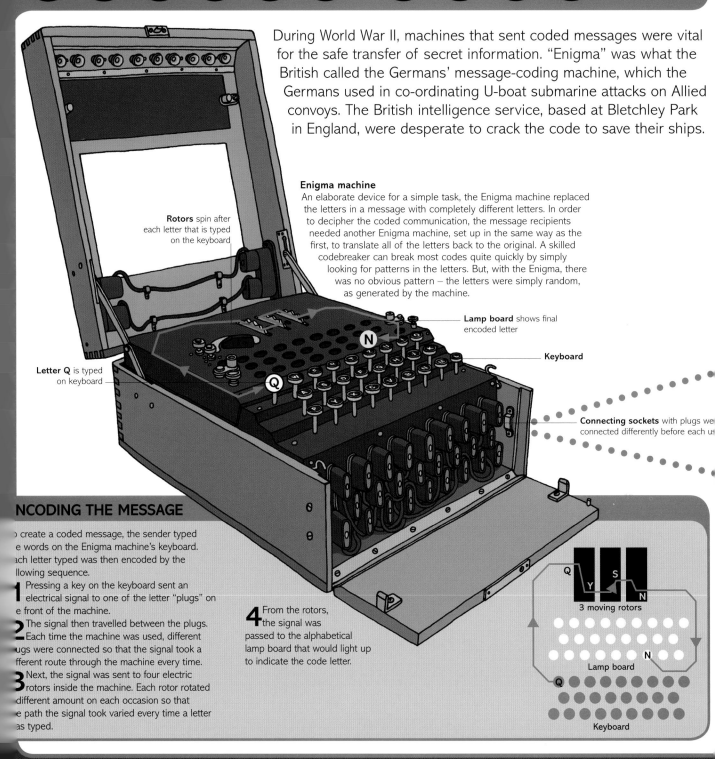

Rotors spin after each letter that is typed on the keyboard

Enigma machine
An elaborate device for a simple task, the Enigma machine replaced the letters in a message with completely different letters. In order to decipher the coded communication, the message recipients needed another Enigma machine, set up in the same way as the first, to translate all of the letters back to the original. A skilled codebreaker can break most codes quite quickly by simply looking for patterns in the letters. But, with the Enigma, there was no obvious pattern – the letters were simply random, as generated by the machine.

Lamp board shows final encoded letter

Keyboard

Letter Q is typed on keyboard

Connecting sockets with plugs we connected differently before each us

NCODING THE MESSAGE

create a coded message, the sender typed e words on the Enigma machine's keyboard. ach letter typed was then encoded by the llowing sequence.

1 Pressing a key on the keyboard sent an electrical signal to one of the letter "plugs" on e front of the machine.

2 The signal then travelled between the plugs. Each time the machine was used, different ugs were connected so that the signal took a fferent route through the machine every time.

3 Next, the signal was sent to four electric rotors inside the machine. Each rotor rotated different amount on each occasion so that e path the signal took varied every time a letter as typed.

4 From the rotors, the signal was passed to the alphabetical lamp board that would light up to indicate the code letter.

3 moving rotors

Lamp board

Keyboard

Cracking the code

The big breakthrough in cracking the code came when the British captured an Enigma machine. As soon as Bletchley Park picked up a message, they set about decoding it. This was difficult because the Germans changed the set-up of their Enigma machines daily. The Bletchley Park codebreakers used an early computer – called a bombe – to work through all the encoding possibilities. At the same time, the codebreakers tried to spot well-known German phrases in the message. It typically took two hours to decipher the communication.

Cracked it, sir!

German message intercepted at 2200 hours: "Await arrival of U-boat 488 and then attack the Allied convoy." Take evasive action.

Warning message

If the convoy received a warning message from Bletchley Park in time, they could either take evasive action or counter-attack the U-boat submarine by dropping underwater bombs called depth charges.

Await arrival of U-boat 488 and then attack the Allied convoy.

Receiving the coded message

When a message from German command was picked up, the U-boat submarine's radio operator keyed the coded message into the submarine's correctly assembled Enigma machine for decoding. The decoded message was then passed to the submarine's captain who would act accordingly.

Puzzle over codes on Bar codes pp.58–59 and Mary Queen of Scots on pp.92–93.

HITLER'S SECRET

During World War II, the German dictator Adolf Hitler was hatching a secret plan to develop a nuclear bomb that could have changed the outcome of the war. There were rumours that a plant in Norway was making "heavy water" for the Nazis. This form of water is used in the making of nuclear bombs. On hearing these reports, Europe's Allied forces decided to carry out a series of daring raids in Norway to sabotage the Nazi plan before a catastrophe could occur.

Operation Freshman

On 19 November 1942, Operation Freshman got underway – 15 men were meant to be dropped from gliders to meet up with the men from Operation Grouse. Bad weather caused the the gliders to crash, and the survivors were caught by the Gestapo (Nazi police). The Grouse men were luckier – they survived the winter by living in a cave and eating reindeer moss.

Top secret

Operation Grouse

In the first operation on 19 October 1942, four men parachuted from an aircraft in Norway and skied all night to the heavy water plant. They memorized a secret question to ensure they contacted the right people in the Norwegian resistance (a secret force fighting Nazi occupation of Norway). The question was "What did you see in the morning?". The correct answer was "Three pink elephants".

Operation Gunnerside

Six more men were dropped by parachute on 28 February 1943 to meet up with the Grouse four. The group of ten travelled through an icy ravine to the plant. They laid explosives, blew up the plant, and then escaped. Four stayed in Norway to help the resistance; the other six skied 400 km (250 miles) to Sweden and freedom.

The sinking

Following the explosion, the Nazis decided to take what was left of the plant to Germany, including the heavy water. On hearing about this, Norwegian resistance fighters drew up a secret plan to sink the *Hydro*, the ferry boat that was to carry the heavy water. On 20 February 1944, a bomb was smuggled on the boat. As *Hydro* crossed Lake Tinnsjo in Norway, the bomb exploded and the boat sank, finally ending Germany's nuclear programme.

Underwater exploration

In 2005, a television company sent a crew down to the bottom of Lake Tinnsjo to explore the wreckage of the *Hydro*. Using robotic underwater cameras, they discovered one of the barrels, which was found to contain heavy water. The discovery provided proof that the Nazis were developing a nuclear programme, though it seems they were only in the early stages of building a bomb.

➔ For more international intrigue, go to Cheyenne Mountain on pp.20–21 and Enigma Code on pp.132–133.

HOAXES

They say there's a sucker born every minute. The world is full of hoaxers, and these are some of the best spoofs that have been pulled. Would you have fallen for any of these tall tales? Be honest, now...

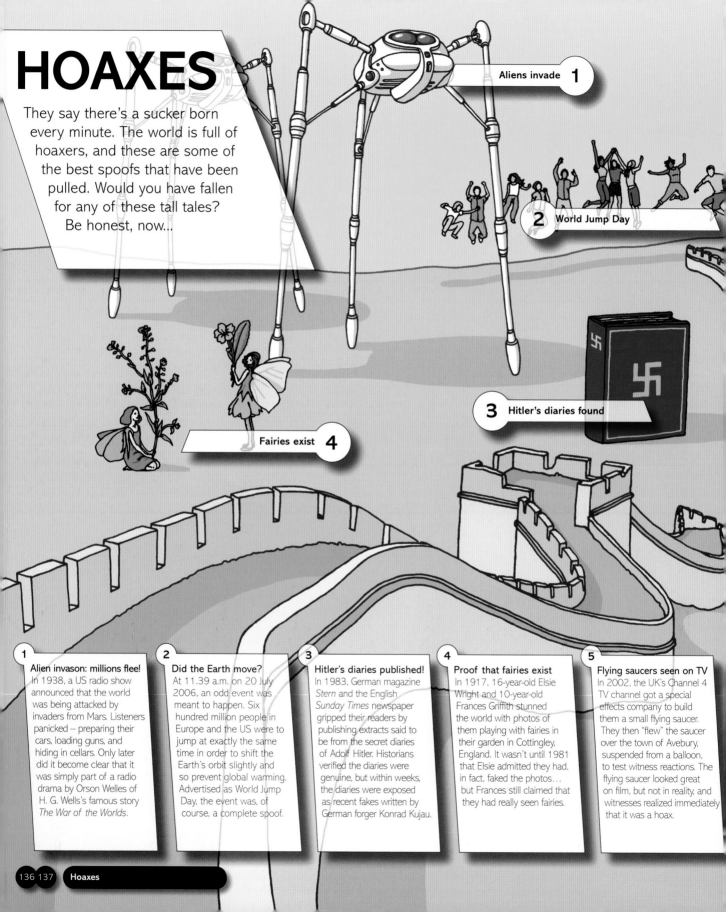

Aliens invade 1

World Jump Day 2

Hitler's diaries found 3

Fairies exist 4

1

Alien invason: millions flee!
In 1938, a US radio show announced that the world was being attacked by invaders from Mars. Listeners panicked – preparing their cars, loading guns, and hiding in cellars. Only later did it become clear that it was simply part of a radio drama by Orson Welles of H. G. Wells's famous story *The War of the Worlds*.

2

Did the Earth move?
At 11.39 a.m. on 20 July 2006, an odd event was meant to happen. Six hundred million people in Europe and the US were to jump at exactly the same time in order to shift the Earth's orbit slightly and so prevent global warming. Advertised as World Jump Day, the event was, of course, a complete spoof.

3

Hitler's diaries published!
In 1983, German magazine *Stern* and the English *Sunday Times* newspaper gripped their readers by publishing extracts said to be from the secret diaries of Adolf Hitler. Historians verified the diaries were genuine, but within weeks, the diaries were exposed as recent fakes written by German forger Konrad Kujau.

4

Proof that fairies exist
In 1917, 16-year-old Elsie Wright and 10-year-old Frances Griffith stunned the world with photos of them playing with fairies in their garden in Cottingley, England. It wasn't until 1981 that Elsie admitted they had, in fact, faked the photos... but Frances still claimed that they had really seen fairies.

5

Flying saucers seen on TV
In 2002, the UK's Channel 4 TV channel got a special effects company to build them a small flying saucer. They then "flew" the saucer over the town of Avebury, suspended from a balloon, to test witness reactions. The flying saucer looked great on film, but not in reality, and witnesses realized immediately that it was a hoax.

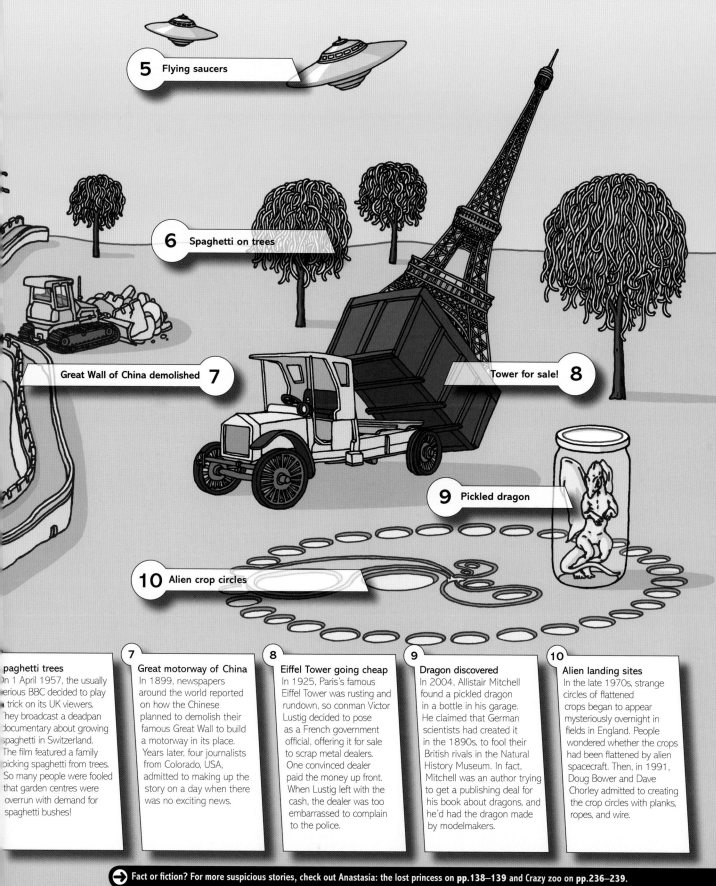

5 Flying saucers

6 Spaghetti on trees

Great Wall of China demolished **7**

Tower for sale! **8**

9 Pickled dragon

10 Alien crop circles

paghetti trees
On 1 April 1957, the usually erious BBC decided to play a trick on its UK viewers. They broadcast a deadpan documentary about growing spaghetti in Switzerland. The film featured a family picking spaghetti from trees. So many people were fooled that garden centres were overrun with demand for spaghetti bushes!

7 **Great motorway of China**
In 1899, newspapers around the world reported on how the Chinese planned to demolish their famous Great Wall to build a motorway in its place. Years later, four journalists from Colorado, USA, admitted to making up the story on a day when there was no exciting news.

8 **Eiffel Tower going cheap**
In 1925, Paris's famous Eiffel Tower was rusting and rundown, so conman Victor Lustig decided to pose as a French government official, offering it for sale to scrap metal dealers. One convinced dealer paid the money up front. When Lustig left with the cash, the dealer was too embarrassed to complain to the police.

9 **Dragon discovered**
In 2004, Allistair Mitchell found a pickled dragon in a bottle in his garage. He claimed that German scientists had created it in the 1890s, to fool their British rivals in the Natural History Museum. In fact, Mitchell was an author trying to get a publishing deal for his book about dragons, and he'd had the dragon made by modelmakers.

10 **Alien landing sites**
In the late 1970s, strange circles of flattened crops began to appear mysteriously overnight in fields in England. People wondered whether the crops had been flattened by alien spacecraft. Then, in 1991, Doug Bower and Dave Chorley admitted to creating the crop circles with planks, ropes, and wire.

➡ Fact or fiction? For more suspicious stories, check out Anastasia: the lost princess on **pp.138–139** and Crazy zoo on **pp.236–239**.

Anastasia:
the lost princess

In 1917, the tsar (emperor) of Russia, Nicholas II, was
overthrown by a bloody revolution. Revolutionary guards
seized the tsar, his wife Alexandra, their four young
daughters, and their son Alexei. Then, on 16 July 1918,
they were taken to a basement in Ekaterinburg and shot.
The assassination of the Russian royal family shocked the
public and many people refused to believe it had happened.
Rumours spread that the youngest daughter, Anastasia, had
escaped. But if so, where was she?

The Romanovs
In 1894, Nicholas II became
tsar and ruled over Russia.
He married the German
Princess Alexandra two
years later. They had
four beautiful daughters
called Olga, Tatiana, Maria,
and Anastasia. The couple
longed for a son as only
a boy could become tsar.
Finally, in 1904, their son
Alexei was born.

Alexei Romanov

Anastasia Romanov

Nicholas II

Maria Romanov

Alexandra of Hesse-Darmstadt

Tatiana Romanov

Olga Roman

Family massacre
On the fateful day that the Romanov family
were shot in the basement, bullets seemed
to bounce off three of the sisters. This
was because the girls were protected
by the diamonds they had sewn in their
clothes. At this point, the guards used
bayonets to kill them. However, a soldier
named Tchaikovsky claimed he had seen
Anastasia moving and rescued her.

ВРАГ У ВОРОТ!!!

ВСЕ НА ЗАЩИТУ
ПЕТРОГРАДА

Sole survivor?
Some stories say that
Alexei was also protected
from the bullets by a diamond
waistcoat and managed to
escape. Soon various men
appeared, claiming to be the
prince. No one took the claims
seriously, because Alexei
suffered from haemophilia –
a condition in which the blood
fails to clot. This makes his
survival unlikely.

Captive audience

The possibility that Anastasia, the youngest princess, had survived captured the public's imagination. The fact that she had stood to inherit a huge fortune also inspired interest. Of all the women who claimed to be Anastasia, Anna Anderson had the most supporters. She was taken to a mental hospital with memory loss in 1920, after attempting to jump off a Berlin bridge. When Anna Anderson died in 1984, many still believed she was Anastasia.

The truth is tested

In the 1980s, the emergence of DNA testing enabled Anna Anderson's claim that she was Anastasia to be tested. Though Anna was now dead, a sample of her DNA from a hospital operation survived. Anna's DNA was tested against a sample from the UK's Duke of Edinburgh – a close relative of the Romanovs. She was not the lost princess, but a poor Polish girl.

Finding the bodies

After the family were killed, the bodies were thrown down a mineshaft, then later brought up and buried in a forest. In the 1980s, three men found the grave but kept their discovery secret. DNA tests in 1998, after the bodies were finally dug up, confirmed they were the Romanovs. Strangely, not one but two bodies were missing – one of the girls and also Alexei's.

The royal burial

In July 1998, the remains of Tsar Nicholas II, his wife, and three of his daughters were finally buried in St Peter's and St Paul's cathedral in St Petersburg. But who was the missing daughter? Russian experts concluded from skull measurements that it was Maria. Others pointed out that all the princesses' bodies found were tall, yet Anastasia was very short. Could Anastasia have survived?

For more lost souls, seek out Bermuda Triangle on pp.40–43 and Haunted places on pp.94–95.

Roswell Alien Tribune

Issue number: 56196892090301012

Price: S1

The Roswell case is the most famous alleged flying saucer incident.

Alien alarm raised as flying saucer discovered in Roswell, New Mexico

US Air Force recovers crashed "flying disc" from local ranch

JULY 1947

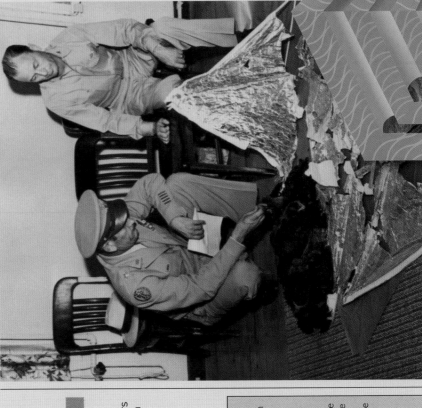

General Roger Ramey (kneeling) and chief of staff Colonel Thomas Dubose present remains of the "weather balloon".

The discovery of the crashed craft was made by prominent local rancher William "Mac" Brazel. He contacted Major Jesse Marcel at the Roswell Army Air Field. Military personnel swooped in and removed the debris to a secure location.

The little town of Roswell is buzzing with rumour and speculation. While some residents feel that there is a rational explanation, others are spreading stories of "little green men". They believe that the discovery is proof that aliens have tried to land in Roswell. A few excited citizens are even planning a welcome party for the aliens!

Air Force General Roger Ramey sought to quash the rumours of a UFO (unidentified flying object). He issued a statement saying that the wreckage was simply tin foil, bits of flowery sticky tape, and strips of rubber from a weather balloon. The Air Force fears that the heightened interest may lead to private military matters being exposed, which would be a threat to US security.

Air Force responds: In 1994, the US Air Force issued their own report on the incident. They revealed that the debris was from a top-secret mission called Project Mogul. The mission did involve balloons, but they were designed to carry a dish with a microphone to detect Russian nuclear tests. They called it a weather balloon to protect the project's secrecy.

Alien dissection

Were eight alien bodies recovered by the military at the Roswell crash site?

JULY 2006

Roswell plumber Ray Danzem claims he saw alien bodies being carried into the base on a stretcher as he worked near the Air Force barracks in July 1947. Mary Bush, who worked at the base's hospital, describes seeing "a creature from another world" and added that she was also called on to assist two doctors as they examined the bodies of three "aliens". Joseph Montoya, one of New Mexico's top politicians, has spoken of how he saw four little men with oversized heads, big eyes, and slit-like mouths near the supposed crash site.

These descriptions match the images in a short film released by Ray Santilli in 1995. The blurry black-and-white footage shows alien bodies being dissected, which Santilli claims was shot by the US military at Roswell. In 2006, though, he admitted the footage was fake.

The Air Force stated that the "bodies" were part of another secret project, called Operation High Dive. This project involved high-altitude parachute tests with dummies that could well have been mistaken for "aliens". Despite this, the debate about what was found at Roswell in July 1947 shows no sign of ending. Military cover-up or a far-fetched story spun out of control? You decide.

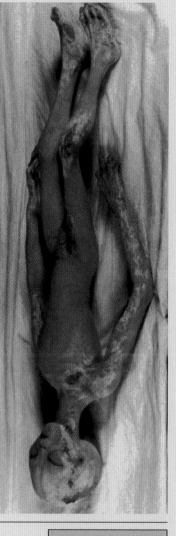

Roswell revisited

More than 30 years after the Roswell incident, the man who made the find speaks about it for the first time

NOVEMBER 1980

The metal at the Roswell crash site resisted hammering and burning according to rancher Mac Brazel (pictured left), who made the discovery in 1947. Other witnesses have backed up his account of the debris's strange qualities. Brazel claims he was ordered to keep quiet about this at the time.

His comments are sure to revive speculation, especially after Major Marcel's recent statement that the debris was "nothing made on this earth" and that the weather balloon story was just a military cover-up.

Air Force responds:
The military reiterated their position that the Roswell case was not a conspiracy. Security measures were only carried out to protect the secrecy of Project Mogul. They pointed out that the reliability of these new claims was questionable, emerging as they had more than 30 years after the event.

CURIOUS SYMBOLS
Strange signs inscribed on the metal pieces at the centre of famous Roswell controversy

Hieroglyph-like symbols were found on the metal debris in the Roswell crash, according to new claims. A sketch (above) was made by Major Jesse Marcel's son. So why was this information not made more widely known and what could the markings mean?

Air Force responds:
Some of the balloon radar reflectors had been made in lofts also used to make women's clothes. The symbols were transferred on sticky tape from fabric.

Are you into aliens? Check out Nazca Lines on pp.32–33, Who are the Men in Black? on pp.48–49, and UFO on pp.200–201.

Lord Lucan

The evening of Thursday, 7 November 1974 began as any other at 46 Lower Belgrave Street, London. At the Lucan family home, the nanny was finishing the final chores of the day, while the children were sleeping. But a chain of events was about to start that would result in a horrific murder, a violent assault, and one of the most famous disappearing acts of all time...

Lord Lucan
Richard Bingham was the 7th Lord Lucan. He was called "Lucky" because of his gambling habit. On the evening in question, there are two reported sightings of Lucan at the Clemont Restaurant at 8.45 p.m. and 9 p.m.

Lucan children
The three Lucan children slept through the attacks at their family home. Lucan was no longer living there, but he was known to want full custody of all the children.

Frances Lucan
Days after, the Lucans' daughter Frances gives a confused account of the evening of 7 November. She says she heard her mother scream, saw blood on her face, and then her mother and father together.

Sandra Rivett
The victim was the Lucan family nanny, Sandra Rivett. As Lucan knew, Thursday was Sandra's night off, but she had agreed to work that night. She is murdered at approximately 9 p.m.

Lady Lucan
Veronica Duncan married Lucan in 1963, but they split up in 1972, because of her depression and his gambling. She is assaulted at about the time the nanny is murdered.

Police
A this point, police are called to 46 Lower Belgrave Street.

Dear Bill,

The most ghastly circumstances arose tonight, which I briefly described to my mother, when I interrupted the fight at Lower Belgrave St and the man left.

V. (Veronica, his wife) accused me of having hired him. I took her upstairs and sent Frances up to bed and tried to clean her up. She lay doggo for a bit. I went into the bathroom, then left the house.

The circumstantial evidence against me is strong in that V. will say it was all my doing and I will lie doggo for a while, but I am only concerned about the children. If you can manage it I want them to live with you – Coutts St Martins Lane will handle school fees.

V. has demonstrated her hatred of me in the past a would do anything to see me accused.

For George & Frances to go through life knowing th father had stood in the dock for attempted murder would be too much. When they are old enough to understand, explain to them the dream of param and look after them.

Yours ever,

Lucky

Statement
In a statement given later, Lady Lucan names her husband as her attacker and the murderer of the nanny.

Accusation
At 9.45 p.m., Lady Lucan enters a pub called The Plumbers Arms shouting, "He's murdered the nanny!"

Lady Lucan says she was struck with a blunt instrument.

Forensic report
Blood groups A and B are found at the crime scene. Lady Lucan is blood group A, the nanny is blood group B.

Blood group **A** found on pipe

Body found
Police find a blood-stained sack with Sandra Rivett's body inside. She has been battered with a blunt instrument.

Lead piping
A length of lead piping at the scene fits Lady Lucan's description of the weapon.

Pathologist
Injuries to Sandra Rivett and Lady Lucan are confirmed as similar.

Letter: 1
Lucan writes to say he stopped a fight between Lady Lucan and an unknown man.

Phone calls
Lucan makes a series of telephone calls immediately after leaving his wife's house.

Though Lucan
attempts to call his friend Bill Shand Kydd, there is no answer on two separate occasions.

Checking up
Lucan makes another call to his mother at 12.15 a.m. to check that she has taken the children to her house.

When Lucan
rings his friend Madeleine Floorman, he's too upset for her to understand him.

Lucan calls his
mother. He says there is a problem at the house and asks her to pick up the children.

Lucan's flat
When Lucan's mother goes to the house, she finds the police there. She explains that the Lucans were separated, and tells them where Lucan has been living. She then leaves with the children.

The Maxwell-Scotts
Lucan travels to Sussex to see his friends Ian and Susan Maxwell-Scott in a car he borrowed from a friend, Michael Stoop. At 11.30 p.m., Lucan arrives, but only Susan is there.

Abandoned car
The car that Lucan had borrowed from his friend Michael Stoop three days before the incident is found abandoned at the port of Newhaven three days later.

Traumatic night
Michael Stoop receives a letter from Lucan. A page missing from a notebook found in the car was used to write it. In the letter, Lucan refers to a "traumatic night of unbelievable coincidences" on 7 November.

Police search
With the new information, police search Lucan's flat. They find car keys, a passport, a wallet, three address books, a driving licence, and a piece of lead pipe.

Lucan's story
Susan retells Lucan's story. He said he was passing his wife's house and saw her fighting with a man. He enters, but the man runs. Lady Lucan goes outside shouting "Murder!" Lucan panics and leaves, too.

No sighting
Although Lucan was claiming to be heading home when he left Susan's house, he was never seen again. There has been no validated sighting of him to this day.

The hunt
The search for Lucan lasted years. Cameras placed on autogyros took aerial photographs and land searches regularly took place.

Bloodstained letters
At Susan's house, Lucan writes two letters to his friend Bill Shand Kydd and posts them. Both envelopes are bloodstained.

Matching samples
When forensic teams take samples from the deserted car, blood groups A and B are found. Lead pipe is also discovered in the car. The blood and the lead pipe are the same as those previously found at the Lucan home.

The theories
■ Some people think Lucan could have committed suicide in Newhaven Harbour. However, 14 divers were sent to search the waters and no body was found.

There is a sale coming up at Christies Nov 27th, which will satisfy bank overdrafts. Please agree reserves with Tom Craig.

Proceeds to go to:
Lloyds, 6 Pall Mall
Coutts, 59 Strand
Nat West, Bloomsbury Branch

Who also hold an Eq. and Law Life Policy. The other creditors can get lost for the time being.
Lucky

Quick exit
After writing the letters, Lucan leaves Susan's house in a hurry saying he must get back. He hastily drives away in the borrowed car.

Same blood
The bloodstains on both envelopes are found to be types A and B again.

■ Although Lucan did not have his passport or wallet with him, it is still possible that he sneaked on to a ferry from Newhaven Harbour without anyone noticing. Local fisherman said they saw a man resembling Lucan.

Guilty verdict
At the trial, the jury took only half an hour to deliver their verdict. They found Lord Lucan guilty of the murder of Sandra Rivett. However, his sentence remains unserved because no one can find him.

■ Following "sightings" of Lucan in Africa, Australia, France, Italy, and the Netherlands, it was thought that he may escaped abroad. But to this day, there has been no confirmed sighting.

Letter: 2
In this letter, Lucan gives details of a sale at Christies, which will help pay off debts.

 For more criminal curiosities check out Hackers on pp.60–61, Safecracking on pp.194–195, and Law tour on pp.206–207.

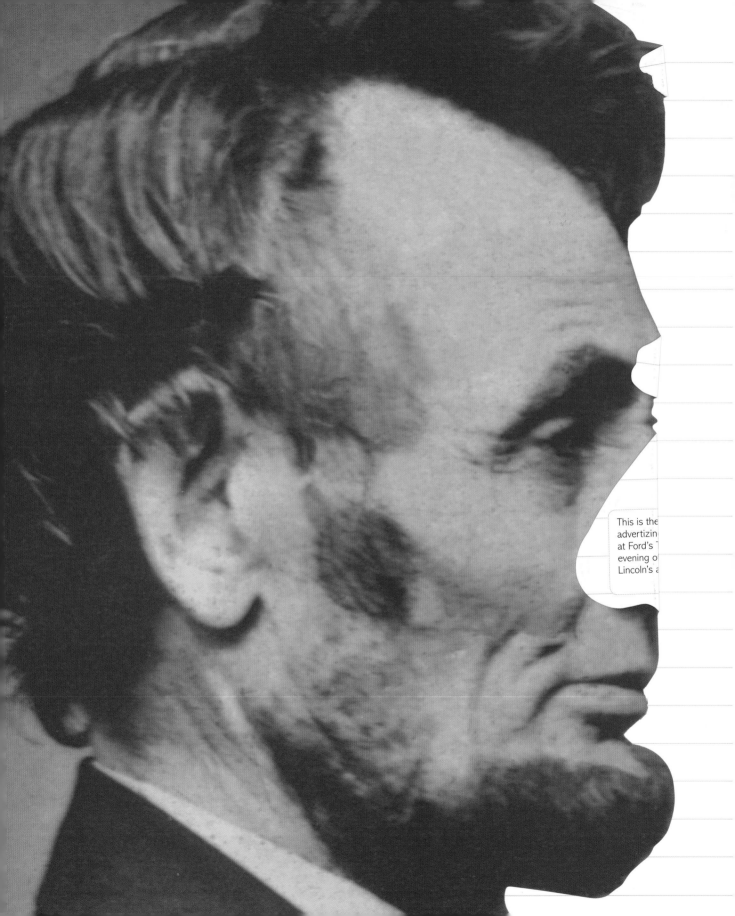

This is the
advertizing
at Ford's T
evening o
Lincoln's a

For more weird coincidences

who was Jack?

A thick mist swirls through the gas-lit backstreets of east London. Suddenly, a shout rings out in the darkness. A woman's body has been found, horribly mutilated. Serial killer Jack the Ripper has struck again! During the autumn of 1888, the Ripper claimed five victims, taunted the press with mocking letters, and evaded police capture. Then, just as suddenly as they began, the murders stopped. But the Ripper's identity remains a mystery.

Victim: Mary Jane Kelly, 25
Murdered: 9 November 1888
Crime scene: Miller's Court, 26 Dorset Street
Circumstances: When Mary Kelly's landlord broke into her bedroom at 10.45 a.m., he found her mutilated body on the bed. One witness claimed to have seen her 45 minutes earlier. Another heard a cry of "Murder!" in the night. She was the last victim.

DORSET STREET, E1

MITRE SQUARE, E1

Victim: Catherine Eddowes, 46
Murdered: 30 September 1888
Crime scene: Mitre Square, E1
Circumstances: Catherine Eddowes was last seen at 1.35 a.m. on the corner of Duke's Street, talking to a young man with a red scarf who looked like a sailor. Her body was found in Mitre Square ten minutes later. She was murdered on the same night as Elizabeth Stride.

BUCK'S ROW, E1

Name: Mary Ann Nichols, 44
Murdered: 31 August 1888
Crime scene: Buck's Row (now Durward Street)
Circumstances: Mary Ann "Polly" Nichols was last seen at 2.30 a.m. walking along Whitechapel Road. Her body was found in a narrow alley about 70 minutes later.

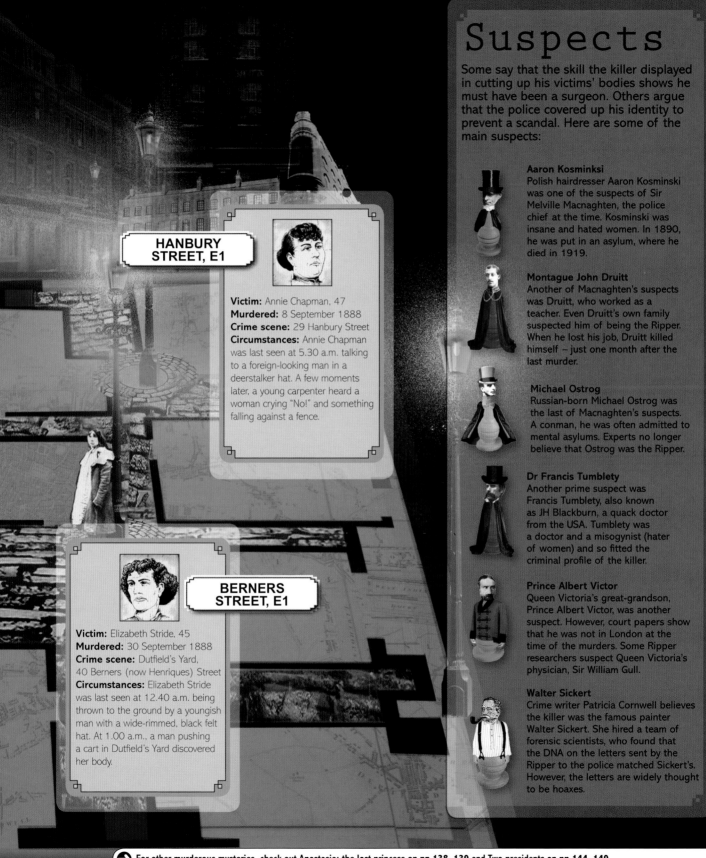

HANBURY STREET, E1

Victim: Annie Chapman, 47
Murdered: 8 September 1888
Crime scene: 29 Hanbury Street
Circumstances: Annie Chapman was last seen at 5.30 a.m. talking to a foreign-looking man in a deerstalker hat. A few moments later, a young carpenter heard a woman crying "No!" and something falling against a fence.

BERNERS STREET, E1

Victim: Elizabeth Stride, 45
Murdered: 30 September 1888
Crime scene: Dutfield's Yard, 40 Berners (now Henriques) Street
Circumstances: Elizabeth Stride was last seen at 12.40 a.m. being thrown to the ground by a youngish man with a wide-rimmed, black felt hat. At 1.00 a.m., a man pushing a cart in Dutfield's Yard discovered her body.

Suspects

Some say that the skill the killer displayed in cutting up his victims' bodies shows he must have been a surgeon. Others argue that the police covered up his identity to prevent a scandal. Here are some of the main suspects:

Aaron Kosminksi
Polish hairdresser Aaron Kosminski was one of the suspects of Sir Melville Macnaghten, the police chief at the time. Kosminski was insane and hated women. In 1890, he was put in an asylum, where he died in 1919.

Montague John Druitt
Another of Macnaghten's suspects was Druitt, who worked as a teacher. Even Druitt's own family suspected him of being the Ripper. When he lost his job, Druitt killed himself – just one month after the last murder.

Michael Ostrog
Russian-born Michael Ostrog was the last of Macnaghten's suspects. A conman, he was often admitted to mental asylums. Experts no longer believe that Ostrog was the Ripper.

Dr Francis Tumblety
Another prime suspect was Francis Tumblety, also known as JH Blackburn, a quack doctor from the USA. Tumblety was a doctor and a misogynist (hater of women) and so fitted the criminal profile of the killer.

Prince Albert Victor
Queen Victoria's great-grandson, Prince Albert Victor, was another suspect. However, court papers show that he was not in London at the time of the murders. Some Ripper researchers suspect Queen Victoria's physician, Sir William Gull.

Walter Sickert
Crime writer Patricia Cornwell believes the killer was the famous painter Walter Sickert. She hired a team of forensic scientists, who found that the DNA on the letters sent by the Ripper to the police matched Sickert's. However, the letters are widely thought to be hoaxes.

For other murderous mysteries, check out Anastasia: the lost princess on pp.138–139 and Two presidents on pp.144–149.

1
2
3
4
5
6
7
8
9
10
11
12
13
14
15
16
17
18
19
20
21
22
X
Y

There are 22 regular pairs of chromosomes. The 23rd pair are X and Y – the chromosomes that determine whether someone is male or female. The stripes on the chromosomes are bands of genes that show up when stained with chemicals and examined under a microscope.

Your body is made of trillions of minute packets called cells. Tucked away inside almost every one is a tiny set of 23 pairs of chromosomes, which look like tangles of wool under a powerful microscope. Each set of chromosomes is a complete instruction manual for the cell to make another human body pretty much like yours – simply by putting natural chemicals together in the right way. The "recipes" for these chemicals are contained in more than 25,000 genes. Scientists have pinpointed the chromosome location of many of the genes, producing a human genome map. They hope to unravel all the genome's secrets so they can pinpoint just which gene gives you red hair and which genes might make you ill if they go wrong.

HUMAN GENOME

Making the map

An international team of scientists from the United States, China, France, Germany, Japan, and the United Kingdom worked on the Human Genome Project, which to date has cost US$3 billion. DNA test samples were gathered from a large number of donors, but only a few were processed. This way the donor identities were kept secret, ensuring no one would know whose DNA had been analyzed. It has even been rumoured that much of the DNA came from a single anonymous male donor from Buffalo, New York, USA, codenamed RP11.

Chromosome 4 has more than 700 genes. If you've got red hair, it's because of one of the genes on this chromosome.

There are more than 3,000 genes on Chromosome 1, with instructions to make more than 3,000 different chemicals. If you're deaf, it may be because a genes on this chromosome has gone wrong.

You could say Chromosome 11 has got smelly genes, because most of the genes for the smell receptors in your nose are found on it.

The X chromosome is one of the sex chromosomes that decide whether you're a boy or a girl. There are more than 2,000 genes on the X. If you've got two matching X chromosomes, you're a girl. But unlike the other chromosomes, the sex chromosomes do not always come in matching pairs…

If you're rather vertically challenged, you can blame Chromosome 3, which is home to the height genes.

If you're immune system – your body's defence against germs – isn't working well, the culprit may be Chromosome 14.

Chromosome 2 has as many as 1,800 genes. It plays a large part in making the chemicals that build up your body's defences against disease.

A little short-sighted? Look no further than Chromosome 9, where you may find the faulty gene responsible.

…The other sex chromosome is Y. If you've got one X and one Y, you're going to be a boy. The Y has just 78 genes, but size isn't everything!

Among the 1,700 genes on Chromosome 19 are the ones that decide whether your eyes will be blue, green, brown, or grey.

 For more mind-bogglers, exercise your brain cells with Fibonacci on pp.86–87 and Dark matter on pp.156–157.

DNA time capsule

Inside every cell in your body are tiny little bundles called mitochondria. These mitochondria are the cell's mini power plants, converting food chemicals into energy. Each mitochondrion also contains a remarkable secret that enables scientists to trace your ancestry back over thousands of years. If we go back far enough, we find we all have the same ancestors.

DNA TIME CAPSULE

The mitochondrion's secret is a snippet of DNA – the chemical instructions for life. However, unlike the main DNA in the centre of a cell, the tiny snippet of DNA in mitochondria (mtDNA) is passed on only from mother to child and remains constant from one generation to the next. Your mtDNA is pretty much the same as your mum's, and her mum's, and so on right back through the generations. Your mtDNA is like a living time capsule in every cell of your body. By taking a sample of mtDNA from the inside of your mouth, scientists can trace your direct female ancestry back thousands of years.

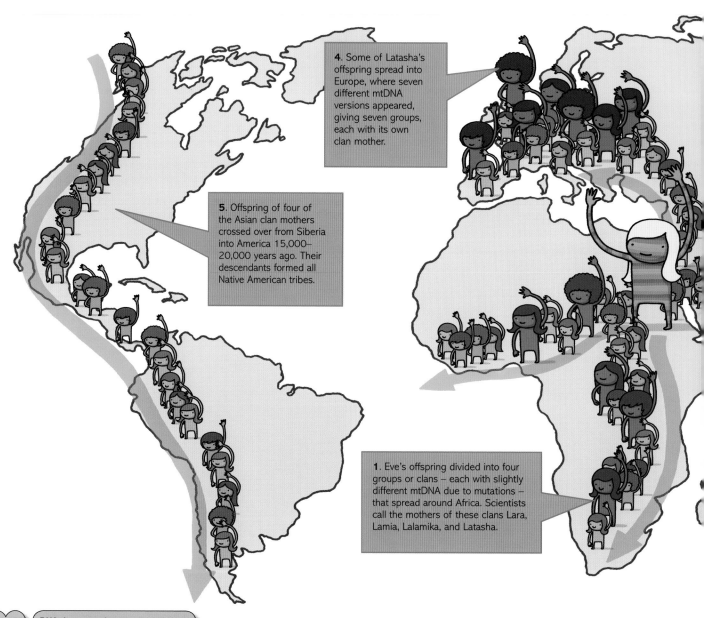

4. Some of Latasha's offspring spread into Europe, where seven different mtDNA versions appeared, giving seven groups, each with its own clan mother.

5. Offspring of four of the Asian clan mothers crossed over from Siberia into America 15,000–20,000 years ago. Their descendants formed all Native American tribes.

1. Eve's offspring divided into four groups or clans – each with slightly different mtDNA due to mutations – that spread around Africa. Scientists call the mothers of these clans Lara, Lamia, Lalamika, and Latasha.

AFRICAN EVE

Over the generations, mtDNA gradually changes or "mutates", but in such a slow and predictable way that scientists have been able to track the changes back through time. They have discovered that every person alive today is descended from a woman who lived in Africa about 140,000 years ago. Scientists call her mitochondrial "Eve" after the first woman in the Bible, but she was not the only woman alive or the first woman, only our most recent common ancestor following the female line. Eve's descendants began to move out of Africa 50,000–70,000 years ago. Using mtDNA scientists have been able to plot how they spread around the world.

AFRICAN EVE'S OFFSPRING

This map shows how all African Eve's descendents spread out around the world. As they moved and had children, they passed on their mtDNA. Mutations gave several different mtDNA versions, so people can be divided into different branches or haplogroups, each with its own "haplo" mother. A particular set of haplomums appeared in each part of the world and most people there are descended from them. If you're African, you are probably descended from one of four African "mums" (red). If you're Asian or native Australian, you likely to be descended from one of seven Asian haplomums (purple). But because people have always moved about there are at least a few people everywhere descended from other haplomums.

THE SEVEN MUMS OF EUROPE

The mtDNA evidence suggests that if you are European you have probably descended from one of seven women. Geneticist Bryan Sykes has given each of these women a name: Ursula, Xenia, Helena, Velda, Tara, Katrine, and Jasmine. Many southern Europeans are children of Jasmine and Katrine, while many northern Europeans are children of Tara, Ursula, and Xenia. Children of Helena and Velda spread throughout Europe.

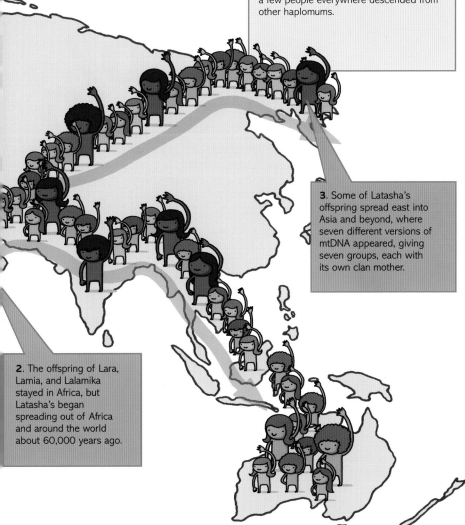

3. Some of Latasha's offspring spread east into Asia and beyond, where seven different versions of mtDNA appeared, giving seven groups, each with its own clan mother.

2. The offspring of Lara, Lamia, and Lalamika stayed in Africa, but Latasha's began spreading out of Africa and around the world about 60,000 years ago.

YOUR SECRET IDENTITY

Every now and then mtDNA does change, and over time humans have split into more than 30 groups, called haplogroups or clans. Each of us belongs to a haplogroup, but the group you belong to is not the same as your race. Racial characteristics can be misleading, and many races contain a mix of haplotypes. The hidden time capsule of mtDNA inside your body cells indicates your true line of female ancestry.

➔ **For more mind-boggling body facts, go to Human genome on pp.152–153 and The body uncovered on pp.166–167.**

Dark matter

In the 1930s, Swiss-American scientist Fritz Zwicky first put forward the idea of dark matter. He had noticed that some galaxies in space spin around too quickly for the gravity of all their visible matter to hold them together. Observations in the 1970s confirmed he was right. So if gravity wasn't keeping the galaxies together, what was?

4%

WHAT IS KNOWN
Less than four per cent of the matter in the Universe is the ordinary stuff we know about – the atoms and molecules that make up the mountains, seas, stars, planets, animals, and even ourselves. So, what makes up all the rest?

96%

WHAT IS UNKNOWN
The remaining 96 per cent of the Universe is made up of invisible matter so mysterious that there is no way to detect it directly. The only reason we know it exists is because of its effect on everything else. It seems there may be two types of hidden matter – dark matter that makes up 23 per cent, and dark energy that accounts for a whopping 73 per cent.

23% DARK MATTER

STAR BURGER
It is now known that all the stars glittering in each galaxy are really embedded in huge "haloes" of dark matter stretching far beyond the visible edge of the galaxy. The stars are like a scattering of salt in the centre of a very big bun of dark matter that cannot be seen. It is the mass of this dark matter that provides the gravity necessary to hold the spinning galaxies together.

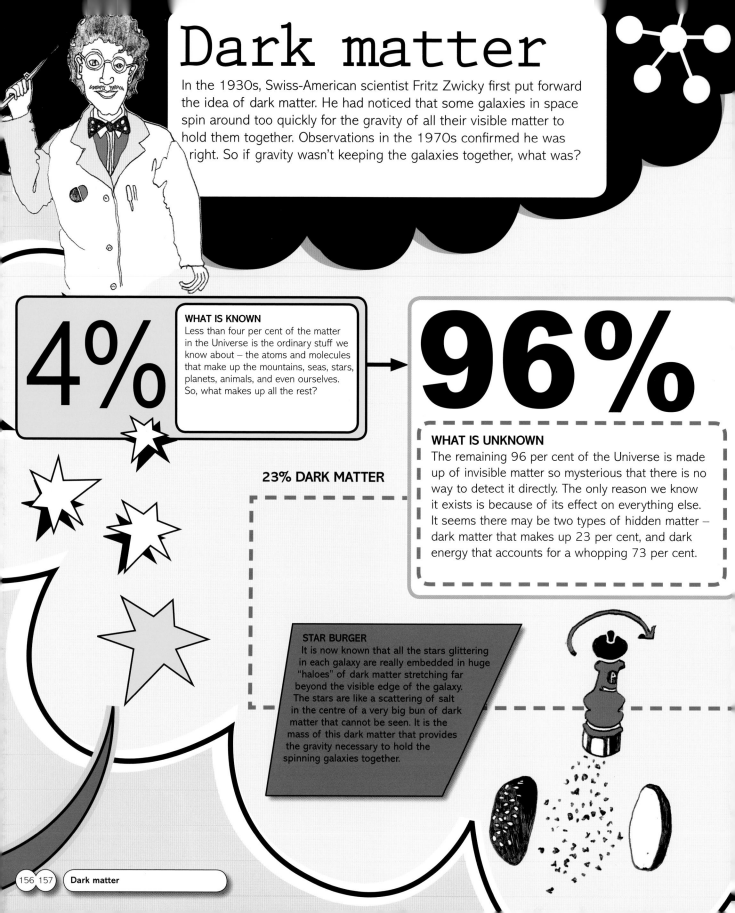

DARK ENERGY

In 1998, astronomers studying bright exploding stars called supernovas realized they could be used to work out how fast the Universe is expanding. While people thought the expansion of the Universe was slowing down, supernovas showed it was actually accelerating. There is a repulsive force pushing the Universe apart that completely counteracts the gravity of ordinary matter pulling it together. This repulsive force is called dark energy.

3% DARK ENERGY

ACROSS THE UNIVERSE

So, it seems there are two mysterious dark forces at work in the Universe. While dark matter is an an invisible force whose gravity helps pull the Universe together, dark energy is a repulsive force that makes the whole Universe expand at an even more rapid rate.

CAN YOU FEEL IT?

Dark matter is like an incredibly thin gas that doesn't move. The stars and planets whizz through dark matter as if through a fog. The solar system is flying through this dark matter fog at more than 220 km/s (136 miles/s). What's most amazing is that dark matter particles are so tiny they simply pass straight through us as the Earth carries us around. In fact, a billion dark matter particles pass through you every single second!

THE REAL DEAL

Astronomers divide the dark matter in galaxy haloes into Massive Astrophysical Compact Halo Objects (MACHOS) and Weakly Interacting Massive Particles (WIMPS). MACHOS are made up of ordinary matter that does not shine, including black holes, burned-out stars, and giant planets, such as Jupiter. However, WIMPS are a mysterious form of matter, made of particles that are completely unknown to science.

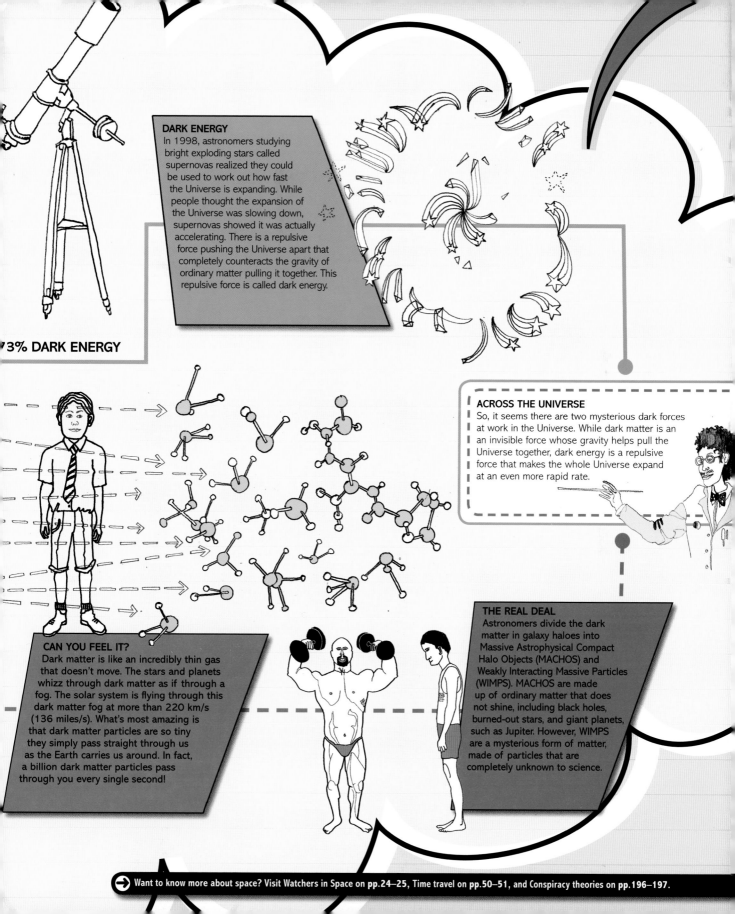

Want to know more about space? Visit Watchers in Space on **pp. 24–25**, Time travel on **pp. 50–51**, and Conspiracy theories on **pp. 196–197**.

All of us change our minds every now and then, but it's our choice. So what if you were forced to change your mind against your will, maybe without you knowing it? This is known as "brainwashing", so named because your own ideas and personality are often washed away in the process. There are many stories of secret agencies and cult religious groups using psychological techniques to wash people's minds, or is it all just spin?

BRAIN WASHING

Three-step cycle

In the 1950s, some American soldiers held as prisoners of war in Korea emerged from captivity as converts to communist beliefs. They decided to stay in Korea even after their release. Many Americans were convinced they had been brainwashed, including psychologist Robert Jay Lifton, who claims it happens in three stages:

1 Breaking you down
The first stage is breaking down your sense of self. Brainwashers verbally attack you for weeks until you're exhausted, telling you that you're not who you think you are. Next they make you feel guilty by continuously reminding you of the bad things you've done. Finally they get you to agree you must be the world's worst person. You end up having a nervous breakdown, asking yourself the questions "Who am I?", "Where am I?", and "What am I supposed to do?"

2 Offering help
As you wallow in a state of confusion, the brainwashers offer to help you. They tell you that you can help yourself by admitting where you've gone wrong, and they explain that this is the root of your suffering.

3 Building you up again
Now your brainwashers are ready to show you a bright new path. Why not forget your bad old ways, they say, and come and join us? We can show you the right road to take, and you'll feel a lot better. So you do as they say. Soon you are utterly convinced that they were right all along. You are a new person. And so the brainwashing process is complete!

WASH-O-TRONIC

13:03

Brainwashing techniques:

Isolation There's nothing like keeping you on your own, away from family and friends, to make you feel vulnerable.

Sleep deprivation When you're very tired, keeping you awake with repetitive music will make you feel disorientated.

Hypnosis By pretending to relax you with soft light, gentle music, and monotonous voices, brainwashers can hypnotize you.

Peer pressure They'll put you in a group of people and then make you feel left out unless you join them.

Removal of privacy With no time or space on your own to think, you don't realize you've been brainwashed.

Verbal abuse They repeatedly hurl insults at you until you can take it no more and beg them to stop.

Disinhibition They make you feel that anything is acceptable, no matter how strange or silly it may seem.

Imitation They encourage everyone to dress in the same way to ensure no one has their own identity.

Chanting and singing They get you to sing and chant together in order to drive all other ideas from your head.

Guilt trips They make you feel incredibly guilty for all the foolish things you got up to in the past.

Threats They scare you with nasty threats whenever you step out of line.

For more brainwaves go to Strange vibrations on **pp.108–109** and Unconscious mind on **pp.180–181**.

Advertising tricks

Adverts are everywhere – on TV, radio, and the Internet, in newspapers, and on enormous billboards. Advertisers pull all kinds of stunts to convince consumers to buy a product, such as using snappy slogans and showing glossy images that promise an ideal lifestyle. Here are some tricks of the trade.

BIGGER BYTES

Advertisers try to convince you that a new gizmo will improve your life. To keep sales flooding in, manufacturers make minor changes to a gadget and relaunch it as a new, improved version.

IDEAL HOME

To sell an item such as a chair, advertisers create a glamorous home to surround it. The chair itself might be dull, but they put the idea in your head that if you buy the chair you're on your way to sitting pretty in your dream home.

LIVING THE DREAM

Advertisers use attractive people to make you link a product with being attractive. Many ads feature celebrities. Advertisers want you to think that by buying a product you will enjoy the blinged-up lifestyle of the rich and famous.

OPEN ROAD

Most people use cars for local trips or dull motorway journeys. So why do car ads show vehicles whizzing along beneath desert sunsets or swooping around mountain passes? It's because they want consumers to think that if they buy the car, that's what life will be like.

CHEAP TRICK
Check the small print at the bottom of an advert promising cheap air flights. Often the budget airline's bargain price only covers a one-way flight and doesn't include the extra airport taxes.

HOLLYWOOD SMILE
Models in ads may look great, but it is often the result of expert lighting to disguise blemishes, and computer manipulation afterwards to take off weight, smooth skin, whiten teeth, and hide wrinkles.

SUNDAE BEST
Food in adverts may look good enough to eat, but in fact is often fake. Ice-cream is made with margarine, powdered sugar, and artificial colourings, and it never melts.

THIRST QUENCHER
Drinks advertisers make sure they incorporate sounds and images that will make you feel thirsty, such as hot, sunny skies, ice cubes clinking in a glass, and liquid pouring from a bottle.

SMELL OF SUCCESS
With smell-o-vision still the stuff of science fiction, perfume ads have to rely on appealing to your other senses. Images are used to portray a perfume as a youthful or sophisticated fragrance.

BOGUS BURGER
To make a burger look tasty in an advert, it is painted with brown food colouring. The bun is sprayed with waterproofing to stop it getting soggy and the sesame seeds are superglued in place. Tasty!

For other persuasive powers go to Magic tricks on pp.78–81 and Brainwashing on pp.158–159.

WHAT'S IN YOUR FOOD?

A chicken burger's not very mysterious, is it? It's just chicken, bread and a bit of salad, right? Look closer at the list of ingredients. Most ready-made food is packed with preservatives and artificial flavourings. Try this for a recipe – it's a lot to swallow:

Basic ingredients

Chicken

Lettuce

Tomato

Cheese

Bread roll

Hidden extras

■ Chemical additives

The average person consumes about 7 kg (15 lb) of food additives a year.

1 **Preservatives** are added to stop food going rotten.

2 **Antioxidants** stop oxygen in the air making the food rancid.

3 **Emulsifiers** are used in sauces to ensure that oil and water stay mixed.

4 **Anti-caking agents** prevent powders in food sticking together to form lumps.

5 **Dyes and colourings** Processing makes food lose its attractive natural colour, so artificial colours are added to make it look tastier.

6 **Flavourings** Food can lose flavour in processing or storage, but manufacturers can choose from a range of more than 4,500 chemical flavours to give the food a delicious synthetic taste instead.

7 **Salt** was originally used as a preservative, but is now added as a seasoning or flavour enhancer.

8 **Sugar** and artificial sweetners are added for flavour.

■ Contaminants

1 **Pesticides** A third of the fruit and vegetables you eat contains residue of the pesticides sprayed on them when they were grown. Mouthwatering!

2 **Growth hormones** Sometimes chickens are injected with chemical hormones to make them grow large quickly.

■ Others

1 **Hydrolyzed proteins** Ground-up, left-over skin and bone are often added to fresh meat to add bulk. They can come from any meat source. So fresh chicken breasts may actually contain beef and pork in the form of hydrolyzed proteins.

2 **Water** Processed bread is 45 per cent water. Fresh chicken is up to 45 per cent water. Water is added to plump up the food – it is cheaper than using more meat.

3 **Hydrogenated fat** Hydrogenated fats in the bread are hard artificial fats that allow products to be baked fast at high temperatures. They are widely thought to cause cancer and heart disease if eaten in large quantities.

4 **Soya** plant increases the protein content of processed meat.

For more chemical concoctions go to Fancy a strawberry milkshake? on pp.164–165 and Alchemy on pp.172–173.

fancy a strawberry milkshake?

You might think the taste of a strawberry milkshake is just strawberries and milk. But if you buy it ready-made, you won't believe what shoots through your straw.

A ready-made strawberry milkshake gets its flavours from more than 60 chemicals, and not a single strawberry! In fact, all ready-made food gets at least some of its flavour from a blend of chemicals. The flavours are brewed up by chemists who send out their special blends to food manufacturers all around the world. The precise blend that goes into each product is a closely guarded secret. Sometimes, it mimics the natural flavour of the food and other times, it offers an entirely new, synthetic taste.

These are the ingredients that go into a "naturally flavoured" strawberry milkshake: **milk-fat and non-fat milk**, sugar, sweet whey, **high-fructose corn syrup**, guar gum, monoglycerides and diglycerides, **cellulose gum**, **sodium phosphate**, carrageenan, citric acid, **E129** and artificial strawberry flavour (amyl acetate, amyl butyrate, amyl valerate, **anethol**, anisyl formate, benzyl acetate, **benzyl isobutyrate**, butyric acid, cinnamyl isobutyrate, **cinnamyl valerate**, cognac essential oil, **diacetyl**, dipropyl ketone, thyl butyrate, ethyl cinnamate, **ethyl heptanoate**, ethyl heptylate, ethyl lactate, **ethyl methylphenylglycidate,**

ethyl nitrate, ethyl propionate, ethyl valerate, heliotropin, **hydroxyphrenyl-2-butanone** (10% solution in alcohol), ionone, isobutyl anthranilate, **isobutyl butyrate**, lemon essential oil, maltol, 4-methylacetophenone, **methyl anthranilate**, methyl benzoate, methyl cinnamate, methyl heptine carbonate, methyl naphthyl ketone, methyl salicylate, **mint essential oil**, neroli essential oil, nerolin, neryl isobutyrate, **orris butter**, rum ether, phenethyl alcohol, rose, undecalactone, vanillin, and **solvent**).

Solvent?
Mmm!

Real strawberries are just not up to the task of flavouring a strawberry milkshake. They are bulky and difficult to store and keep fresh, as well as being costly to grow and ship. Also, their flavour is far too subtle for many people, and they aren't sweet enough to hook you instantly with their taste. So goodbye, berry!

→ Want to know more about the crazy stuff in your chow? Check out What's in your food? on pp.162–163.

Your brain cells started dying off as soon as you were born. Fortunately, you've got billions of brain cells, and replacements are created throughout your life. The brain is more than 80 per cent water. **Tiny mites live at the base of your eyelashes. They have eight legs each and look like alligators! They're actually good for you because they gobble up germs.** You spend half an hour every day blinking – every blink takes 0.3–0.4 seconds. **Nose hairs act like a net to trap and remove nasty particles from the air.** It's impossible to sneeze with your eyes open.

Your body sheds tens of thousands of skin flakes every minute. Over a lifetime a body loses 20 kg (44 lb) of skin flakes. Feeding on our skin flakes (and preventing a flake mountain from forming) are millions of tiny dust mites, each no bigger than a full-stop. **Human fingertips are so sensitive that they can feel an object move even if it only stirs a thousandth of a millimetre.** Some cells, like skin and blood, are only a few weeks old, while others (nerves and bone) may be as old as you are.

Your body is made up of trillions of living cells, of which there are more than 200 different types. The instructions for a cell are on 46 chromosomes in its nucleus. Each of the two strands of DNA that make up a chromosome are about one metre (three feet) long, which is pretty amazing seeing as it curls up so small it can only be seen under an electron microscope. **Electricity constantly shoots through your body, transmitted by the cells that make up your nervous system, and controlled by the brain.** Air is sucked into and pushed out of our lungs by the action of surrounding muscles: the diaphragm and rib muscles. We breathe faster when we exercise because our muscles need more oxygen, faster! **One American man hiccupped non-stop from 1922 to 1990.** In an average lifetime, the heart beats about 2.5 billion times to pump blood around the body. **The first blood transfusion took place in 1667 between a lamb and a human.** An average-size adult has 5 litres (10.5 pints) of blood flowing through their body. **The heart pumps 640 litres (169 gallons) an hour, that's 8,000 litres (2,113 gallons) per day, and 3 million litres (792,500 gallons) per year – more than enough to fill an Olympic-sized swimming pool!** Unravelled and stretched out, an adult's blood vessels would extend across 160,930 km (100,000 miles) – that's long enough to go around the Earth four times.

Approximately 10 per cent of the population are left-handed. No-one knows for sure what causes it, but more men than women are left-handed. **The hand has 27 bones. Eight bones make up the wrist, the palm contains five, and 14 bones make up the fingers and thumb. Half of all 206 bones in your body are in your hands and feet.** Uncut fingernails will continue to grow and grow. The longest uncut fingernails ever measured reached the staggering length of 68.6 cm (2 ft 3 in).

THE BODY UNCOVERED

In the five minutes it will take you to read this, your heart will beat 350 times, you'll blink 30 times, and each of your blood cells will have travelled around your body five times. While you read, you are forming new cells and shedding skin flakes, your hair and nails are growing, your nose hairs are filtering the air you breathe, your eyes are processing the words, and your brain is working out what they mean, Phew! No wonder you need so much sleep!

Food spends up to six hours in your stomach being digested. Your stomach has to produce a new layer of mucus every two weeks otherwise it will digest itself. **Roundworms and tapeworms can infect the small intestine, where they grow, reproduce, and feed on food that is being digested. Tapeworms in humans can grow up to 10m (30 ft) long.** Bacteria in your colon paint your poo brown, and produce the gases that make you fart. **Centuries ago, doctors believed that uroscopy (urine-gazing) was a good way of diagnosing disease. This involved tasting the urine. Yum, bottoms up!**

You are taller in the morning than you are when you go to bed. Walking or standing during the day compresses your joints and spine causing a small difference in height. **When you sleep, you lose up to 42 g (1.4 oz) in weight every hour.** The average adult body contains enough fat to make seven bars of soap. **The largest muscle in your body is the one you are sitting on. The gluteus maximus, or buttock muscle, helps us stand upright.** Bones are weight for weight six times stronger than steel. **Your toenails grow four times slower than your fingernails.** Your bones only make up 10 per cent of your total body weight.

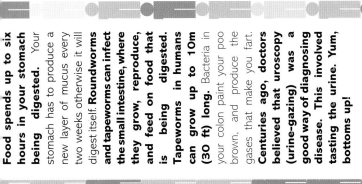

Want to get even more brainy about your body? Go to Human genome on pp.152–153 and DNA time capsule on pp.154–155.

DIRT

Your home may look clean and tidy, but it is really a house of horrors. About 10 million tiny lumps of grit, dead skin, rubber, and ash lurk in every cubic metre of air. If bacteria are kept warm and well-fed at your place, the happy souls will increase in number by splitting in half. They do this every 20 minutes, so in just nine hours, a single bacterium produces 100 million copies of itself. It seems you've got a lot of uninvited guests...

Bedroom bugs
■ Human skin flakes make up 80 per cent of the dust in beds and carpets. House dust mites feed on these skin flakes.
■ Up to 10 million dust mites share your bed each night.
■ The average house dust mite poos 20 times a day. About 10 per cent of the weight of a two-year-old mattress is dead dust mites and their faeces. Sleep tight!

Magnified dust mite

Pesky paintwork
■ Fungus can get into any cracks in paint and reproduce. This results in either dry or wet rot fungus, both of which can make wood crumble.

Carpet critters
■ The average household carpet is five times filthier than a busy street.
■ Moths lay their eggs in the wool of clothes and carpets. These eggs hatch into larvae, which eat the wool and leave holes.
■ Nestling under carpets are beetles. Called "woolly bears", they eat through carpets.

Bathroom beasts
■ Although the average toilet contains less bacteria than the kitchen sink, each time you flush, a cloud of 10 billion bacteria and viruses is sent up into the air.
■ Toothbrushes are packed with bacteria.
■ Bacteria called thermophiles set up home in your hot water system.
■ Mould thrives in damp places. Any black spots on bathroom tiles are mouldy growths.
■ Wingless insects called silverfish dwell in wet places, such as inside baths and under sinks.

Plant pests
■ Red spider mites live on house plants and feed on the leaves.

Wood worries
■ Tiny holes in wood flooring are caused by woodworm, the larvae of tiny beetles. Woodworm feed on wood until they grow into adult beetles.

Magnified flea

Furry foes
■ Fleas live on the fur of cats and dogs, but their eggs drop into carpets.
■ In a few hours of grooming, a cat will release several billion droplets of spit into the air.

Homework horrors
■ The average personal computer has 400 times more bacteria than a toilet.
■ Telephones are absolutely filthy! Each handset is covered in more than 100,000 bacteria.
■ Paper mould grows quickly on old books and wallpaper.
■ Bookworms are small lice that live in books and eat the paper.

Fungus on bread

Kitchen creepies
■ The water contained in an average sink sponge contains about 50 million bacteria.
■ There are billions of mould spores in the air, ready to settle and spread on rotting food.
■ Green, grey, or black fungus grows on bread. This fungus is made from mats of tangled threads called hyphae.
■ Larger mites feed on cheese and their munching creates a grey crust. Yum.

If you love dishing the dirt, take a look at What's in your food? on **pp.162–163** and Nuclear waste on **pp.170–171**.

THE SOLUTION?

Many scientists think burying the waste deep below ground, sealed in special canisters is the best option, but there are many factors to consider to keep it safe for 100,000 years.

☢ No-one can be sure the canisters will stay leakproof.
☢ Earthquakes might cause the canisters to crack.
☢ Water trickling through the ground or microbes that live underground might corrode the canisters.

Some scientists think the waste could be made safer by vitrification – mixing it into glass. Glass is airproof and waterproof and chemically inert (inactive).

WHERE TO BURY IT?

In most places in the world, the ground is too wet, too unstable, or too near where people live. So, in the USA, they are thinking about burying it beneath a mountain in the Arizona desert called Yucca Mountain. In Europe, stores are being built in very hard old rock in Sweden and Finland, and surrounding the canisters with a special material called bentonite that swells to seal them in and cushion them against shocks.

BAD IDEAS

Some people suggested blasting the waste into space. If the rocket crashed the result could be disastrous – at best spreading radiation far and wide, at worst creating a nuclear explosion.

Another idea is to dump it in the sea. No container can stay leakproof forever, so the sea could become disastrously polluted by radioactive waste.

DEVIOUS!

Many countries have been getting rid of their waste by shipping it to other countries and paying them to deal with it.

WHERE IS IT NOW?

Already, a staggering quarter of a million tonnes of spent fuel is sitting in pools of water to keep it cool and catch the radiation it emits. In these pools, the waste fuel is divided by special radiation-absorbing boron panels to prevent a nuclear reaction starting. By 2020, there will be almost twice that amount of spent fuel and many new pools will need to be built or another solution found.

NUCLEAR WASTE

Nuclear power stations use the heat from rods of uranium fuel to generate energy. So far, so good? Well, this is only half the story. After the heat is used, the rods of spent fuel are left behind. The rods are dangerously radioactive and will give off deadly radiation for 100,000 years – and nobody really knows what to do with them.

For other explosive issues go to Alchemy on **pp.172–173** and Spontaneous combustion on **pp.184–185**.

Alchemy

The ancient science of alchemy dates back thousands of years. Cloaked in mystery, it has always been viewed with suspicion. Young alchemists were sworn to secrecy when they became trainees, and alchemists wrote their notes in riddles, symbols, and codes so that no one but an alchemist could decipher them. As a result, they are often viewed as con artists or fools. In fact, the alchemists' work laid the foundations for modern medicine and science, especially chemistry.

Alchemists experimented with substances in the medieval equivalent of a laboratory, but they also studied astrology and magic. They had three main goals:

● To discover the "philosopher's stone" – the ultimate pure, essential, and "incorruptible" material.

● To change base metal into gold. If they could find the philosopher's stone, its power would enable them to turn corruptible, base metal, such as lead, into incorruptible gold, which never corrodes. Bling it on!

● To discover the "elixir of life" – a remarkable liquid that would stop the ageing process corrupting living things. In other words, the secret of eternal youth. Cool!

Scientific achievements

In Medieval times, no one knew more about substances than alchemists. This knowledge had immense practical value and paved the way for a number of scientific breakthroughs.

Ore refining

As alchemists searched for ways to purify impure metals, they discovered many of the processes of extracting metals from ores that are still used today. Ores are the raw rock materials in which metals are found, mixed in with many unwanted substances.

Medicines

The alchemist Paracelsus realized the need to understand the chemistry of the body and its illnesses. Building on his alchemical knowledge, he introduced the idea of finding simple chemical drugs to remedy the chemical imbalances in the body caused by illness, as well as the use of specific doses.

Chemical elements

The idea of the basic chemicals or "elements" that are so central to science today came from the alchemists. In fact, Robert Boyle, the scientist credited with first promoting the idea, was secretly an alchemist.

Experiments

A key part of modern scientists' work is carrying out experiments – this idea was developed by the 13th-century alchemist and monk Roger Bacon.

Incredible inventions

In addition to researching chemical substances, alchemists were also responsible for a number of important inventions.

Gunpowder
Saltpetre, sulphur, and carbon – the main ingredients of gunpowder – were also key substances in the search for the philosopher's stone. Needless to say, it was only a matter of time before alchemists made a big bang! Chinese alchemists are thought to have discovered gunpowder first. Medieval alchemists, such as Roger Bacon and Albertus Magnus, developed the invention.

Inks and dyes
More than 4,000 years ago, Indian alchemists are thought to have devised the recipe for Indian ink still used today. It was made from soot floating in water, with gum arabic (a type of gum used to thicken mixtures).

Glassworks
Alchemists may well have invented glass; they certainly made many improvements to the glass-making process, including the invention of "decolourizers", such as manganese dioxide, which took out impurities such as iron to leave the glass crystal clear.

Eyeglasses
Alchemists provided most of our early knowledge of lenses and optics, and it was the alchemist Roger Bacon who invented spectacles in the 13th century.

Modern revelations

In recent years, scientific discoveries have shown that there may be more to some of the alchemists' most astounding claims than was ever realized.

Transmutation of gold
Modern nuclear chemistry has demonstrated how one element can be transmuted (changed) into another. In 1980, nuclear scientist Glenn Seaborg changed lead to gold in microscopic quantities inside a nuclear reactor. This involved huge amounts of energy, and recently, some scientists have made unverified claims that they transmuted lead to gold in low energy, cold nuclear fusion experiments.

Transmutation of living things
The discovery of genetic modification techniques has shown that, like chemical elements, living material can be transmuted, too, by swapping parts of its DNA. Scientists are also working on the chemistry of ageing, and many believe they will soon be able to prolong youth and extend life dramatically.

Psychology
The alchemists believed that all objects possess a spirit, and that there is a deep link between all things, which is expressed in symbols. In the 1930s, Carl Jung developed his revolutionary idea of the Collective Unconscious – the symbolic ideas that we all inherit – and soon realized he was looking at something very similar to alchemy.

➔ For more scientific secrets, see Nuclear waste on pp.170–171 and Unconscious mind on pp.180–181.

HERMES TRISMEGISTUS

The first great alchemist, Trismegistus, lived in Egypt about 4,000 years ago. Most of his secrets were lost, but legend has it that the Emerald Tablet, said to contain his instructions for alchemists, was found in a cave clutched in his dead hands.

ROGER BACON

English monk and alchemist Roger Bacon (1214–1294) invented spectacles, revealed the role of air in burning, and anticipated many inventions of the future, such as powered ships, motor cars, and aircrafts. Despite his achievements, his reputation as a magician brought him into conflict with the Church and he spent many years in prison.

JOHN DEE

As a youngster, John Dee (1527–1608) was arrested for reading the horoscopes of English King Henry VIII's two daughters, Mary and Elizabeth. Then, as a leading alchemist, mathematician, and expert in navigation, Dee was made chief astrologer and scientific adviser by the newly crowned Queen Elizabeth. Later in life, a frustrated Dee tried to acquire scientific knowledge through magic.

Alchemists and wizards

For thousands of years, alchemists kept their work secret and many were thought to be wizards and magicians. Then, in the 1600s, people learned of their quest for the philosopher's stone that would turn base metal into gold. Alchemy quickly attracted all kinds of conmen and was soon discredited. The brilliance and scientific achievements of some alchemists was then quickly forgotten.

PARACELSUS

Swiss-born Paracelsus (1493–1541) travelled widely, seeking out alchemists and physicians from whom he could learn. He believed an alchemist's first task was to make medicines, not gold, and he pioneered the idea that illnesses could be treated by small doses of chemicals – the basis of medicine today.

NICOLAS FLAMEL

This French alchemist was said to have discovered the secret of the philosopher's stone and apparently succeeded in making gold. When Flamel (1330–1417) died, a thief broke into his tomb to get at the secret – but is said to have found the tomb empty.

AGRIPPA

A dark legend surrounds the name of Agrippa (1486–1535), who, on his deathbed, is said to have released a terrible black dog to prey upon the world. This black dog is the same Grim that features in the *Harry Potter* books.

TRITHEMIUS

After publishing his book *Steganographia*, Trithemius (1462–1516) was accused of dealing with the occult, and his book was banned by the Church for preaching black magic. In 1993, *Steganographia* was finally deciphered properly and shown to be the first ever book on secret codes… written in a brilliant code!

 For more magical mysteries, make your way to Magic tricks on pp.78–81 and Alchemy on pp.172–173.

In 2002, scientists decided to test the brainpower of highly ranked memorizers at the World Memory Championships. The tests revealed that the memory champions' brains were no different from anybody else's. Moreover, they performed no better in intelligence tests than "average" people. What the researchers did discover, though, was that nine out of ten of the memory champs were using the secret techniques shown here.

Can you imagine memorizing the order of every single playing card in a pack? Memory champ Andi Bell can do it in just 32.9 seconds. What's more, in 2003, he memorized the order of the cards in ten packs – all 520 cards – in just 20 minutes. Such feats seem so astounding that it is easy to assume that the people who perform them must have very special brains, or are just amazingly clever. In fact, most memory champs are simply using a variety of secret tricks to help them memorize things, some dating back thousands of years to the time of Ancient Greece.

NUMBER IMAGES

One trick to remember numbers, developed in Ancient Greece, is to link each number to a memorable image with a vaguely similar shape to the number. You can choose your own image, but here are some suggestions.

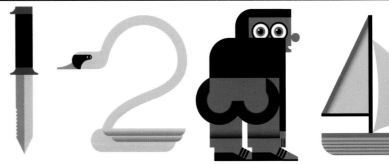

Themistocles

Seneca

Throughout history there have been a number of great memorizers, whose reputed feats are so astonishing that we cannot be entirely sure they are true. It is claimed that Themistocles knew the names of 20,000 citizens of Ancient Athens, but he was a slouch compared with Seneca who knew the names of all the citizens of Ancient Rome.

Italian 17th-century memorizer Antonio Magliabechi spent his entire life surrounded by books. When he was given charge of the 40,000 volumes of the Grand Duke of Tuscany's library in Florence, it is reported he memorized every single word of every single volume. To test Magliabechi's abilities, an author gave him a manuscript and asked him to read it as quickly as possible. After Magliabechi returned the manuscript, the author pretended that he had lost it, and asked Magliabechi to help him remember what he could. To his amazement, Magliabechi wrote down the entire book without missing a single word or punctuation mark. Pretty unforgettable!

Magliabechi

Turn over

NUMBER CRUNCHER

07964034512

If someone showed you their mobile phone number once for just three seconds, do you reckon you could remember it?
Try looking at the number above for three seconds. Close the book immediately and try to write it down.
Bet you got the wrong number.

Now group the numbers and say them aloud to yourself twice:

079 640 345 12

Shut the book and try writing it down. How did you do this time? Easy, eh? Memory experts call this technique chunking.

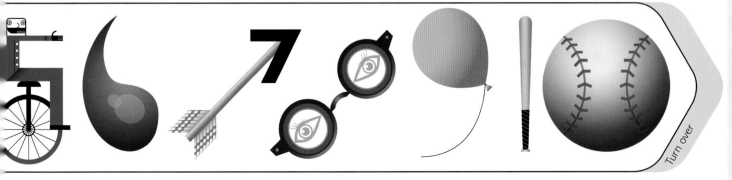

Once you've got the number images firmly in your head, you can use them to help you remember all kinds of things. You'll be amazed by how effective it is. Try to memorize this shopping list using number images. Simply combine the objects on the shopping list with the number images to create a memory tag for each object.

The amazing thing about this trick is that the memory tags stay in your brain for ages, so it's great for things you want to remember for a long time.

5 eggs
1 bag of sugar
2 bags of flour
8 bottles of milk
4 apples
10 chocolate biscuits
6 fish fingers
9 oranges
3 bananas

A monocyclist balancing 5 eggs

A knife piercing a bag of sugar

A swan enveloped in a cloud of flour

A bottle of milk wearing spectacles

A sailing boat with 4 apples on board

A baseball player smashing a chocolate biscuit with his bat

A fish weeping over the loss of his fingers

Orange balloons

A banana skin stuck to the seat of someone's trousers

The most popular trick used by memory champs is the method of places. The idea is to take a route you know really well, such as your route to school, then in your imagination link the objects you want to remember to places along the route. The images here show how you could link points on your route to tasks to remember for the school fête. By linking the points to the route, you will find it easier to remember what tasks to do and in what order.

1 Task: borrow a table for the fête. Imagine yourself in the kitchen, lifting a huge table.

2 Task: recruit a friend to help at the fête. Imagine an unbelievably long line of your friends queueing at your door.

3 Task: collect items to sell at the fête. Imagine yourself picking up items strewn all along your garden path.

4 Task: make a banner. Imagine your garden gate with the biggest, most colourful banner flying over it.

5 Task: borrow a cashbox to keep fête takings in. Imagine finding the biggest cashbox ever on the corner of your street.

6 Task: make a flier to advertise the fête. Imagine seeing every headline on a newspaper stall announcing your fête.

7 Task: clean up your sale items for the fête. Imagine everyone in the bus queue cleaning items with rag and polish.

8 Task: separate out any valuable objects. Imagine sitting on the bus holding on to enormous jewels and dumping any junk.

9 Task: make price labels for the sale. Imagine you school bus stop plastered with price labels.

10 Task: hand over your takings. Imagine standing at the school gate handing in a huge trunk of money.

→ **For more brain-busting facts go to Strange vibrations on pp.108–109 and Brainwashing on pp.158–159.**

Unconscious mind

You may think you know what you're doing, but your unconscious mind, the part of your mind you are unaware of, can play some very strange tricks. Goodnight, sleep tight… or will you?

SLEEP PARALYSIS (Finding upon waking that your body is completely paralyzed): Scientists believe this o— because during normal "dreaming sleep" the body is paralyzed to stop you from acting out your dreams an injuring yourself. Sleep paralysis occ— when the brain wakes up, but the b— is still frozen in a dream.

DREAMING Some scientists think dreaming helps convert the short-term memories of the day to long-term memories. Others suggest it's the brain's daily housekeeping, or a reworking of problems. Some people believe dreams have meanings and messages, such as predicting the future.

NIGHTMARE (Unpleasant or even horrific images, sounds, and sensations experienced while dreaming): During a nightmare, your brain is as active as when you are awake. Scientists believe it is caused by stress. Others blame diet, such as eating cheese before going to bed (although experts discount this). People once thought nightmares were the result of evil magic.

DÉJÀ VU (Weird sensation that somehow you've been through the same experience before): Scientists think this may be caused by an overlap in the memory process, whereby the experience is registered in your unconscious brain a split second before you register it consciously. So when you become aware of it, your brain already has a memory of it. Some people think déjà vu is the memory of dreams. Others believe that it is a memory from a previous life!

SLEEPWALKING (Doing normal waking activities while asleep): Walking in your sleep is common, but some people may talk, eat, bath, dress, or even drive a car. One person even committed a murder. Scientists believe it starts when the sleepwalker wakes suddenly during Slow Wave Sleep (SWS), when the brain is ticking over very slowly. Children and men are more likely to sleepwalk than women.

Want to uncover more mind mysteries? Go to Strange vibrations on pp.108–109 and Memory tricks on pp.176–179.

Reincarnation

Many religions believe that a part of us lives on after we die. Some people are convinced we are actually born again to live a new life in a new body. There is no real evidence for reincarnation, but there are many instances of people claiming to remember past lives including details they couldn't possibly know. Many cases of reincarnation feature famous people; others are much more obscure, but are often more intriguing.

Bard reborn To be or not to be William Shakespeare, that is the question for many people who claim to be reincarnations of the famous English playwright. It's not hard being the bard though. So much is known about him already, there are no details that only the "real" Shakespeare reincarnated could reveal.

All in an accent Some people believe that in a past life they were on board *Titanic*, the great ocean liner that hit an iceberg and sank in 1912. American William Barnes claimed he was the ship's designer Tommie Andrews. Barnes spoke in a Scottish accent when "remembering" it, but Andrews was, in fact, Irish. Oops.

DNA denial A lot of stories of reincarnation are attached to the Romanovs, the Russian royal family that was assassinated in 1918. American Donald Norsic claimed that in his past life as the Russian tsar, he escaped to the Sahara. But his claims were disproved in 1994 when DNA tests showed the Romanovs really did die in Russia.

Going under One way of trying to find out if you've lived past lives is by hypnosis. While in a trance, some patients tell stories of past lives. Most experts think the mind is making it all up.

Fact or fiction Welshwoman Jane Evans recalled seven past lives under hypnosis. In one, she claimed to be a Jewish woman living in 12th-century York in England. She described details of life then — and also of being killed in a church crypt during a terrible massacre of the Jews. A history professor testified as to how accurate her knowledge of historical details was, but the church she described, St. Mary's Castlegate, did not have a crypt. Then several months later, during renovation, a crypt was discovered. However, it was found that Jane's story resembled a historical novel she had read in school. At least she learned something there.

War bore Roman emperor Caracalla (186–217 CE) believed he was a reincarnation of the famous Greek war leader Alexander the Great (356–323 BCE) and fancied himself as a military hero. In reality, Caracalla was a cruel and brutal dictator.

French fancy In 1894, medium Hélène Smith claimed she was the reincarnation of the French queen Marie Antoinette, who was guillotined during the French Revolution in 1793. The multi-talented Hélène also believed she could communicate with Martians!

Children from a past life

Englishwoman Jenny Cockell was haunted by dreams of a life in a cottage as an Irish country woman called Mary Sutton. This woman had apparently died 20 years before Jenny was born, leaving eight children. After years of research, Jenny located Mary Sutton's children, by then all grown up, of course. Mary's children did not believe that Jenny was their mother reincarnated, but instead thought that their mother was speaking through Jenny from beyond the grave.

Mind your language

Tales of reincarnation are much more strange when they are about the lives of ordinary people. It is particularly odd when the person under hypnosis knows a foreign language they claim they cannot speak or read when awake. Famous Hollywood actor Glenn Ford recalled five previous lives when hypnotized. One life was as a French cavalry officer in the 1600s. While recalling the officer's life, he spoke fluent 17th-century French, even though when awake Ford spoke only a few words of French.

Born-again children?

Canadian psychiatrist Ian Stevenson (1918–2007) conducted extensive research with children who apparently remember past lives. He believed children remember their past lives well between the ages of two and four, but the memories fade as they grow older. He once introduced a child to his mother from a previous life and the child asked her if she had finished the sweater she was knitting him when he died. After recording 3,000 stories around the world, Stevenson was convinced reincarnation was true, but could not explain how it happened.

➜ Is there life after death? Examine more evidence in Haunted places on pp.94–95 and Spooky! on pp.96–97.

Spontaneous combustion

If someone went up in a puff of smoke in front of you, leaving only a pile of ashes, a charred foot, and some smouldering slippers, would you believe your eyes? According to some people, this freaky phenomenon – known as spontaneous human combustion (SHC) – can really happen. Most scientists say that it is scientifically impossible, but others have tried to explain it with scientific theories. So, what is SHC? Is it a tragic but natural phenomenon, or is something spooky going on?

Theory 1: The wick effect

One possible explanation for SHC is the "wick effect". This theory suggests that a person's clothing and body fat can act like the wick and wax in an inside-out candle, with the body fat sustaining the burning once the clothes catch fire.

Case 1: Mary Reeser's strange death in St Petersburg, Florida, USA, in 1951, earned her the name "The Cinder Lady". When she was found, all that remained of her was a pile of ashes along with a charred left foot and slipper. Strangely, her skull was found shrunken in the ashes. Was she sitting too close to the fire, or did she spontaneously combust from within? Nearby plastic objects were slightly melted, but otherwise there was no damage to her flat.

Case 2: In 1982, 61-year-old Jeannie Saffin burst into flames in front of her family in their kitchen in London, England. Her father managed to douse the fire, but Jeannie was badly burned. Strangely, the rest of the kitchen was undamaged, and the only parts of her body that were badly burned were the unclothed parts, such as her face, neck, and hands. She died eight days later and her burns remain unexplained.

Theory 2: Static flash
Another theory is that SHC occurs from a static flash of electricity. In a carpet, for example, static electricity could build up and create a spark, igniting a person's clothing as they walk across the carpet.

Case 3: One of the most recent cases occurred in August 1998, when Agnes Phillips was out for the day with her daughter, Jackie Park, in Sydney, Australia. Left asleep in the car while her daughter nipped to the shop, Agnes was consumed by smoke and then flames. She was dragged from the car by a passer-by, who put out the flames. Despite suffering very severe burns within minutes, Agnes remained remarkably calm, only complaining of being "too hot". No-one knows where the fire originated – the car was in perfect condition and the engine was turned off.

Case 4: In November of the same year that Agnes Phillips suffered her fate, the remains of 67-year-old widow Gisele (whose surname has not been disclosed) were discovered in her farmhouse near Honfleur in Normandy, France. Bearing a striking resemblance to the 1951 case of "The Cinder Lady" in Florida, all that remained of Giselle was one slippered foot. The wheelchair that she had been sitting in was also reduced to ashes. The cause of the fire and of Gisele's combustion continues to mystify police today. There was no sign of a break-in, and the rest of the house remained untouched by the fire, apart from the odd bit of soot here and there.

For more unexplained phenomena go to Haunted places on **pp.94–95** and Weird weather on **pp.228–229**.

BODY LANGUAGE

You might think that the only things you say are the words that come out of your mouth, but your body secretly sends messages all the time, too, with little signs and movements. This is called body language. You may sometimes be aware of what your body is saying, but most of the time, your body sends the messages without you knowing. What's more, when other people pick up your body's messages, they're not always aware of it either. So, in future, watch your language!

Tilting head: Interest

Rubbing hands: Anticipation

 Secure **Insecure** **Lying**

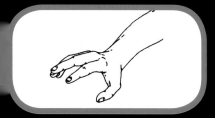
Sitting with legs crossed and foot kicking slightly: Boredom

Standing with hands on hips: Readiness, aggression

Pulling or tugging at ear: Indecision

Biting nails: Insecurity, nervousness

Touching and slightly rubbing nose: Rejection, doubt, lying

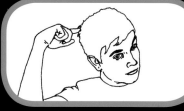
Patting or playing with hair: Lack of self-confidence

Stroking chin: Trying to make a decision

Sitting with hands clasped behind head: Confidence, superiority

Walking with hands in pockets and with hunched shoulders: Dejection

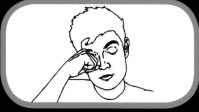
Tapping or drumming fingers: Impatience

Rubbing eye: Doubt, disbelief

Steepling fingers: Authoritative

Pinching bridge of nose with eyes closed:
Negative evaluation

Sitting cross-legged: Relaxation

Looking down with face turned away:
Disbelief

Arms crossed on chest: Defensive

*Hand to cheek: Contemplating

Locked ankles: Apprehension

How to spot a fibber

People may think they are accomplished liars, coolly answering even the trickiest question, but you can be sure that their body language is giving them away…

Staring

Slight delay in speech-body alignment

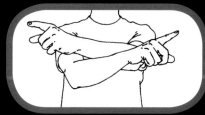

Sending conflicting signals

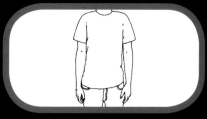

Holding body rigid

Avoiding eye contact

Rubbing eyes more often

Smiling but only with mouth, not eyes

Adjusting clothing

Dilated pupils

Sitting behind barriers, such as books
or crossed arms

Blinking more often

Shrugging and grimacing

 For more body basics, visit The body uncovered on pp.166–167 and Unconsious mind on pp.180–181.

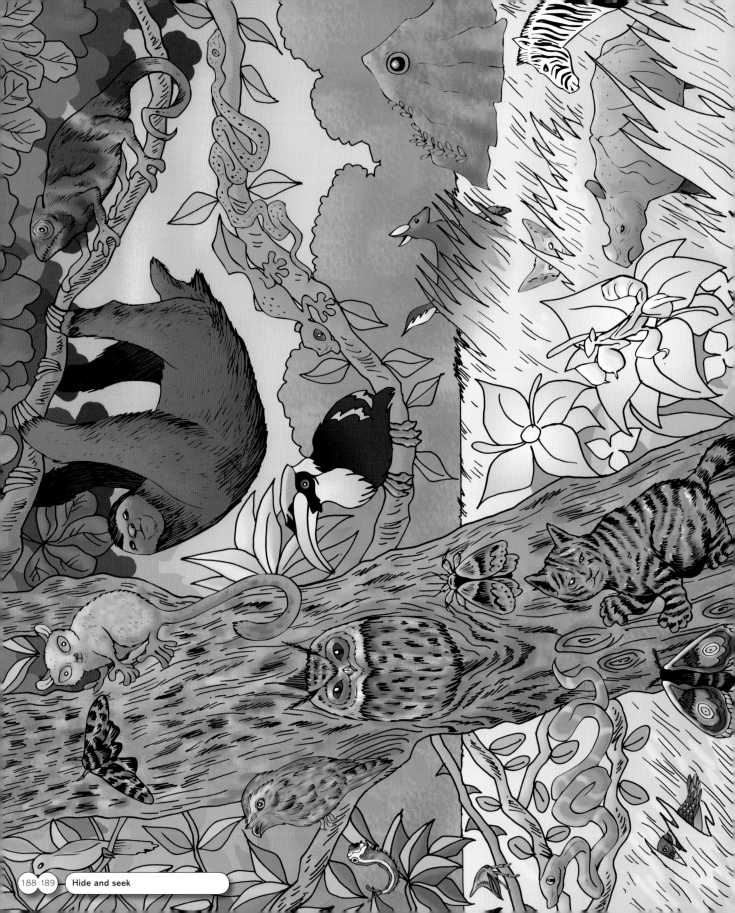

Hide and seek

hide & seek

How many hidden things can you spot in the picture?

→ Seek out other hidden things at Secret writing on pp.110–111 and Magic Eye on pp.220–221.

CamouflaGe

Did you spot all the things hidden in the picture on the previous page? Many creatures boost their survival chances by blending in with the colour of their surroundings, making it harder for predators to see them. This is "protective colouration", or camouflage. Another way animals avoid the eye is "disruptive colouration" – when an animal is so patterned that it is difficult to make out its overall shape.

The **scops owl** is hard to see against tree bark, especially with its orange eyes closed to a thin slit.

Lesser chameleons change colour according to their mood, not for camouflage.

Indian rhinoceros skin hangs in heavy folds that look like armour plate, deterring predators.

The **lemur's** subtle variations in colour make it hard to see.

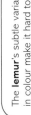

The **long-tailed nightjar** is almost indistinguishable from leaf litter on the forest floor.

The **horned frog's** colouration keeps it hidden on the forest floor.

Ambush bugs look like flower parts and lie in wait for prey, such as butterflies.

When lying still on the woodland floor, the **dead leaf butterfly** is virtually impossible to spot.

Unfortunately for its prey, the **spotted bush snake** can't be spotted!

Wildlife photographers sometimes disguise their **cameras** as mounds of dung.

Wolf spiders have a drab colour that matches their dusty habitat.

Crocodiles look just like floating logs when lying in wait for their prey.

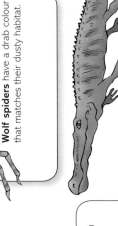

Three-toed sloths are so slow moving that predators can hardly see them in the trees.

An **orchid mantis** looks just like an orchid flower, so its prey doesn't see it coming.

With its wings folded, this **kitten moth** blends in with the tree where it rests.

The **grey partridge** has camouflaged plumage (feathers) like all ground-nesting birds.

A **zebra's** stripes disrupt its outline, making it hard to see in the tall African grass.

Soldiers wear camouflaged uniforms to blend into their surroundings, so they are harder for the enemy to spot.

Flower crab spiders blend into the flowers to catch their prey unawares.

The **deadleaf mantis** sits stock still before pouncing on its prey.

Resembling a leaf, this **leaf-tailed gecko** is hard to see when resting by day or hunting by night.

Unsuspecting victims can't spot the **palm viper** lying in wait amid palm fronds in Central America.

Anthill lookouts are used to hide nature photographers.

Tribal hunters often paint their skin or use leaves to camouflage themselves.

Peppered moths rest on trees where their mottled colouring stop them being seen by birds.

Using camouflage, **triangle web spiders** remain unseen until their prey is trapped.

The **thorn bug** looks just like a rose thorn – and can prick any bird that tries to eat it.

The **tawny frogmouth** relies on its plumage to make it look like part of the tree.

Marsh frogs are brown like marshland mud.

When wet, a **hippopotamus** is blue-grey, hiding it underwater from crocodiles.

In West Africa, some tribal people use **hornbill** heads when hunting to disguise themselves as birds.

The North American **bobcat**'s stripes and spots make it hard to see in thick undergrowth.

A **puss moth caterpillar**'s tail has a fake face to fool birds into going for the wrong end.

Rattlesnakes are grey or brown to blend in with their desert surroundings.

Water buffalo have a few stripes or spots that break up their outline.

A **cheetah**'s spots mean its prey can't see it easily in the African grasslands.

Leaf litter toads hide in the rotting vegetation by streams in tropical forests.

The **fennec fox** has a pale beige coat that reflects heat and hides it in the sand of the Sahara desert.

White-tailed deer change from pale grey in winter to mottled brown during summer.

Giant spots on an **emperor moth**'s wings resemble owls' eyes, scaring off predators.

With its bright green plumage, the **green leafbird** is hard to spot in its rainforest home.

➜ Like finding hidden things? Go to Holbein's *The Ambassadors* on pp.82–83 and Arnolfini Marriage on pp.84–85.

Fake

In their rough state, diamonds look quite ordinary, but once cut and polished by a jeweller, they acquire a brilliant flashing dazzle called "fire" that no other gems have. They are also very rare, so it is no wonder that people are prepared to pay a fortune for a dazzling diamond. These big spenders are the motivation for fraudsters to create convincing fakes – could you spot a serious sparkler and a cheap imitation?

Champion diamond

Colour, clarity, cut, and carat are the four indicators of a quality diamond. Diamonds vary in colour, but colourless ones are the most highly valued. A colour grading system runs from D to Z, with D, E, and F the colourless ones. The clarity of diamonds varies from I3 (imperfect 3, when the diamond appears cloudy – contains inclusions) to VS| (very slight inclusions) and FL (flawless). A diamond's weight is measured in carats.

Diamond-making

Natural diamonds come from carbon, forged under extreme heat and pressure deep in Earth's core, up to three billion years ago. They were brought to the surface during volcanic activity.

Piece of carbon

More recently, scientists have found out how to make diamonds synthetically. Like natural diamonds, the synthetic versions are made from pure carbon so they are real, but just not natural.

The High Temperature High Pressure (HTHP) method of producing synthetic diamonds involves cooking and crushing carbon under extreme heat and pressure. HTHP diamonds are rarely good enough to make valuable gems, but they are useful in industry. Their incredible hardness makes them ideal for cutting edges and drill bits.

The CVP (Carbon Vapour Deposition) method involves building up layers of carbon from hydrocarbon vapour. CVP creates gems so convincing that even expert jewellers are fooled into thinking they are natural diamonds.

Uncut diamond in rock

diamonds

Diamond-faking
With diamonds fetching such high prices, it makes sense for fraudsters to have a go at getting in on the action. Although diamonds are made from pure carbon, it is possible to use other materials to make a realistic fake. Cubic zirconia, diamond nexus, moissanite, and strontium titanate are just some of the options for imitations. Experts are rarely fooled by these alternatives, but good fakes can result in people making purchases, convinced they are buying the real deal.

Diamond-testing
Tests can be carried out to verify whether a diamond is genuine or an imposter:

1. Line test – draw a black line on white paper, then put the diamond on the line. If you can't see the line, the diamond is either genuine or an excellent fake.

2. Hardness test – fakes can be scratched by a real diamond.

3. Density test – cubic zirconia is a denser substance than diamond.

4. Sparkle test – fakes don't sparkle in the same way that real diamonds do.

5. Thermal conductivity test – fakes don't conduct heat as well as diamonds.

6. X-ray spectroscopy – by shining X-rays through a diamond, the pattern of light can reveal the truth.

For more sparkle and shine, go to Lost treasure on pp.26–27 and Hidden gold on pp.34–35.

SAFECRACKING

Given enough time and the right tools, a safecracker can break into just about any safe. Most safes have a combination lock, which can only be unlocked by dialling the correct sequence of numbers. However, safecrackers know many techniques that don't involve number crunching. Electronic safes have keypads instead of dials, but cracking the digital codes is easy for computer-savvy thieves.

Winning combination

The best way to break into a safe is to know the combination. A surprizing number of people forget to change the standard combinations set by the safemakers, or even leave the number written down somewhere.

6-75-9-23

Torching

Sometimes a safecracker may get a bit hot under the collar trying to burn out a lock with an oxyacetylene burner, or, if he has state-of-the-art gear, a plasma cutter or thermic lance.

Rear drilling

The cracker can always drill in through the back. Two holes are needed – one for the borescope, and one for a very long screwdriver to unscrew the lock from the inside.

Blow it up!

A safecracker's last resort is quick, but it's also very noisy and may destroy whatever is inside. The thief pours nitroglycerine (a highly explosive liquid) into the door frame. Then he inserts a fuse, lights it, and swiftly stands back.

Manipulation

A good safecracker can work out the correct combination by listening with a stethoscope. Each number in a combination relates to a different wheel, located behind the dial. A cracker can listen for the faint clicks as the wheels are moved into place. When the correct combination is dialled, wheel notches line up and the safe can be opened.

ELECTRONIC SAFES

Crackers can spray an electronic keypad with ultraviolet ink then shine a UV flashlight on it to reveal fingermarks.

onal drilling

her option is to drill down diagonally above to insert a fibre-optic viewer, d a borescope, for watching the ls while trying out combinations.

Front drilling

A safecracker may simply drill out the lock. After drilling through to the lock wheels, the cracker inserts a rod to push the fence (bolt) that locks them out of the way.

Clever computer software programs linked up to a safe will run through all of the possible combinations until finding the right one. Lazy crackers can put their feet up and wait for their computers to unlock the loot!

Safekeeping

Of course, if all else fails, a safecracker can always steal the entire safe and crack it in his own time…

BOOM!

For more inside info on criminal capers, get in to Hackers on **pp.60–61** and Private eye on **pp.106–107**.

CONSPIRACY THEORIES

Many people think that landmark events in history are not as they seem. They believe, and try to prove, that an event is part of a conspiracy – a plan to conceal the true facts.

Some people argue that there should have been a star-studded sky in the background of this photograph.

The stars and stripes flag was blowing, yet there is no breeze on the Moon.

Sceptics believe this surface resembles the desert in Nevada, USA.

MOON LANDING

On 20 July 1969, US astronaut Neil Armstrong stepped onto the Moon's surface with the now-famous words, "This is one small step for man, one giant leap for mankind". When mission partner Buzz Aldrin joined him on the Moon, Armstrong took this photograph. But did they really make history with their Moon landing? Conspiracy theorists believe it was faked. They think the USA were so keen to beat the Russians to the Moon that they staged the landing in the desert in Nevada. They also ask where the stars are in the photos, and how the flag could move when there is no wind on the Moon. In response, scientists point out that the distance to the Moon can now be accurately measured from Earth by shining a laser beam at the reflectors that were left there by the astronauts.

TITANIC DISASTER

On 14 April 1912, the ocean liner *Titanic* sank on her maiden voyage across the Atlantic Ocean, claiming 1,500 lives – or at least that's what the history books tell us. Some people say the ship that went down was really her sister ship *Olympic*. A few months earlier, *Olympic* was damaged in a collision. Conspiracy theorists say the owners patched *Olympic* up, swapped her name plates with *Titanic,* and sent the ship on a voyage with the intention of sinking it slowly and claiming huge sums in insurance. Unfortunately, the ship hit one of the unlit rescue ships that the owners had in position ready for the "accident". The owners said it hit an iceberg to prevent their plan from being uncovered. Theorists also point out that ship-owner J P Morgan was meant to be on board, but cancelled, blaming an illness, and 500 Belfast crewmen refused to board the ship despite being in need of work. Divers who have explored the ship's wreck, however, are convinced it is *Titanic*.

THE BLACK DEATH

Between 1347 and 1351, a terrible outbreak of disease called the plague swept across Asia and Europe. Nicknamed the Black Death, it ravaged city after city, killing in excess of 25 million people – more than a third of Europe's population. We now know the disease is spread by the fleas on black rats, but at the time rumours of a conspiracy were rife. Some people thought the water in wells had been deliberately infected to spread the disease. Others said that India knowingly sent ships with infected rats to Europe. None of these rumours had in any truth in them, but what does seem likely is that the Tartars (a people from Central Asia) who were besieging Kaffa (now Feodosiya, a port town in the Ukraine) helped introduce the disease to Europe by hurling infected corpses from their boat into the town.

 To uncover more plots, go to Great escapes on **pp.68–71** and Mary Queen of Scots on **pp.92–93**.

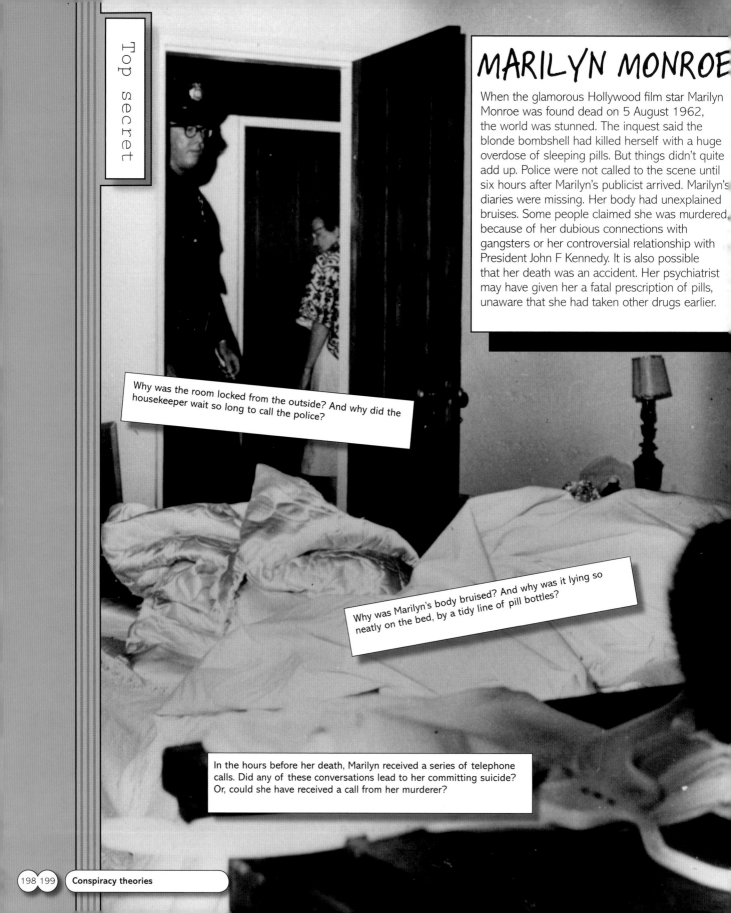

MARILYN MONROE

When the glamorous Hollywood film star Marilyn Monroe was found dead on 5 August 1962, the world was stunned. The inquest said the blonde bombshell had killed herself with a huge overdose of sleeping pills. But things didn't quite add up. Police were not called to the scene until six hours after Marilyn's publicist arrived. Marilyn's diaries were missing. Her body had unexplained bruises. Some people claimed she was murdered, because of her dubious connections with gangsters or her controversial relationship with President John F Kennedy. It is also possible that her death was an accident. Her psychiatrist may have given her a fatal prescription of pills, unaware that she had taken other drugs earlier.

Why was the room locked from the outside? And why did the housekeeper wait so long to call the police?

Why was Marilyn's body bruised? And why was it lying so neatly on the bed, by a tidy line of pill bottles?

In the hours before her death, Marilyn received a series of telephone calls. Did any of these conversations lead to her committing suicide? Or, could she have received a call from her murderer?

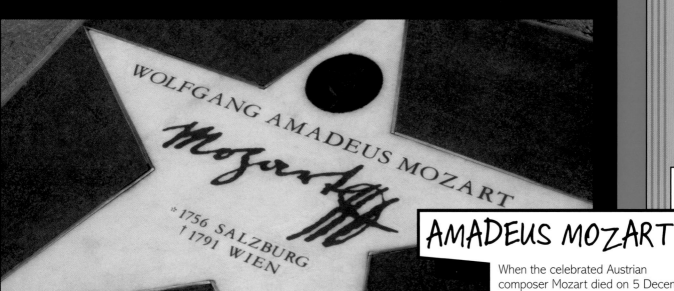

AMADEUS MOZART

When the celebrated Austrian composer Mozart died on 5 December 1791, aged just 35, rumours spread that he had been poisoned. On his deathbed, Mozart said he suspected this was the case. Could jealous rival composer Antonio Salieri have poisoned him? In 1823, rumour had it that Salieri had gone insane and admitted to the poisoning. Perhaps the society of Freemasons were responsible, since Mozart, a Freemason himself, had revealed their secrets in his opera *The Magic Flute*? Recently, experts have concluded that he died from eating rotten pork, or from rheumatic fever. Spookily, his last work was music for a funeral.

POPE JOHN PAUL I

When John Paul I became pope on 26 August 1978, he was nicknamed "the smiling pope", due to his friendliness and popularity. So it came as a huge shock when he was found dead only 33 days later. Millions of Italians were convinced he had been poisoned. Was it true that the new pope was about to reveal a conspiracy of Freemasons in the Vatican? Or were Vatican conservatives worried that this pope was too liberal? According to the Vatican, a heart attack was the cause of death. Yet, strangely, there was no autopsy, and, unusually, the body was embalmed less than 12 hours after he died.

➜ Uncover more mysteries in Kremlin on **pp.66–67** and Turin Shroud on **pp.90–91**.

The United States is the ultimate hotspot for UFOs. More UFO sightings have been recorded here than anywhere else. This picture of a UFO over Central Park in New York City meets the criteria of the classic UFO – it has a clear geometrical shape and a shiny surface, and appears to be hovering low over the ground.

UFO

Since World War II, countless people have reported seeing mysterious flying discs and flashing lights in the sky. Could these unidentified flying objects (UFOs) be alien craft from outer space keen to pay Earth a visit? Critics say close encounters of the alien kind are really just sightings of secret military aircraft. Others insist that we might not be alone in the universe...

In 1965, this picture was taken by Paul Villa near the Volcano Mountains in Canada and it remains one of the clearest UFO images to date. Villa claims that he has been taught telepathy by aliens ever since he was a child and that this photoshoot was previously arranged with them for the purposes of capturing their craft on film. Ok, then.

Some of the most extraordinary UFO photographs have been taken by pilots flying alone, at high altitude. In 2000, British pilot David Hastings took this photograph from the cockpit, during a flight over the Mojave Desert in the US.

World War II fighter pilots regularly reported seeing UFOs during flights. Nicknamed "foo fighters", these unexplained balls of light in the sky moved suddenly and rapidly. Critics dismissed them as exploding bombs or secret enemy weapons.

UFOs often appear as bright, flashing lights in the sky, as shown in this photograph taken in Sao Paulo, Brazil, in 1984. Their powerful light makes details impossible to detect. Sceptics rule these images out as merely reflected city lights, aircraft, or camera faults.

Is it a bird? Is it a plane? No, it's two lampshades reflected in a window! This hoax picture of UFOs over the Eiffel Tower in Paris, France, shows how easy it is to make a fake. Smudges on film, model spacecraft on string, and computer enhancement can all create convincing images.

This photograph was taken in New Zealand in 1979 and shows what seems to be an illuminated spacecraft. Amazingly, the photographer did not see it until he processed the camera film. So, is it a UFO or just a spot on the film?

For more encounters of the alien kind, visit Who are the Men in Black? on pp.48–49 and Roswell Alien Tribune on pp.140–141.

Also known as the Royal Institute of International Affairs, this group is named after Chatham House in London, England. The goal of the organization is to research and debate international issues. The Chatham House Rule prevents the identity of any speaker or any other participant at a meeting from being revealed to non-members.

Chatham House

Every year since 1954, a group of about 100 corporate and political leaders have met in secret to talk about world problems. There is never any publicity or reports on what has been discussed.

Bilderberg Group

Freemasons

The Freemasons began as an organization for stoneworkers in 14th-century England. Today it is an international society with millions of members. Symbolic rituals form part of their meetings and they are rumoured to have a secret handshake to recognize other members.

The Mafia is a criminal secret society that originates from the Italian island of Sicily. There are Mafia networks all over the world, often linked to violence and organized crime. Each group is called a family and is run by a boss or "don". Sometimes the families fight each other for supremacy.

Mafia

Rosicrucians

Rosicrucians claim they possess a secret wisdom handed down from ancient times. They get their name from the Latin words for their symbol — a rose (*rosa*) with a cross (*crux*). No one is allowed access to their library or details of their activites.

The Triads formed in the 1760s in China to fight the Qing dynasty of emperors. When the Qing was finally overthrown in 1911, the Triads turned to crime and are now involved in everything from counterfeiting to drug-trafficking. They got their name because of their symbol — a triangle and swords.

Triads

The Ku Klux Klan is a secret society in the USA that seeks white Christian supremacy through violent action. Divided into chapters, known as "klaverns", they target black people and Jews. Klan members disguise themselves in white robes and hoods.

Ku Klux Klan

Secret societie

Sons of Liberty

In the 1760s, the Sons of Liberty formed in the American colonies to begin the fight for independence against British rule. In 1773, members threw tea into Boston harbour rather than pay the British tea tax. That's one big cuppa!

The IRB, or Fenians, got together in the late 1800s to encourage Irish people all around the world to fight against British rule in Ireland. Led by Michael Collins, the IRB fought in the Irish War of Independence from 1919–21, which eventually led to the creation of the Republic of Ireland.

Irish Republican Brotherhood

The KGC was formed during the American Civil War to join the South in a "golden circle" of slave-owning states with Mexico, Central America, and the Caribbean. They disagreed with the North's belief in the abolition of slavery.
The KGC were called "Copperheads" because of their copper-coin badges.

Knights of the Golden Circle

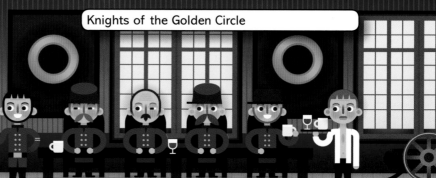

Illuminati

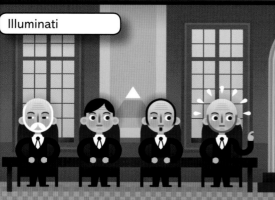

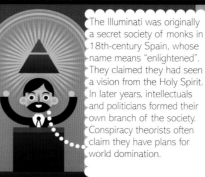

The Illuminati was originally a secret society of monks in 18th-century Spain, whose name means "enlightened". They claimed they had seen a vision from the Holy Spirit. In later years, intellectuals and politicians formed their own branch of the society. Conspiracy theorists often claim they have plans for world domination.

Floor: Chatham House, Bilderberg Group, Sons of Liberty, Irish Republican Brotherhood
Floor: Knights of the Golden Circle, Freemasons
Floor: Mafia, Rosicrucians, Illuminati
ement: Triads, Ku Klux Klan, Hellfire Club, Carbonari

In the 1740s, English baron Sir Francis Dashwood established the Hellfire Club. Members met in caves and abandoned abbeys to hold secret parties and perform black magic.

Hellfire Club

In the early 1800s, young Italians got together in secret to organize the fight against foreign rulers and unite Italy. They came to be known as *carbonari* (charcoal-burners), because they met like the men who burned charcoal in the forests – far away from prying eyes.

Carbonari

➜ For more secretive goings-on, sneak a peak at Hackers on **pp.60–61** and Conspiracy theories on **pp.196–199**.

FORBIDDEN CITY

For five centuries, from 1420 to 1912, Chinese emperors ruled from behind the high walls of a vast wooden palace in Beijing. Called the Forbidden City, only the emperor, his family, and his senior officials could enter. Other intruders risked a horrible death if caught. Only now are the secrets of this mysterious palace finally being revealed.

Empress Cixi
In 1861, Empress Cixi took control of China after the death of her husband, Emperor Xianfeng. Cixi was a ruthless ruler during her 47-year reign. She conducted all her interviews with courtiers from behind a yellow screen so no-one could see her face.

Meridian Gate

Gate of Supreme Harmony

Hall of Supreme Harmony

Hall of Complete Harmony

Deadly design
According to legend, Emperor Qianlong (1711–1799) wanted the palace's four watchtowers to be built to match towers he had imagined in a dream. The first builders failed to do this so Qianlong had them beheaded.

Dangerous dangler
Hanging from the middle of the ceiling in the Hall of Supreme Harmony is a large pearl called the XuanYuan Mirror. According to legend, it will drop down and strike dead anyone who tries to seize control of China.

Carved dragons
Dragons were believed to have magical powers. There are carvings and pictures of dragons everywhere in the Forbidden City, but the most famous adorn the palace rooftops. These dragons are believed to attract clouds and rain to protect the wooden buildings from fire.

Bending to please
Whenever the emperor appeared, everyone, even the very highest court official, was expected to "kou tow" – touch their foreheads to the floor. Anyone who failed to do so would be punished by death.

Cycle circuit
Puyi, who became the last emperor of China at the age of three, loved the bicycle given to him by his tutor and had holes cut in palace doors to ride through.

Hall of Preserving Harmony

Gate of Divine Prowess

Royal number
The number nine has always had special significance for the Chinese. As the highest single digit number, it was considered the royal number, and features in many ways in the palace. For example, the studs on the gates are arranged in nine rows of nine.

One less wife
Guangzu became emperor in 1875 at the age of four, but it was always his aunt, Empress Cixi, who ruled the roost. It was Cixi who introduced the beautiful young Zhen Fei to him to be one of his wives. But Zhen Fei was a tough cookie who encouraged Guangzu to rebel against his aunt. Outraged, Cixi had Zhen Fei wrapped in a carpet and thrown down the palace well.

Don't eat this
The emperors were afraid their enemies would try to kill them. To ensure their food had not been poisoned, a small piece of silver was placed inside each dish. If it changed colour it indicated the presence of an acid poison. The emperors also employed tasters to test a sample of their food first.

➜ For other mysterious places, go to Cheyenne Mountain on pp.20–21, Kremlin on pp.66–67, and Vatican on pp.88–89.

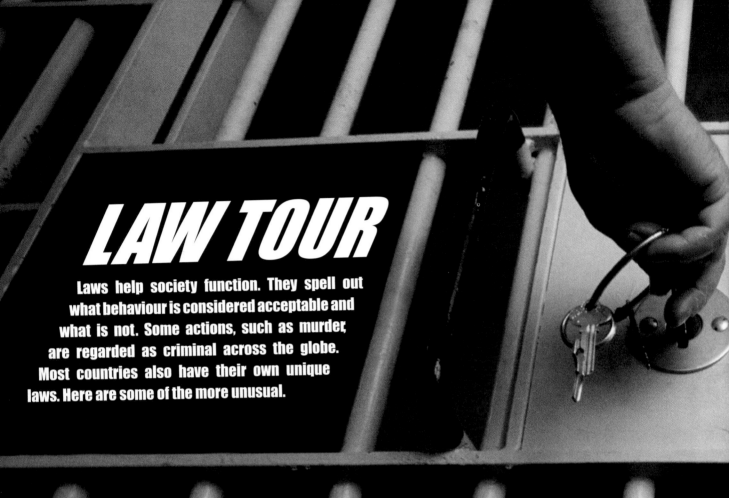

LAW TOUR

Laws help society function. They spell out what behaviour is considered acceptable and what is not. Some actions, such as murder, are regarded as criminal across the globe. Most countries also have their own unique laws. Here are some of the more unusual.

This is to stop them from mixing freely with men in the strict Muslim country.

↑

Women are not allowed to drive cars in Saudi Arabia.

Whalebone was used to make corsets, which was a wardrobe essential for fashion-conscious queens.

↑

Whales captured in the sea around England are the property of the monarch.

Substituting margarine for butter is prohibited, unless requested by the customer.

↑

You'd better believe it's butter in Wisconsin, USA. Margarine is off the menu.

This law dates from 1313, but fortunately most politicians are thick-skinned and haven't missed the added protection.

↑

Members of Parliament in the UK are forbidden from wearing suits of armour in parliament.

This law was passed 160 years ago to help combat antisocial behaviour in the rapidly expanding cities.

↑

In England, a law forbids people from flying kites in the street. Spoilsports.

Stay home if you have the sniffles in Washington, USA. You can not walk about in public if you have a cold.

It is a misdemeanor to be in a public place if you have a contagious or infectious disease.

An old law in Mexico states that bicycle riders may not lift either foot from the pedals.

The law was passed to ensure cyclists don't lose control of their bikes, but how do they dismount without breaking the law?

Cutting down a cactus in Arizona, USA, could land you in jail for 25 years.

The saguaro cactus is an endangered species so local lawmakers have taken measures to protect it.

Ordering a pizza to be delivered to a friend without them knowing can be a costly prank in Louisiana, USA.

A US$500 fine can be levied on anyone found guilty of ordering goods or services for another person without their permission.

The sale of chewing gum is prohibited in Singapore.

Gum is banned to counter the sticky problem of chewed gum residues on pavements and in subway stations.

In Athens, Greece, only cars with odd-numbered licence plates can drive in the city on odd-numbered days.

Residents have got around this legislation by buying congestion-busting even-numbered plates a second car so they can drive on both days.

Water guns can not be used in the New Year's celebrations in Cambodia.

Some pesky revellers have been known to fill water guns with sewage and spray passing traffic. Yuck! Smells like trouble.

Don't even think about training a bear to wrestle in Alabama, USA.

It is against the law, so you will just have to grin and bear it... and maybe find a more humane hobby.

Watch out for cows in the streets of India. They have right of way.

Cows are sacred to the Hindu religion and are allowed to roam free.

Residents in Kentucky, USA, face a fine and dye a duckling blue and offer it for sale.

However, they can keep on the right side of the law by offering six for sale at once.

Don't hang out your washing in an English town.

Breaking this 1847 law could land you a hefty fine – and someone might run off with your smalls!

→ Want to learn more about lawbreakers? Go to Everyday surveillance on **pp.56–57** and Safecracking on **pp.194–195**.

PARIS UNDER

Spooky stations
The Paris Metro system links to a network of quarries, tunnels, and sewers. Some Metro stations were abandoned and sealed off during the last century, leaving a legacy of so-called "ghost stations" with their original 1940s tiling and posters.

There are more rats in Paris's sewers than there are people living in the city itself.

Stinky tunnels
The sewers are so extensive that, laid out in a line, the tunnels would stretch 2,000 km (1,300 miles). Paris used to run boat tours in the sewers, but the boats were eventually banned after bank robbers used them for a successful escape. Construction of the modern sewers was started in the 1800s. Before then, sewage was allowed to flow directly into the River Seine. Lovely!

Underground scene
Although entering the tunnels is illegal, urban adventurers still risk going deep underground. During World War II, the tunnels were used by both the Nazis and the French Resistance, but today they are often the scenes of parties and even graffiti art exhibitions.

Secret cinema
In 2004, French police found a fully kitted-out cinema in a cavern leading off from one of the tunnels. Rows of seats were carved into the rock, facing a full-sized projection screen.

Rocky remains
Stone-mining remains that date back to Ancient Roman times have been found, deep underground. The mines were dug so far beneath the surface to reach the best deposits of the hard rock.

GROUND

Beneath the city of Paris lies a secret world. Catacombs, sewers, Roman-era quarries, and the modern Metro system all link together to form a vast network of underground tunnels.

Dead end
The first person known to have ventured into the secret passages was Philibert Aspairt, who descended into the unknown in 1793, never to return. His skeleton was found 11 years later He had died only metres from the exit.

Monkey business
When the maze of sewers was mapped in the 19th century, many strange things were found, including the skeleton of an orangutan that had escaped from the zoo!

Blockage ball
Giant balls are used to clear any blockages in the sewers. The balls' size fits the tunnels perfectly, so that when water pressure builds up behind them, they are forced through the build-up of sludge.

Urban myths claim that crocodiles live in the sewers!

Bone home
The Paris catacombs were created in 1786, as the city's burial grounds were beginning to overflow. Six million skeletons were discreetly transferred to the Roman limestone quarries where they were stacked up in elaborate patterns.

Door law
There are only a few entrances to the tunnels from the surface, and their location is kept top secret. Explorers who venture into the tunnels are pursued by the police, hot on their heels, who sometimes block up the entrances.

For other secret places, tiptoe to Cheyenne Mountain on **pp.20–21**, Kremlin on **pp.66–67**, and Forbidden City on **pp.204–205**.

The divisions of the Templars
The Knights Templar were not just soldiers, they were monks too, and led very spartan lives. There were four divisions. At the top were the knights with their heavy armour, white habit, and red cross. The sergeants were the light cavalry. The rural brothers were the managers, and the chaplains catered for the order's religious needs.

Jacques de Molay, the last Templar, is said to have put a curse on the French king and the pope when he was burned at the stake in 1314.

ENGLAND

GERMANY

King Philip IV of France brought an end to the Templars, but he was killed within a month of Jacques de Molay's dying curse.

Templar banks
One reason for the Templars' huge wealth was because they became the first modern bankers. When pilgrims travelled to the Holy Land, the Templars offered to look after their finances. This soon developed into a large-scale business and the Templars were also the first to introduce the use of cheques.

FRANCE

SWITZERLA

Geoffrey de Charney, who burned at the stake alongside Jacques de Molay, possessed the now famous Turin Shroud.

The red cross – the symbol of the Knights Templar

SPAIN

PORTUGAL

The Templars' seal

Holy Grail
In Christian legend, the Holy Grail is the lost cup used by Jesus at the Last Supper, which is said to possess miraculous powers. There are many stories of where it might be, and the search for it is at the heart of the tales of the knights of King Arthur. The Knights Templar are said to have found it at the Temple Mount in Jerusalem.

The end of the Templars
Between 1307 and 1309, the Templars disappeared suddenly and mysteriously. King Phillip IV of France and the pope had moved to suppress the order. The knights were arrested and burned at the stake for blasphemy. Some say it was because they had simply become too big for their boots. Others say it was because of the secrets they knew.

KNIGHTS TEMPLAR

Around 1118, French knight Hughes de Payens and eight other knights formed a little band dedicated to protecting Christian pilgrims travelling to the Holy Land. From this little band grew the extraordinary order of the Knights Templar – so-called because they were based at the Temple Mount in Jerusalem. The order lasted almost 200 years before it was crushed.

The Ark of the Covenant
In the Hebrew Bible, the Ark is the sacred box containing the stone tablets on which the Ten Commandments are written. Most historians say it was destroyed, but a few think it was preserved in the Temple Mount, where it was found and hidden away by the Templar Knights. Some believe the Ark is now hidden away in a church in Axum, Ethiopia.

The Temple Mount
Many legends about the knights revolve around what they might have found on Temple Mount. Some think they discovered proof that Jesus survived crucifixion, married Mary Magdalene, and had children. There is very little evidence for this. The only thing they could have found is the Turin Shroud, which was first revealed by the family of Geoffrey de Charney, one of the last Knights Templar.

GREECE

TURKEY

CYPRUS

Hughes de Payens founded the Templars in 1118.

Jerusalem

Want to know more mysteries of the past? Investigate Who crossed the Atlantic first? on pp.30–31 and Turin Shroud on pp.90–91.

ATLANTIS

In 360 BCE, the Greek philosopher Plato told a story about an idealistic place called Atlantis that was drowned beneath the sea in a terrible catastrophe. Ever since, people have been captivated by the idea of this "lost civilization". Did Atlantis really exist? If so, where was it? With the aid of modern underwater survey equipment, today's Atlantis hunters are busy exploring beneath the waves.

1 — Bermuda

2 — The Azores

3 — Spartel Island

4 — Cornwall, England

5 — Andalucia,

MOVIE
Does my head look big in this?
Smile for your public, darling.

214 219

Stage backdrop

Main stage filming

Take 9!

Greenscreen filming

Editing suite

Stage entrance

Set the stage

Indoor stages have padded, soundproofed walls to stop any outside noise getting in, and special doors allowing people to enter and exit silently. Red and green lights at the stage entrance indicate whether filming is in progress (red) or if a rehearsal is underway (green). Indoor stages are so big that an elaborate set for each movie scene can be built. The film will not necessarily be shot in the order it appears in the final cut. More often, the director will shoot all the scenes that take place on one particular set, such as the hero's office, in one go. The set is then dismantled and replaced with a new set. Some scenes are shot with a greenscreen as the backdrop, which can be replaced in the editing suite so the actor can appear to be hurtling through space or coming face to face with aliens.

Key people

1. The director oversees how the story is told.
2. The cinematographer directs the cameras.
3. Camera operators use either hand-held or freestanding cameras.
4. The boom operator puts the microphone in the right place to pick up sound.
5. Lighting specialists ensure the lighting is appropriate for the scene.
6. Actors sometimes perform against a greenscreen instead of a real backdrop.
7. In the editing suite, film editors add other elements to the greenscreen film footage, such as a new background.
8. Computer operators control cameras on the main stage to record close-ups and scenery.

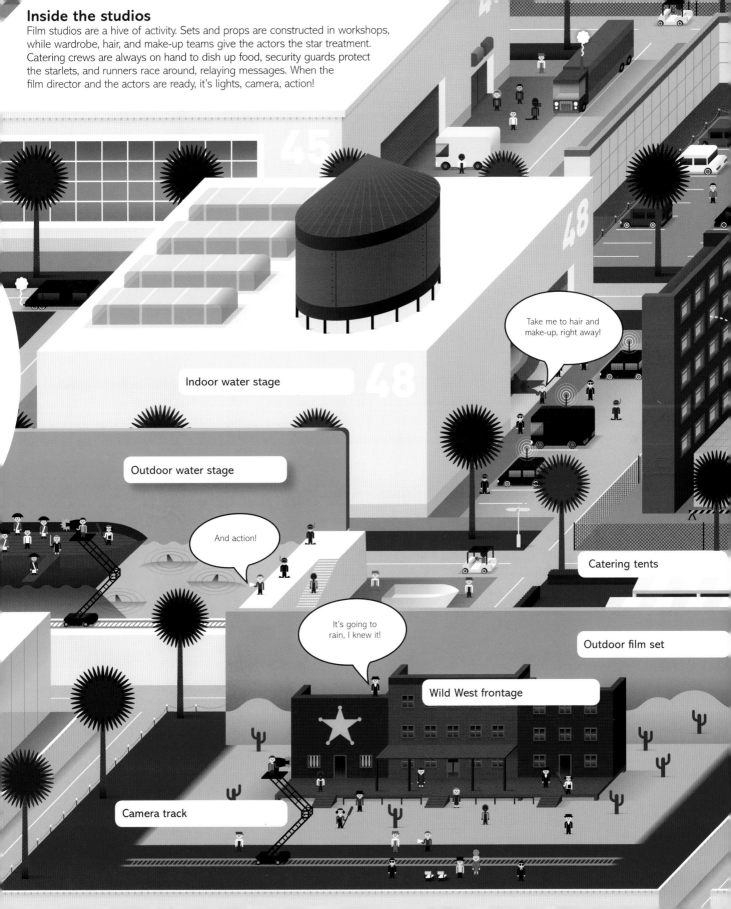

Inside the studios

Film studios are a hive of activity. Sets and props are constructed in workshops, while wardrobe, hair, and make-up teams give the actors the star treatment. Catering crews are always on hand to dish up food, security guards protect the starlets, and runners race around, relaying messages. When the film director and the actors are ready, it's lights, camera, action!

① Bimini Roads: In 1938, American clairvoyant Edgar Cayce said that remains of Atlantis may lie under the sea near Bermuda. Then, in 1968, divers found mysterious lines of stones there (the Bimini Roads). Some people think the stones were a drydock – a basin that can be flooded (so that ships can be floated in) and then drained (so that the ships can be mended) – built by Chinese explorers in the 1400s.

② The Azores: Could this collection of islands in the mid-Atlantic be the remnants of a lost continent? The islands are the tips of a chain of underwater mountains.

③ Spartel Island: On the seabed of the Straits of Gibraltar lies Spartel Island, which was drowned when ice from the last Ice Age melted and caused the seas to rise. French geologist Dr Jacques Collina-Girard thinks it may have been Atlantis, but mapping the island failed to reveal any artificial structures and showed it to be much smaller than previously thought.

④ Cornwall, England: A team from Moscow University believes they've found Atlantis in a relatively shallow area of the seabed, called Little Sole Bank, 161 km (100 miles) off the coast of south-west England.

⑤ Andalucia, Spain: German doctor Rainer Kühne believes satellite pictures of marshes in southern Spain reveal traces of the famed circular walls of Atlantis. The marshes were flooded around 800–500 BCE.

⑥ Thera: Geologists know that the island of Thera in the eastern Mediterranean blew up in a huge volcanic eruption about 1600 BCE. Could this have caused a massive tsunami to destroy the Minoan civilization on Crete? If so, could it have inspired the Atlantis legend? Minoan civilization did come to a mysterious end at about this time.

⑦ Manisa, Turkey: After studying ancient texts, British archaeologist Peter James concluded that Atlantis was near modern day Manisa in Turkey. Manisa, he believes, is the site of an ancient city ruled by the mythical king Tantalus, who Plato mentioned. The city was called Tantalis (a misspelling of Atlantis?) and was said to have been destroyed by an earthquake.

⑧ Black Sea: American explorer Robert Ballard has recently found prehistoric house beams deep down on the sea floor in the Black Sea. These houses may have been drowned after the last Ice Age. Could they be the remains of Atlantis?

⑨ East of Cyprus: American explorer Robert Sarmast has made detailed three-dimensional computer maps of the Mediterranean sea floor east of Cyprus. He believes they show a landmass just like the Atlantis described by Plato.

➡ For more secrets of the seas, go to Who crossed the Atlantic first? on **pp.30–31** and The mystery of the Mary Celeste on **pp.44–47**.

Indoor water stage

Underwater scenes

Specially built tanks are needed for water scenes. The water in the tank is kept warm, so everyone feels comfortable during filming. For cleanliness, the water is continuously replaced and filtered. Camera operators work underwater inside the tank, using scuba diving equipment, while the director and a diving co-ordinator view the filming through a glass window. They use microphones to speak to the camera operators. Some actors dive into the water and do the scenes themselves, but if the scene is dangerous, a trained stunt double who looks like the actor will do the scene instead. A wave machine is used to create dramatic waves, or if gentle waves are called for, a barrel is rolled in the water.

Set construction

Every scene shot at the film studio needs a set. Before filming starts, workshops are busy for months, and even years, making the sets. Many are made of plaster, which can be moulded, then painted and dressed to suit the movie's requirements. Forests, houses, and statues can all be moulded in plaster. Once they are on film with paint and proper lighting, no one can tell that they are fake. Plaster is preferable to the real thing because it is light, easy to move, and can be adapted to the exact shape that the set designer requires. Most studios also have a carpenter's workshop, where wooden props, backdrops, and supporting frames are constructed. Elaborate scenes and special effects can be created on computers, using CGI (computer-generated imagery).

Carpenter's workshop

Foley studio

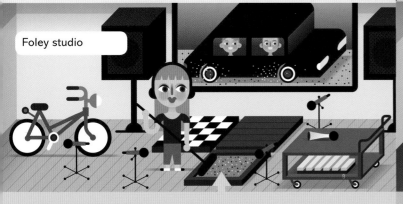

Editing suite

Sound recordings

It is often impractical to record all the sounds necessary for a scene during the actual filming, so extra sounds are created in a recording theatre. The original dialogue may need to be changed, added to, or re-recorded. Editing teams mark up the change, then the actor is brought in to recreate the line. Sound effects are also added. Background noises can build up a scene, such as singing birds or busy traffic. "Hard" sound effects come from what is actually seen on screen, such as a car driving past. Foley sound effects are detailed natural sounds, created in a special studio using a range of props, that come from the movements you see on screen. These sounds must synchronize precisely.

Post-production

Once the film has been shot, all the material goes to post-production to be put together by the film editor, whose first task is to create a very basic version of the film, called a rough cut. It is called a cut because editors used to literally cut up bits of film and stick them together. Now, they use computers. In the rough cut, the best shots are linked together in the correct order. Using this, the editor trims scenes, blends them together, and introduces linking shots to make a smooth-flowing fine cut. When the fine cut is finished, it goes to the sound department to have the soundtrack added, including dialogue, sound effects, and music.

For more showbiz secrets see Magic tricks on pp.78–81 and At the theatre on pp.98–105.

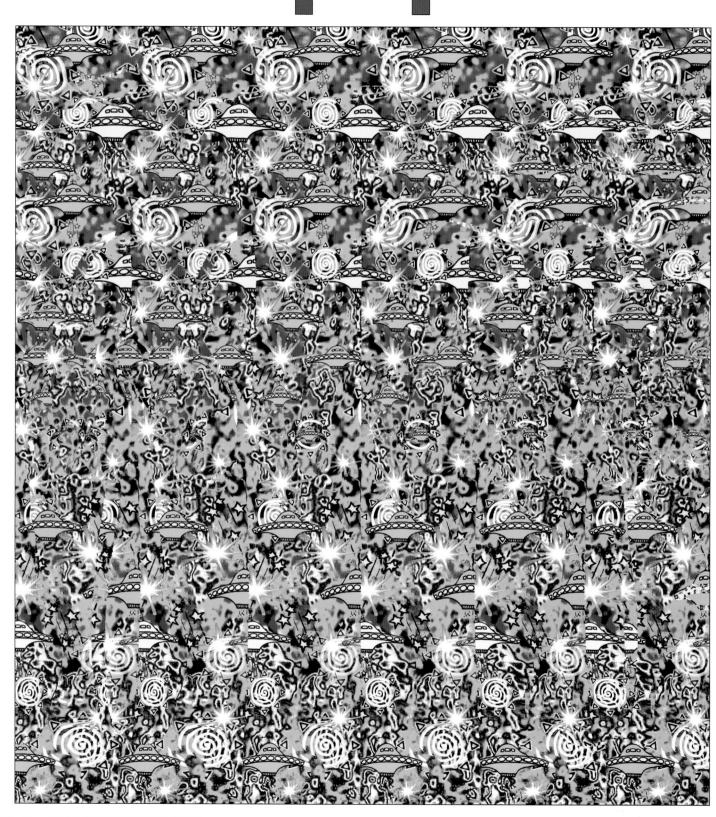

Magic Eye

Can you see the hidden picture?

→ For more tricks of the eye, look at Holbein's *The Ambassadors* on **pp.82–83**, Optical illusions on **pp.222–223**, and Fractals on **pp.226–227**.

OPTICAL ILLUSIONS

Seeing is believing, they say, but that's not always the case. Sometimes your eyes can fool you completely. As we grow up our brains learn to take shortcuts to help us make sense of what we see. Without these shortcuts life would be impossible. But sometimes these shortcuts can trick your brain into seeing things wrongly – or even seeing things that are simply impossible! These tricks are known as optical illusions.

Rubin's Vase
This is a picture of a white vase – or is it? Look again. Can you see two silhouetted faces, staring at each other? This illusion is called Rubin's Vase after Danish psychologist Edgar Rubin, who developed it in 1915.

Saxophone girl
This is a cartoon silhouette of a cool musician with a big nose playing the saxophone, isn't it? Have another look. Perhaps it's a girl in strong lighting, her face in deep shadow on the left. His sax is actually her nose and chin! Weird.

TRICK PICTURES

What you see depends on how your brain interprets it. In a trick picture, you can see two different things. The pattern of lines and tones doesn't change, but your brain can interpret them completely differently.

Old crone or young beauty?
What do you see here – an old woman or a young girl? The old woman's nose is the girl's cheek and chin, her eye the girl's ear, her mouth the girl's neckband. Once you see both, your eye flickers between them, confused.

Hidden skull
Most trick pictures are simple, but this one's quite elaborate. It looks like a picture of two children with the arch of a bridge in the background. But there's a gruesome skull here too, and those children's heads are it's holllow eyes. Disturbing!

TRICKS OF THE EYE

Even if you are a good judge of distance, the chances are you'll be fooled by these illusions. Your brain can pick up on visual clues to tell how straight something is, how far away it is, and so on. But the clues don't always give your brain the right answer!

Tile teaser
It looks as if the tiler must have been crazy when he stuck these tiles on a café wall. Yet believe or not, all the tiles are exactly the same size and the rows are completely parallel. The illusion, created by offsetting the tiles in each row, is so powerful you'll have to use a ruler to be convinced.

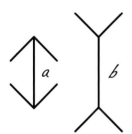

Long and short
Which of these two lines is longest, a or b? The chances are you said b, but they're actually both the same length. Your eye is fooled by the inward-pointing arrows in b into thinking it's actually longer. It's not. Measure it!

Room for confusion
This girl seems a giant next to her brother. In fact, the boy is simply further away. You think they're at the same distance because the room (an Ames room) is constructed to fool your eye – the walls and tiles are in fact at very odd angles.

Matching tones
Which of the two squares, A or B is lighter in tone? The chances are you said A is much darker. Amazingly, they are both same tone. But your eye imagines B to be lighter because it appears to be in the shadow of the cylinder.

IMPOSSIBLE THINGS

Skillful artists can create pictures of objects that look realistic enough, but would be completely impossible to make in reality. Pictures like these are called paradox illusions.

Crazy chess
Many artists have tried their hand at drawing impossible things. This one shows chess boards at different angles. Look at any small area and it all looks sensible enough. But how on earth does it all fit together? Checkmate!

Impossible triangle
At first glance this looks like a triangle made out of three blocks of wood. But could you join up three blocks and actually make a triangle just like this? It's impossible!

→ **Check out other visual tricks at Holbein's *The Ambassadors* on pp.82–83 and Magic Eye on pp.220–221.**

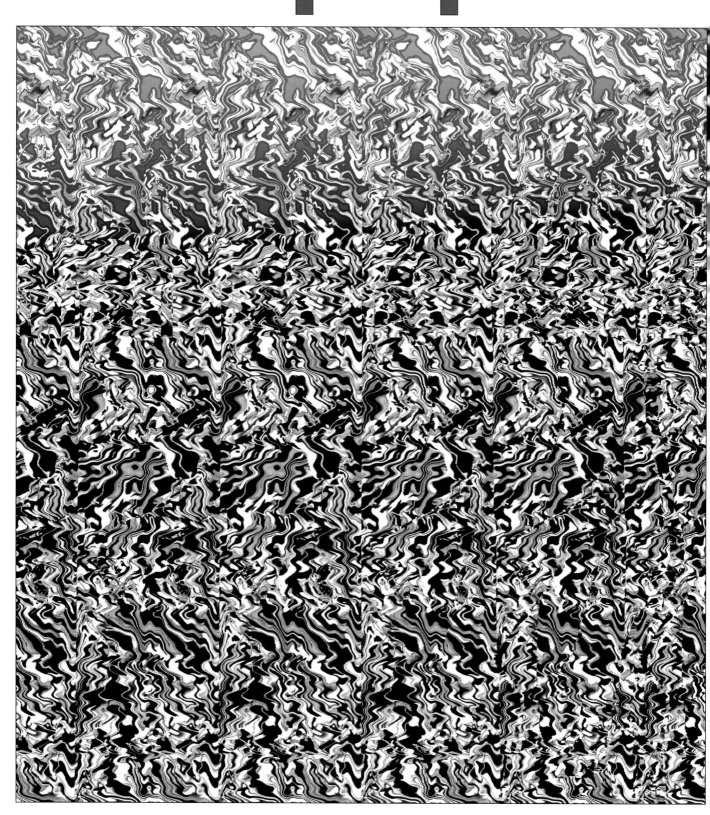

Magic Eye

Magic Eye
You can see it if you try...

This may look like a mind-boggling pattern, but this is a Magic Eye image. If you look at in the right way, you will see an incredible three-dimensional picture. Here's how:

Hold the printed pattern up, with the centre right in front of your nose. It looks blurry, doesn't it? Now concentrate, as though you are looking through the pattern and past it into the distance. Very, very slowly start to move the pattern away from your face until the two squares directly above the image become three squares. If you see four squares, just keep moving the pattern further away from your face until you can clearly see three squares. If you can only see one or two squares, start again – your patience will pay off. When you see three squares, keep the pattern exactly where it is and watch as a hidden image magically appears before your very eyes. Once you've spotted the image and seen the perspective, you can look around the entire three-dimensional image. The longer you spend looking, the clearer the illusion becomes. Good luck!

If you still can't see these two secret images, go to Revealed on pp.244–245 for the solutions, but no cheating!

For more hidden images, go to The almighty dollar on pp.16–17 and Turin Shroud on pp.90–91.

A fractal is a special kind of mathematical pattern. If you zoom in closer, you see the pattern repeated on a smaller scale. As you zoom closer and closer, you see smaller and smaller versions of the pattern. The swirl here is made up of countless smaller swirls.

These two parts of
the fractal are identical
except in size.

If you look closely at a frond
of the whole fern. Fractals can also

Fractals can be generated by computer, but they also occur in nature.

from a fern, you will see that its pattern is a miniature version

be seen in the shapes of cauliflowers, clouds, snowflakes, lightning forks, and many other things.

➜ **For other peculiar patterns, see Fibonacci on pp.86–87 and Magic Eye on pp.220–221.**

Weird weather

Even the forecasters can't predict this kind of weather.

Today's forecast: cloudy with a chance of frogs.

 Raining frogs In 1873, Kansas City, USA, was blanketed by a shower of frogs! Then, in 1968, Acapulco in Mexico was splattered with maggots. And as recently as 1996, Tasmania was slimed with a shower of jellyfish. No one can quite explain these odd showers; the theory is that the animals are sucked up by tornadoes or water spouts and dropped off elsewhere.

 Red sprites Scientists have discovered that lightning does a lot more than just flash between the clouds and the ground. Above a thundercloud, you can see much more, including giant red lightning pillars called "sprites", huge pancakes of lightning named "elves", and beams that shoot up from the top of the cloud, known as "blue jets".

 Hailstones Inside thunderclouds, layers of ice freeze on ice crystals to create hailstones. Normally, they're no bigger than peas. But in 1888, hailstones as big as tennis balls fell on Moradabad, India, killing 246 people. And on April 15, 1986, hailstones weighing more than 1 kg (2 lbs) crashed onto Dhaka, Bangladesh.

 Dust devils In deserts, tubes of whirling dust sometimes dance across the hot sand, almost as if they're alive. Arabs call them *jinns*, or genies, and Navajo tribes in the United States call them *chiindii*, or ghost spirits. But these dust devils are an entirely natural phenomena caused when very hot ground heats the air above it, sending hot air shooting up through cooler air and taking dust with it.

 Fire devils Even scarier relatives of dust devils are "fire devils". In this case, the source of heat is a fire. It may be a forest fire, burning plants, or even a house on fire. Hot air shooting up from the flames spins as it hits cooler air above, pulling up terrifying ropes of fire that whirl furiously into the sky.

 Bloody snow People have long described pink snow that turns blood red when you step on it. In 1818, ships saw ice cliffs in the Arctic that seemed to be streaming with blood. In fact, the snow is stained by microscopic red algae called *Chlamydomonas nivalis*.

 Ball lightning Just what are those strange glowing balls of light that zip across people's lawns or float into their bedrooms? Some scientists think ball lightning is balls of plasma (hot, electrically charged gas) spawned by thunderstorms, or plasma trapped by aerosols (floating dust or droplets). Others think it could be glowing silica (a crystal compound), vaporized when lightning strikes soil.

 Lightning attack US park ranger Roy Sullivan (1912–1983) was living proof that lightning can strike twice in the same place. Sullivan was first struck by lightning on his big toe. Another strike cost him his eyebrows. Then lightning burned his shoulder, two more strikes sizzled his hair, while another damaged his ankle. A seventh strike scorched his chest.

 St Elmo's fire During thunderstorms, sailors may see pink balls of fiery light dancing on the masts of their ships. Sailors call this light St Elmo's fire, after their patron saint, but similar balls can appear above church spires, aircraft wings, and even cattle horns! They are caused by a build-up of static electricity, which heats up the air and turns it to a plasma.

 **Water spouts** Many people have reported seeing hissing monsters with long necks rearing up out of water, including the infamous Loch Ness Monster in Scotland. But all the sightings are far more likely to be water spouts – small tornadoes that skip across water and snake up into the cloud, often with a roaring, swishing sound.

 Ice balls Sometimes blocks of ice falling from the sky come from the frozen flushed toilet water of planes flying overhead. Shudder! But ice can fall when there are no planes around. A chunk the size of a tree trunk fell on Ord in Scotland in 1849. About 50 big chunks, some as big as refrigerators, fell on Long Beach, USA, in 1953. Most scientists suspect that these enormous ice chunks may be just very, very big hailstones.

➜ **For more strange goings-on, visit the Bermuda Triangle on pp.40–43 and Spooky! on pp.96–97.**

All around the world, mysterious ancient stone structures, known as megaliths, can be found. But what was their purpose? Some people believe they were simply religious sites or tombs, but could they also have been sophisticated astronomical devices, designed to plot the movements of the Sun, the Moon, and the stars through the sky, and predict astronomical events?

Standing

Stonehenge

Built between 4,000 and 5,000 years ago, Stonehenge in England is the most complex of all the ancient stone structures. In the 1960s, astonomer Gerald Hawkins described Stonehenge as a primitive computer, used to predict eclipses of the Sun and Moon. He proved that the central "altar" stone and the "heel" stones beyond the circle lined up at the winter solstice.

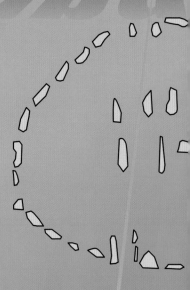

What are solstices?

Throughout the year, the place where the Sun rises and sets shifts slowly along the horizonas Earth circles the Sun, and the days lengthen or shorten. The longest day is known as the summer solstice. The winter solstice, the shortest day, was of great significance to ancient peoples, since it marked the point where days got lighter and the weather warmer.

Circles

As sunrise shifts across the horizon during the year, the angle its rays strike across the land move round too. This may be why standing stones were sometimes arranged in circles. As the sunrise shifted, the shadow of a stone in the middle would strike a different stone in the circle. So the circle could have acted as a calendar, telling people what time of year it was.

Passage

Chambers buried beneath soil were probably tombs, but their entrance passages often seem to have been aligned with remarkable accuracy to coincide with astronomical events. Just as the shifting sunrise made the shadow of the centre stone move around a stone circle, soit shone down the passageway to illuminate different parts of the chamber.

Stones

Nabta Playa

The oldest of all the stone circles is at Nabta Playa in Egypt. It dates back almost 7,000 years, thousands of years before the pyramids or Stonehenge. The stones of this circle seem to line up with the point on the horizon where the Sun rose on the summer solstice 6,800 years ago. This may have been important to the people of Nabta Playa because it marked the time when the rainy season began, an important event for growing crops. Like Stonehenge, this was probably a giant calendar.

Newgrange

Newgrange in Ireland dates from about 3200 BCE. This ancient tomb is reached by a long, narrow passageway that slopes upwards to block off any light, keeping it in darkness. However, just above the entrance is a tiny window, and every year on the morning of the winter solstice, four minutes after sunrise, a beam of sun passes through the window and up the passage to light up the inner chamber. Five thousand years ago, this would have happened exactly at sunrise.

Small window allows sunlight to flood into the passage and light up the tomb on just one day each year.

Tomb remains in darkness all year until the winter solstice.

→ Explore other ancient mysteries at Nazca lines on pp.32–33 and Giza secrets on pp.120–121.

Missing links

Most people believe that all species of life on Earth are continually evolving, as they have done for millions of years. Tiny changes in each generation make them increasingly better equipped to survive in particular conditions, while those species less well equipped die out. Fossils enable scientists to work out how various species developed over time, yet there are still many gaps in their knowledge. Scientists might think that birds evolved from dinosaurs, or that humans evolved from apes, but the hunt for those final "missing links" continues. Look at this monster mix of long-extinct creatures. Can you guess which present-day animals each has been linked to? Turn over to find out.

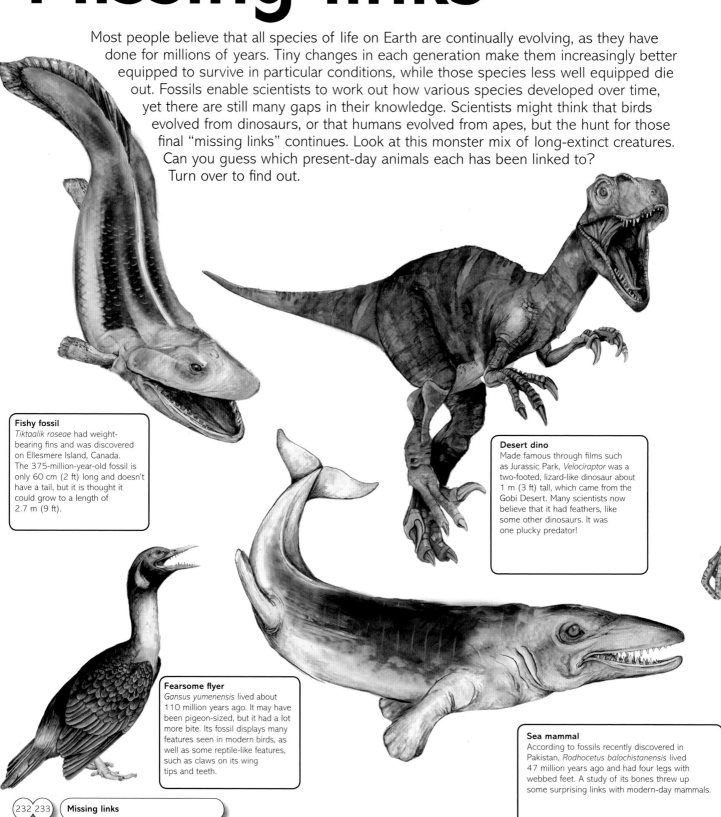

Fishy fossil
Tiktaalik roseae had weight-bearing fins and was discovered on Ellesmere Island, Canada. The 375-million-year-old fossil is only 60 cm (2 ft) long and doesn't have a tail, but it is thought it could grow to a length of 2.7 m (9 ft).

Desert dino
Made famous through films such as Jurassic Park, *Velociraptor* was a two-footed, lizard-like dinosaur about 1 m (3 ft) tall, which came from the Gobi Desert. Many scientists now believe that it had feathers, like some other dinosaurs. It was one plucky predator!

Fearsome flyer
Gansus yumenensis lived about 110 million years ago. It may have been pigeon-sized, but it had a lot more bite. Its fossil displays many features seen in modern birds, as well as some reptile-like features, such as claws on its wing tips and teeth.

Sea mammal
According to fossils recently discovered in Pakistan, *Rodhocetus balochistanensis* lived 47 million years ago and had four legs with webbed feet. A study of its bones threw up some surprising links with modern-day mammals.

Winging it
Archaeopteryx lithographica lived about 150 million years ago. It had feathers but also teeth, claws, and a flat chest bone. Although it has wings, it is not thought to have been a strong flier.

Monkey business
Discovered in Spain in 2002, the ape-like *Pierolapithicus catalaunicus* fossil is thought to be related to both the great apes (chimps and gorillas) and smaller monkeys. The fossil has been dated as 13 million years old and had a wide, flat ribcage, flexible wrists, a sloped face, and short fingers and toes.

Grip and rip
Excavation in Utah, USA, led to the discovery of the 1.4-m-(4-ft-6-in-) tall dinosaur *Falcarius utahensis*, which lived 125 million years ago. Its blade-like serrated teeth suggest it could have had a plant diet, but its relatives ate meat, and like them it had sharp, curved claws about 10 cm (4 in) long. Ouch!

Mystery mammal
The 50-million-year-old *Pakicetus inachus* was clearly a land dweller, with its four well-defined limbs, though it probably waded in streams. However, this Asian fossil mammal possesses several features that set it apart from other land animals – the position of ear bones, the structure of the middle ear, and the shape of its teeth.

Family affair

Hippos are four-legged land animals in the same group as pigs and giraffes, while whales swim in the sea like fish. Seems unlikely they'd have anything much in common – but appearances can be deceptive. Studies of cell chemistry suggest whales are more closely related to hippos than to any other living mammal. The discovery of *Rodhocetus* revealed a creature with a spine typical of that of a whale, but with the same unique limb structure seen in cows and hippos. *Pakicetus* also possesses several whale-like features. Both are descendents of a common ancestor – a relatively unspecialized mammal that also eventually gave rise to the ancestor of the hippos.

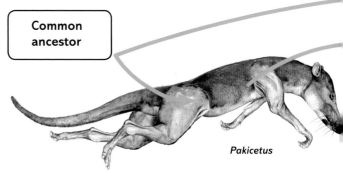

Common ancestor

Pakicetus

The greatest ape?

Some apes, like gorillas and orangutans, are so much like humans that scientists group them all together as the great apes. All great apes must have evolved from a half-human, half-ape creature. Yet, although scientists have found many bones from human ancestors with ape-like features, dating back millions of years, they couldn't find this missing link. Then, in 2004, a fossilized skeleton of an ape-like creature was found in Spain and named *Pierolapithecus* after the village of Pierola where it was found. Some scientists believe it is the missing link, but not everyone agrees.

Pierolapithecus

Gorilla

Human

The fishapod

Scientists are sure that life began in the sea, and land animals appeared when fish crawled onto the land. Yet there was a missing link. Strangely, there were no fossils of fish that liked to crawl on land. Then, in 2004, American scientists exploring the Canadian Arctic found the snout of a flat-headed animal sticking out of a cliff. It turned out to be a fossil of a creature the local people named *Tiktaalik*. When they dug the whole animal out, the scientists found it had fins and scales like a fish, but it's leg-like fins could have helped it walk on land. It seems they might have found a missing link.

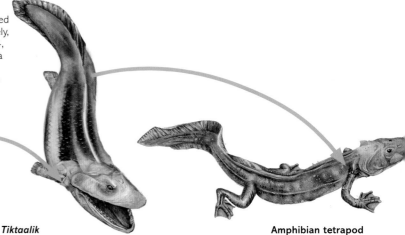

Fish

Tiktaalik

Amphibian tetrapod

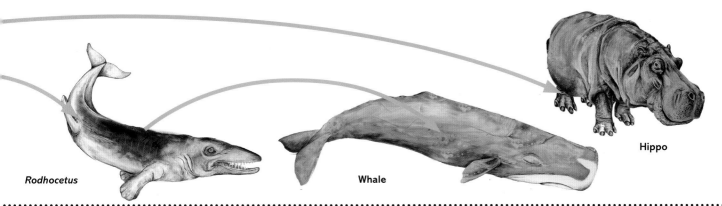

Rodhocetus

Whale

Hippo

Dinosaur bird 1 – The first bird

Discovered in Germany in 1860, *Archaeopteryx* was a "transitional" animal, neither a true reptile nor a true bird. *Archaeopteryx* lived about 150 million years ago. It had feathered wings like a bird, yet it had claws, teeth, and a tail like a dinosaur. At the time it was discovered, the British scientist Thomas Huxley hailed it as proof that evolution occurs, since it seemed to show that birds, such as the pheasant shown here, evolved from dinosaurs. It is most likely that *Archaeopteryx* evolved from a dinosaur such as *Deinonychus* or *Velociraptor* (see below). The commonly held belief that birds evolved from the winged dinosaur *Pterodactyl* is untrue, since *Pterodactyls* were flying lizards and have no connection to birds.

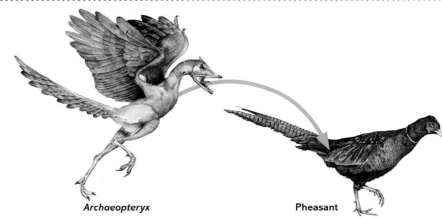

Archaeopteryx

Pheasant

Dinosaur bird 2 – Feathered dinosaur

Birds are amazingly similar in bone structure to the fearsome predator *Velociraptor* (not a missing link itself, *Velociraptor* was the start of a chain of evolution leading to birds). So how did vicious *Velociraptors* evolve into timid sparrows and thrushes? Scientists were convinced there must have been a half-bird, half-*Velociraptor*. The breakthrough came in 2005, when scientists found in Utah, USA, a mass graveyard of hundreds of little fossil dinosaurs, which they named *Falcarius utahensis*. They don't know whether *Falcarius* ate meat or plants – it may have eaten both. But it had shaggy feathers like an emu and a beak like a bird. The origin of the humble chicken, perhaps?

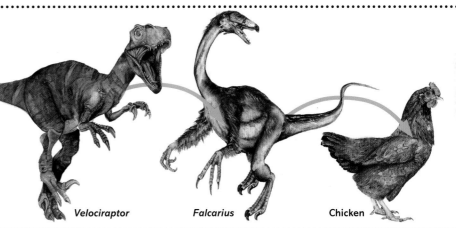

Velociraptor

Falcarius

Chicken

Dinosaur bird 3 – The first modern bird

Falcarius and *Archaeopteryx* showed how dinosaurs could become birds – but they were so different from modern birds that it seemed there must be yet another missing link. Then, in 2006, scientists found fossils of a bird in Gansu province in China. This bird, which they called *Gansus yumenensis*, looked like a present-day diving bird. So now scientists believe all modern birds may have first evolved in water.

Archaeopteryx

Gansus

Loon diving bird

➜ For more weird wonders of nature, go to Hide and seek on **pp.188–191** and Crazy zoo on **pp.236–239.**

Elasmotherium (AKA Giant unicorn)
Habitat: Grassy plains of Russia and Siberia

Unicorns are usually considered to be mythical creatures… but were they real? Bones of an elasmotherium – a long-extinct rhino lookalike with slender legs and a single horn – have been unearthed in the Russian steppes. Medieval travellers journeying across Asia wrote about encounters with a similar animal. Did this creature inspire the legendary unicorn tales?

Loch Ness Monster (AKA Nessie)
Habitat: The waters of Loch Ness, Scotland

Does a long-necked monster lurk in the murky depths of Loch Ness? Based on thousands of reported sightings, blurry photos, and shaky films, Nessie believers say she may be a plesiosaur – a gigantic dinosaur-like creature thought to have become extinct 65 million years ago. Nessie naysayers point out that tests with the latest scientific instruments failed to find any large creature in the loch.

Nandi Bear (AKA Kerit)
Habitat: The bush of western Kenya, Africa

The Nandi bear, named after the Nandi people of Kenya, is said to be a ferocious creature that gobbles up its victim's brains, ignoring the rest of the body. However, bears became extinct in Africa long ago. So who is this mind-munching monster? Some scientists speculate that it is a chalicotherium – a gorilla-like mammal with huge claws. Others think it's an oversized hyena.

Mongolian death worm
Habitat: Gobi Desert, Mongolia

Almost 1.7 m (5 ft 6 in) long and as thick as a human arm, this incredibly unpleasant worm-like creature lives in the desert sands. Its Mongolian name, *Allghoi khorkhoi*, means "blood-filled intestine worm" because it resembles the bloody guts of a slaughtered cow. If its looks alone don't put you off, try this: Mongolians insist that the worm spews out an acidic spray that can kill in an instant. If that doesn't work, it can zap you with an electric shock. Nice.

TICKETS

CRAZY ZOO

Psst… want to see the craziest zoo ever? Step inside, and hear the real stories of some unreal animals.

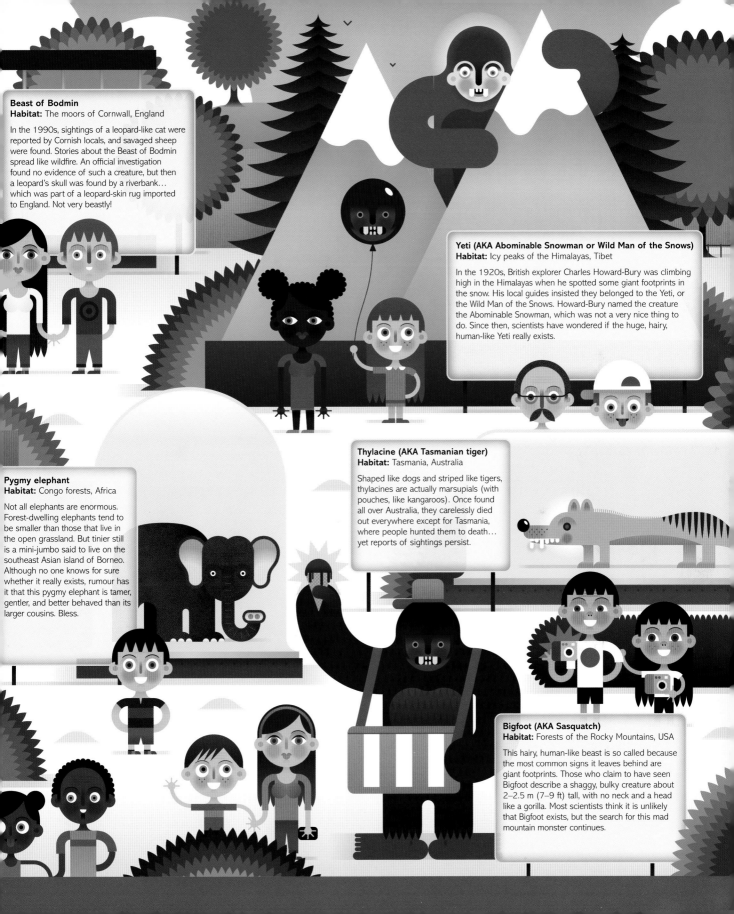

Beast of Bodmin
Habitat: The moors of Cornwall, England

In the 1990s, sightings of a leopard-like cat were reported by Cornish locals, and savaged sheep were found. Stories about the Beast of Bodmin spread like wildfire. An official investigation found no evidence of such a creature, but then a leopard's skull was found by a riverbank… which was part of a leopard-skin rug imported to England. Not very beastly!

Yeti (AKA Abominable Snowman or Wild Man of the Snows)
Habitat: Icy peaks of the Himalayas, Tibet

In the 1920s, British explorer Charles Howard-Bury was climbing high in the Himalayas when he spotted some giant footprints in the snow. His local guides insisted they belonged to the Yeti, or the Wild Man of the Snows. Howard-Bury named the creature the Abominable Snowman, which was not a very nice thing to do. Since then, scientists have wondered if the huge, hairy, human-like Yeti really exists.

Thylacine (AKA Tasmanian tiger)
Habitat: Tasmania, Australia

Shaped like dogs and striped like tigers, thylacines are actually marsupials (with pouches, like kangaroos). Once found all over Australia, they carelessly died out everywhere except for Tasmania, where people hunted them to death… yet reports of sightings persist.

Pygmy elephant
Habitat: Congo forests, Africa

Not all elephants are enormous. Forest-dwelling elephants tend to be smaller than those that live in the open grassland. But tinier still is a mini-jumbo said to live on the southeast Asian island of Borneo. Although no one knows for sure whether it really exists, rumour has it that this pygmy elephant is tamer, gentler, and better behaved than its larger cousins. Bless.

Bigfoot (AKA Sasquatch)
Habitat: Forests of the Rocky Mountains, USA

This hairy, human-like beast is so called because the most common signs it leaves behind are giant footprints. Those who claim to have seen Bigfoot describe a shaggy, bulky creature about 2–2.5 m (7–9 ft) tall, with no neck and a head like a gorilla. Most scientists think it is unlikely that Bigfoot exists, but the search for this mad mountain monster continues.

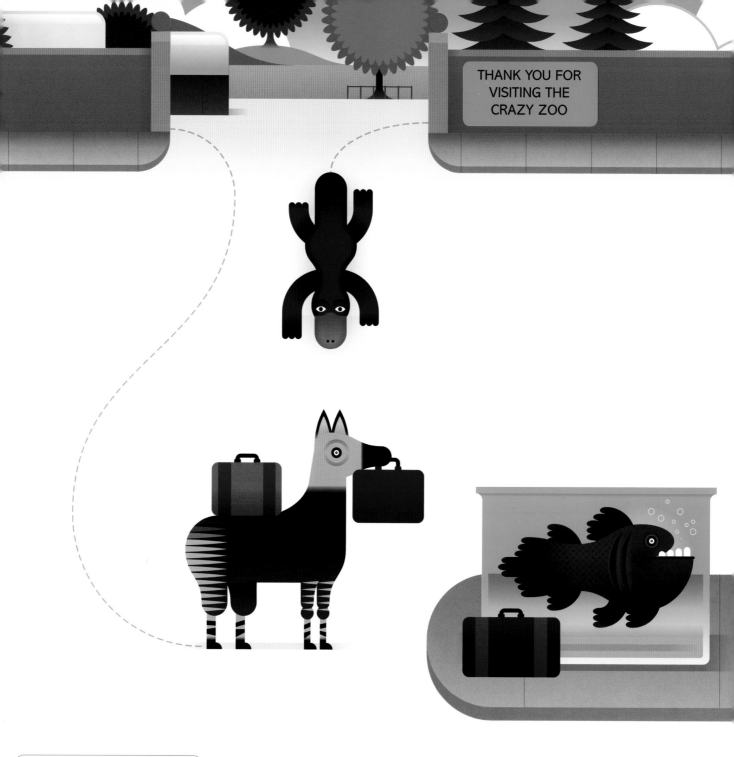

THANK YOU FOR
VISITING THE
CRAZY ZOO

The ones that got away

 A beaver-like creature with a bill like a duck? A mammal that lays eggs? "Impossible!" said scientists. When specimens were brought back to Europe from Australia in 1799, they were called hoaxes, until the existence of the **duck-billed platypus** was confirmed in 1800.

 The Ancient Egyptians knew of the **okapi**, which looks like a zebra but is really a type of giraffe. European explorers in Africa in the late 1800s heard rumours of an African unicorn. The okapi evaded them until 1907, when its existence was proved.

WAIT HERE FOR
BUS TO REALITY

The **coelacanth** was one of the first fish, dating back more than 400 million years. Scientists thought it died out with the dinosaurs 65 million years ago, because no more recent fossils had been found. In 1938, a coelacanth was found in the sea near South Africa.

Giant squids were thought to be the biggest of all squids – until 22 February 2007, when a fishing boat sailing near Antarctica caught something bigger. Called the **colossal squid**, this new species was more than 10 m (33 ft) in length and weighed 494 kg (1,089 lb).

→ Fact or fiction? For more intriguing stuff, have a look at Time travel on pp.50–51 and UFO on pp.200–201.

Forms:
can take different forms, including a bat, mist, and dust

On the menu:
the blood of the living, whether people or animals

Preferred haunts:
this homebody likes to hang out in its own castle or tomb

Active:
usually at night and always when hungry

Strengths:
superhuman senses, and mind-control over victims

Weaknesses:
can't look in a mirror, fear of garlic, sunlight, and crucifixes

Distinguishing features:
large fangs; deathly pale skin; red eyes; never casts a shadow

To kill a vampire:
drive a wooden stake through its heart, or expose it to sunlight

In death:
a vampire finally passes from the undead to the dead

Vampire attack:
victims either die or become the undead

To become a vampire:
get bitten by one

DID YOU KNOW?
- A trapdoor in a theatre stage is called a vampire.
- Some legends say even fruit and vegetables will become vampires if bitten by one!

By the light of a silvery moon, two legendary creatures of the night prepa for a fight with some serious bite. In the blood-red corner is the vampire, eyes blazing and fangs gleaming, while in the werewolf's neck of the woc

VAMPIRES
VERSUS

Definition:
the undead – a person who should have passed on but who still inhabits the world of the living

Legend origins: Vlad the Impaler in 15th-century Romania; Bram Stoker's novel *Dracula*

...aws glint in the moonlight and a spine-chilling howl echoes through the ...ght. How will these monsters measure up, and who will put the frighteners ...you? Feel the fear factor to decide the ultimate master of terror...

WEREWOLVES

Definition:
a person who shape-shifts into a scary, hairy man-wolf

Legend origins: stories from medieval times told by people living near woods and wolves

Forms:
can take only one form

On the menu:
people – either living or dead

Preferred haunts:
a graveyard visit is the firm favourite

Active:
full moons bring out these hairy folks

Strengths:
stamina and speed; cunning and agility

Weaknesses:
definitely stands out in a crowd, plus silver causes werewolf skin to burn

Distinguishing features:
long, narrow ears; sharp claws; thunderous howl

To kill a werewolf:
shoot a silver arrow or fire a silver bullet

In death:
a werewolf becomes a human again

Werewolf attack:
few can survive this savage attack

To become a werewolf:
be a 7th son of a 7th son, or born on 24 December

DID YOU KNOW?
- 80% of Russian farmers believe in werewolves.
- In the 1990s, a string of man-eating wolf attacks were reported in Uttar Pradesh, India.

 For more monsters and spooks, see Spooky! on **pp.96–97** and Crazy zoo on **pp.236–239**.

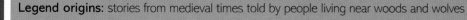

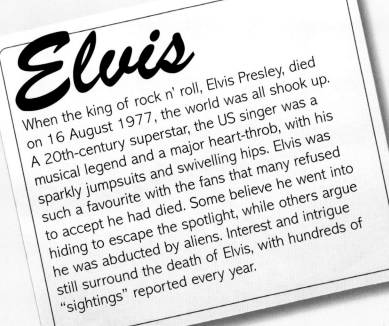

Elvis

When the king of rock n' roll, Elvis Presley, died on 16 August 1977, the world was all shook up. A 20th-century superstar, the US singer was a musical legend and a major heart-throb, with his sparkly jumpsuits and swivelling hips. Elvis was such a favourite with the fans that many refused to accept he had died. Some believe he went into hiding to escape the spotlight, while others argue he was abducted by aliens. Interest and intrigue still surround the death of Elvis, with hundreds of "sightings" reported every year.

New identity
Elvis received multiple death threats, but it was also claimed that he was in danger from a company with links to organized crime. Having lost money to the company, he assisted the government in exposing the dodgy deals. Some say Elvis was given witness protection in exchange for his information, and that he used the fake identity to start a new life.

Heavyweight coffin
Elvis was a fan of junk food, and in his later years, his waistline was whopping. But when his coffin weighed in at 400 kg (900 lb), even a diet of hamburgers and fries couldn't explain it. Suspicious minds said Elvis was not in the coffin at all – it was a wax body made to look like him. An air-conditioning unit put inside the coffin to stop the wax melting would explain the extra load.

Rave from the grave
In 2002, an independent label released an album called *Kingtinued*. The singer sounded like Elvis, and the credits said it was his voice. Yet many of the songs are recent hits, with lyrics that were not written until after 1977. Computerized voice analysis confirmed this recording was an exact match with Elvis. Is the legend still a singing sensation somewhere or is it a convincing impersonator?

Afterlife holiday
Shortly after news broke of Elvis's death, a man calling himself Jon Burrows (the name Elvis used to travel under) bought a one-way ticket to Buenos Aires, Argentina. This has fuelled the rumours that Elvis faked his own death to end the fame game.

Gift of Graceland
A sprawling Memphis mansion called Graceland was the Presley family home for almost 20 years. Elvis had a burning love for the property, which he left to his daughter, Lisa Marie. Now open to the public, Graceland welcomes about 600,000 visitors a year, and it's a hot spot for Elvis "sightings". A year after his death, a photograph was taken of the man himself in the grounds of Graceland. So was it an Elvis impersonator, a visit from beyond the grave, or Elvis alive and well?

Preparations on hold
Just before his death, Elvis "the Pelvis" was due to go on a big US tour. He usually planned a whole new wardrobe when concerts were coming up, but this time, there were no requests for glittering jumpsuits or blue suede shoes. Many were surprised that he had not ordered new costumes, especially considering his recent weight gain. Did swivel-hips know something the rest of the world didn't?

The camera never lies
This is the Elvis the fans love so tender, but it was a different story at the viewing of the body. A mini-camera was smuggled in and the pictures shocked his fans. The eyebrows, nose, chin, and fingers did not look Elvis-y, and a sticky sideburn was hanging off his face! At the autopsy, organs were removed, including his brain, and experts say this is what changed his appearance.

Tombstone typo
Another debate raged over the spelling of Elvis's name on his gravestone. His birth certificate and passport stated that his middle name was Aron, but on the stone, an apparent misspelling meant it read Aaron. In truth, Elvis changed his middle name to Aaron before he died. A devout Christian, Elvis believed this spelling was more Biblical. Still, some people cite the grave mistake as a sign that Elvis is alive. And let's not forget that "Elvis" is an anagram of "lives"...

For more famous disappearances see Anastasia: the lost princess on pp.138–139 and Lord Lucan on pp.142–143.
For more famous disappearances see Anastasia: the lost princess on pp.138–139 and Lord Lucan on pp.142–143.

REVEALED

The almighty dollar There are 13 symbols hidden on the dollar bill. See below for any that you didn't get.

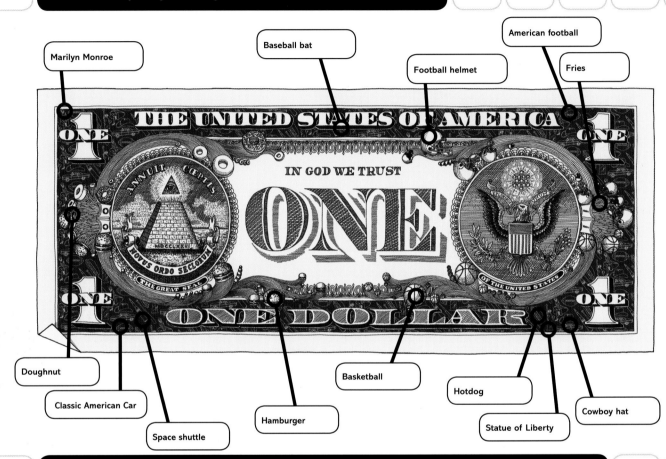

Marilyn Monroe

Baseball bat

American football

Football helmet

Fries

Doughnut

Classic American Car

Space shuttle

Hamburger

Basketball

Hotdog

Statue of Liberty

Cowboy hat

Lost treasure The numbers and letters in the clues indicate how many squares to move, and in which direction: North (up the page), South (down the page), East (right across the page), and West (left across the page).

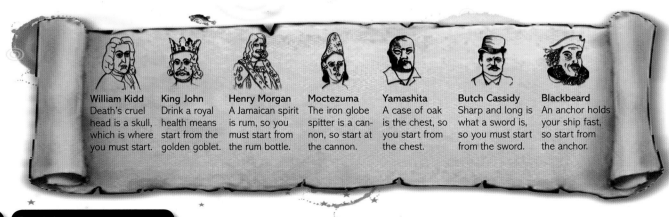

William Kidd Death's cruel head is a skull, which is where you must start.

King John Drink a royal health means start from the golden goblet.

Henry Morgan A Jamaican spirit is rum, so you must start from the rum bottle.

Moctezuma The iron globe spitter is a cannon, so start at the cannon.

Yamashita A case of oak is the chest, so you start from the chest.

Butch Cassidy Sharp and long is what a sword is, so you must start from the sword.

Blackbeard An anchor holds your ship fast, so start from the anchor.

Magic Eye

Found yourself going cross-eyed trying to see the images? On p.220, an alien should jump out at you, as shown here, surrounded by hovering UFOs...

...and on p.224, you should see a werewolf by the light of the Moon. Go back to the Magic Eye pages and try again after reading the instructions once more on p.225.

GLOSSARY

additive
A chemical added to food during processing to do anything from making it last longer to giving it extra flavour.

alchemy
An ancient form of study from which the science of chemistry developed. Alchemists sought the philosopher's stone that would turn plain metal to gold.

bar code
The black and white stripes printed on most products you buy that identify the product when scanned by a laser at the check-out.

base metal
For an alchemist, base metal was any metal of low value, typically lead.

body language
All the gestures, movements, and facial expressions we make with our bodies that give away our feelings to other people.

brainwashing
Manipulating someone's thoughts and feelings with clever psychological games to make them do or think something they never would have done or thought otherwise.

camouflage
Concealing something by disguising it to look like its surroundings. Soldiers might camouflage something by covering it in leaves. Animals have natural camouflage.

chromosome
A thin coil of DNA inside living cells that carries the genes that give the instructions for life.

cipher
The substitution of one letter or symbol for another in a message to hide it from prying eyes.

codename
A name given to an activity or person to disguise who or what they really are.

conspiracy theory
The idea that there are people more powerful than ordinary people who are conspiring to change world events and hide the truth.

dark energy
A mysterious repulsive force only recently discovered by scientists that is pushing all the matter in the universe apart at an ever accelerating rate.

dark matter
Invisible matter in the universe that can only be detected by its effect on ordinary matter.

DNA
Short for dioxyribonucleic acid. This is the chemical whose structure is a code carrying the complete instructions for life.

escapology
The art of escaping from things, such as shackles, often as a form of entertainment for spectators.

espionage
Another word for spying.

Fibonacci sequence
A sequence of numbers in which each successive number can be discovered by adding together the two previous numbers in the sequence.

fire
A brilliant dazzle given off by diamonds.

fossil
The remains of a plant or animal preserved from long ago, typically by being turned to stone.

fractal
A special kind of mathematical pattern that occurs naturally but can be generated on a computer. The same pattern is repeated on smaller and smaller scales.

gene
The chemical code on DNA that controls a specific characteristic of an animal's body or a plant.

genome
The complete range and location of genes on an animal or plant's DNA.

geoglyph
A giant pattern marked out on the ground, typically in ancient times.

greenscreen
A special green-coloured screen used in movie making to provide a completely blank background onto which background scenery can be dropped digitally after the actors have finished shooting.

hacker
A computer wizard who uses his skill to gain illegal access to someone else's computer.

hieroglyphics
Picture writing used by the Ancient Egyptians and painted on the walls of their tombs and temples.

hypnosis
A sleep-like state induced by slow rhythmic voices or movements. While under hypnosis, people can respond to questions and are very easily persuaded to do things by the hypnotist.

knight
A soldier in medieval times who wore armour and rode on horseback. Most knights followed a strict code of behaviour called chivalry.

latitude
How far north or south something is in the world. Latitude is measured in degrees north or south of the equator.

longitude
How far east or west something is in the world from a line called the meridian, drawn through Greenwich in London to the north and south poles. Longitude is measured in degrees east or west of this line.

map projection
The way the curved surface of the world is shown on a flat map. It is called a projection because the shapes on the curved surface are projected onto the flat map.

mitochondria
Tiny little structures inside most living cells that generate energy by converting food chemicals.

morphic resonance
A theory that suggests that everything that happens in the world leaves a trace in the form of invisible vibrations. These vibrations may enable us to communicate telepathically.

optical illusion
When your eyes are fooled into seeing something that is not really there, or is different from how it actually looks.

paranormal
Something that cannot be explained in terms of normal scientific knowledge.

Pharaoh
An Ancient Egyptian king.

philosopher's stone
A special substance sought after by alchemists but never found that would transform ordinary base metals into gold.

psychic
Someone who claims to be, or is thought to be, sensitive to supernatural forces.

radar
A device for revealing things by sending out radio waves and picking up any that reflect back off things in their path.

radiation
Radiation means the process of spreading energy, either in the form of waves or particles. Atoms give off particles as they break down naturally. This radiation can be very dangerous.

reincarnation
The idea that after you die you can be reborn in another body and live another life.

safecracker
A person who illegally breaks into private safes to steal the valuables.

serial killer
A murderer who goes on killing again and again.

solstice
The time of year when the sun is at its highest or lowest in the sky, creating the longest or shortest days.

spontaneous combustion
The idea that a person can burst into flames from the inside out, without any obvious reason.

stealth plane
A plane that uses all kinds of devices, such as a special shape and special paint, to avoid being detected by radar.

surveillance
Continual secret observation of someone or some people.

telepathy
The idea that we can communicate thoughts and feelings directly from one mind to another without using any of our normal senses.

UFO
This stands for Unidentified Flying Object. UFOs are mysterious flying objects in the sky that cannot be identified, but some people think they may be alien spacecraft.

vampire
In European folklore, a mysterious dead person who rises from his grave by night to suck the blood of the living. He is sometimes transformed into a bat.

vexillologist
Someone who studies flags.

werewolf
According to folklore, someone who is believed to be transformed into a ferocious wolf when the moon is full.

wire tapping
Making a connection to someone's telephone line in order to listen in on their conversations.

wizard
A wise man who is supposed to have magical powers.

INDEX

INDEX

INDEX

Acknowledgements

Dorling Kindersley would like to thank the following for their help in creating this book:

Additional contributors
Steven Carton for *Flag it up* and *Numbers*
Niki Foreman for *The body uncovered*, *Create your own state*, and *Mind the gaffe!*
Andrea Mills for *Elvis*, *Lord Lucan*, *Magic Eye*, *Vampires versus werewolves*, *Spooky!*, and *UFO*
Consultants
Kim Bryan, Jacqueline Mitton, and Jon Woodcock
Additional designers
Nina Brennan and Ken Jones

Thanks also go to:
Steven Carton for research and factchecking
Julie Ferris for proofreading
John Noble for the index
Pete Millsom for re-touching
Traci Salter for DTP assistance

Great Ormond Street Hospital for their kind permission to reproduce the character of Peter Pan for *At the Theatre*
Pinewood Studios, England, for their help and inspiration in planning *Movie Studios*
The Royal Opera House, Covent Garden, for their help and inspiration in planning *At the Theatre*

The publisher would also like to thank the following for their kind permission to reproduce their photographs:

(Key: a-above; b-below/bottom; c-centre; l-left; r-right; t-top)

14 Alamy Images: Mario Ponta. 16–17 Corbis: Visions of America/Joseph Sohm (background). 31 Beinecke Rare Book and Manuscript Library, Yale University: (t). 32 Alamy Images: Kevin Schafer (b). Corbis: Yann Arthus-Bertrand (t). 33 South American Pictures: Robert Francis (bl); Tony Morrison (br). SuperStock: SGM (tr). 34 Corbis: BSPI (c). 34–35 Corbis: Louie Psihoyos.

35 Corbis: Charles O'Rear (t). 50–51 Masterpiece Models: Alex Castro (c). 52–53 akg-images: Topkapi Saray Museum. 54–55 Masterfile: Nora Good. 62–63 Science Photo Library: Pasieka. 66–67 Google Earth: DigitalGlobe. 72–73 The Wayne Namerow Houdini Collection. 74 Library Of Congress, Washington, DC. 76 Getty Images: Time Life Pictures/Mansell. 77 Library Of Congress, Washington, DC. 82 The Art Archive: Eileen Tweedy/National Gallery London. PunchStock: Stockbyte (frame). 83 The Art Archive: Eileen Tweedy/National Gallery London (bl) (br) (cl) (cra) (crb) (tl). National Gallery, London: (tr). 84 The Art Archive: Eileen Tweedy/National Gallery London. 85 The Art Archive: Eileen Tweedy/National Gallery London (c). 88–89 Google Earth: DigitalGlobe. 90–91 Corbis: P. Deliss/Godong. 94 courtesy Monte Cristo Homestead: (c). www.stonepages.de: (tl). 94-95 Alamy Images: WoodyStock. 95 Alamy Images: allOver photography (c); Robert Harding Picture Library Ltd (cr). britainonview.com: (t) (cl). TopFoto.co.uk: Charles Walker (b). 96 Fiona Broome/www.HollowHill.com: (l). TopFoto.co.uk: (r); Charles Walker (c). 97 Fiona Broome/www.HollowHill.com: (l) (br). News Team International: (tr). TopFoto.co.uk: Fortean Picture Library (bc). 106–107 Corbis: Michael Prince. Getty Images: Photonica/Barnaby Hall (c). 110–111 TopFoto.co.uk: Charles Walker (c). 116 akg-images: Erich Lessing/British Museum (tl) (br). 116–117 akg-images: Erich Lessing/British Museum. 117 akg-images: Erich Lessing/British Museum (tl). The Art Archive: Dagli Orti/Heraklion Museum (cr). The Trustees of the British Museum (tr). Corbis: Sandro Vannini (br). 128 Alain Guilleux/http://alain.guilleux.free.fr: (r). Science & Society Picture Library: (l). 129 © 2006 Antikythera Mechanism Research Project : (br). PA Photos: AP/Thanassis Stavrakis (tr). TopFoto.co.uk: Fortean Picture Library (l). 134 Corbis: (r). courtesy Norsk Hydro: (l). 135 Alamy Images: Travis Rowan (br). courtesy Norsk Hydro: (bl) (tr). 138 Alamy Images: Mary Evans Picture Library (br). Getty

Images: Time Life Pictures (l/Alexandra) (l/Anastasia) (l/Maria) (l/Nicholas) (l/Olga) (l/Tatiana). popperfoto.com: (l/Alexei). 138–139 popperfoto.com. 139 Corbis: Bettmann (tr). Reuters: (br). TopFoto.co.uk: Picturepoint (cr). 140 Corbis: Bettmann (t). 141 PA Photos: AP (tc). Science Photo Library: (bl). TopFoto.co.uk: Picturepoint (r). 142 Mirrorpix: (c). TopFoto.co.uk: Picturepoint (l) (br); UPP (tr). 143 Alamy Images: Phil Talbot (l). Getty Images: Angela Deane-Drummond (r). 144 Corbis: Anthony Berger. 145 Corbis: Bettmann (l). Getty Images: Kean Collection (br). Google Earth: © The Sanborn Map Company, Inc (2007) (tr). 146 courtesy FBI Laboratory. 147 Corbis: Sygma/Lee Corkran. 148 Corbis: Bettmann (tr). Google Earth: © The Sanborn Map Company, Inc. (2007) (bl). PA Photos: AP (br). 149 Corbis. 150–151 The Art Archive: John Webb (map). 162–163 Photolibrary: Tim Hill. 168 Corbis: Bob Sacha (tl). 168–169 Elizabeth Whiting & Associates: Di Lewis. 171 Corbis: Roger Ressmeyer. 192–193 Photolibrary: Phillip Hayson. 196 National Aeronautics and Space Administration. 197 Corbis: Ralph White (t). Getty Images: Lonely Planet Images/Martin Moos (b). 198 Getty Images: Fox Photos/E. Murray. 199 Alamy Images: Simon Reddy (t). Getty Images: Keystone (b). 200 Getty Images: Steve Weinrebe (tr). Mary Evans Picture Library: (tl) (cr). 201 Mary Evans Picture Library: (tr) (bl). TopFoto.co.uk: Fortean Picture Library (bc) (br); National News/Jerry Daws (tl). 204–205 Google Earth: DigitalGlobe. 206–207 Corbis: Charles O'Rear. 220 © 2007 Magic Eye Inc.. 222 Mary Evans Picture Library: (br) (bl). 223 Edward H Adelson: (cr). Corbis: William Whitehurst (bl). Science Photo Library: Mauro Fermariello (tr). 224 © 2007 Magic Eye Inc.. 226-227 Science Photo Library: Gregory Sams. 230 Alamy Images: Rolf Richardson (bl); Mike P Shepherd (br). 231 Corbis: Geray Sweeney (br). 243 Corbis: Bettmann (cra); JAI/Walter Bibikow (crb). 245 © 2007 Magic Eye Inc.: (l) (r)

Acknowledgements

Ali Pellatt has some secrets: she eats baked beans cold from the tin, she is a massive Birmingham City supporter who collects children's encyclopedias, and she has a soft spot for scraggly old cats and dogs.

Hennie Haworth has always loved doodling – inspired by geometric shapes, bright colours, and gadgets – and recently scribbled her way through an illustration degree. Her favourite things are the colour yellow and mobile homes.

Gilman Calsen's artistic side didn't show itself until he was 15 years old, when his brother gave him a 3-D modelling computer program for Christmas. He loves the outdoors and wears a size 14 shoe!

Steebz from KHUAN loves drawing on computers because computer paint doesn't stain his clothes. He likes all art throughout the entire human history and he has a big secret: his Dad's a caveman and his Mum's a vampire! That's why he's hairy all over and only comes out at night.

Alain Goffin has been illustrating since he doesn't know when! He's recently been working on a comic strip about the life of an industrial designer who is plunged into the surprisingly secret world of hang-glider construction.

Neal Murran's crayon drawing won a competition when he was five years old. He owns 900 crayons today and his favourite one is blue. He likes picnics but dislikes clowns. When he was little his Dad told him not to eat play dough because a monster would grow in his stomach. Disregarding this and ending up in hospital, the first thing he asked the nurses was, "Where's my monster?"

Mr Bingo has been drawing for as long as he can remember. He likes Scrabble™, dogs who wear clothes, and old postcards. He dislikes litter, and has a big secret: his haircut is the same as his mum's!

Craig Conlan watched a lot of cartoons and read a lot of comics as a boy. They inspired him to become an artist when he grew up. In secret, he still watches a lot of cartoons and reads a lot of comics. He likes Frankenstein and blueberry muffins. He dislikes jazz music and intensely dislikes Brussell sprouts.

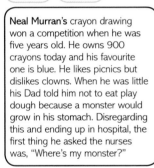

Jude Buffum is better known as the beard-sporting half of the Philadelphia-based Headcase Design in the USA. From his secret underground lair, he enjoys creating illustrations, designing books, and teaching his Boston terrier to mix cocktails.

Led Pants started this illustration stuff soon after working at an animation company. He doesn't much like drawing on the computer ("I think it's watching me") although he does like drawing in general (as well as gardening and climbing rocks). His secret is that he is a nurse practitioner at a psychiatric school for teenagers. If you were wondering, his full name is Leopold Ezra Dizzelpop Pants... or so he says.

Irene Jacobs first started illustrating when she was little. Flattery sustained her skill as she liked to hear that she ma[...] beautiful pictures. Today, she still loves drawing: "It's a way [...] express what impresses you". Her secrets are locked in her [...] which she always used to lay [...] hair over so that she'd know [...] anybody had opened it.